This War Is For A Whole Life

The Culture of Resistance Among

Southern California Indians, 1850–1966

By

Richard A. Hanks, PhD

Ushkana Press

DOROTHY
RAMON
LEARNING CENTER, INC.

Ushkana Press

Ushkana Press is the publishing arm of Dorothy Ramon Learning Center, Inc. The nonprofit, 501(c)(3) public-benefit corporation works to save and share all Southern California's American Indian cultures, languages, history, music, and other traditional arts. Central to the lives of all Southern California's diverse communities and visitors, Indians and nonIndians alike, the Learning Center inspires and advances discovery, understanding, and continuance of these tribal cultures integral to our national heritage.
P.O. Box 1510, Banning, CA, USA 92220
www.dorothyramon.org and www.ushkana.org/www.dorothyramon.blogspot.com

Learning Center President & Founder, Ernest H. Siva
Editor, Pat Murkland
Thank you for major contributions to design and layout, Robin S. Hanks
Thank you for the cover illustration, David Fairrington, www.davidfairrington.com

First edition, September 2012
Printed in the United States of America
ISBN 978-0-9754496-4-6 All rights reserved.

Contents

FOREWORD

I remember attending Adam Castillo's funeral. My mother had told me he had played Schubert's "Ave Maria" on the violin at his wife's funeral. Who was going to lead the Mission Indian Federation now that he was gone? It was the first time I saw grown men cry.

The author, Richard Hanks, revisits a time of great turmoil in the lives of the Indians of Southern California. The issues of loss of land and life that accompanied the invasion of settlers into their homelands were dealt with by a strong, resilient people. This strength comes from a world view of ancient wisdom and tradition. The belief in a higher power is the key.

Often overlooked by mainstream academia, stories of individual leaders speak of the heroic efforts made on behalf of native sovereignty and human rights. Many of these leaders included non-Indian allies, who understood the plight of their brothers and wanted to do something about it.

We are thankful that author Richard Hanks took the time and effort to tell the stories of long-forgotten individuals who played a part in influencing events affecting a lot of our families. Their relatives will undoubtedly be surprised and rightfully proud in many cases. This is an important book!

—Ernest H. Siva

Southern California leaders: Front row, from left, Santos Manuel (with top hat), possibly Francisco Morongo, Chief Cabezon (arms folded), possibly Pedro Chino; second row: Juan Ramon, unknown, Will Pablo (leaning).
Courtesy of Weinland Collection, Huntington Library, San Marino, CA

DEDICATION

On behalf of all of those who assisted in this work, I dedicate this book to the Indian children of Southern California whose heroes were stolen from them. It is my hope that they will come to know the names of those ancestors who fought and died to preserve the Indian culture of the area and understand what a heroic story it truly is.

—Richard A. Hanks

Acknowledgements

An endeavor such as this manuscript is a journey of discovery. As with any journey into new waters, success often depends on the assistance and generosity of others. I especially thank those who gave of their stories, recollections and time to help me find my way.

I sincerely thank the tribal council of the Gabrieleño Band of Mission Indians who set me on this path. Machado sisters, Dorothy Mathews, Debra McIntire, Susan Frank, cousin Valkyrie Houston and Dorothy's husband, Harold Mathews (Cahuilla), selflessly shared resources and information with me and more importantly their friendship and faith that this project would actually be done.

Thank you, Professor Clifford Trafzer, who gave me the opportunity and offered needed guidance. Anthropologist Lowell Bean for his insights and much appreciated conversations. Scholar Lisa Woodward for generously sharing her research and knowledge. Archivists Kevin Hallaran and Bill Bell for their encouragement and discovery of vital facts which added to the story. Pat Murkland for her talent and support of the project and Joan Hall for building the index for this work, and for being a kindred spirit.

My deep thanks, in particular, go to all the Native Californians from throughout the reservations of Southern California who so thoughtfully gave of their time and experience and permitted me to benefit from their wealth of knowledge and understanding: people such as Robert Levi, Joe Guacheño, Gloria Wright, Pauline Murillo, Mary Magee, Francis De Los Reyes, Paul Cuero, Manuel Hamilton, Ann Hamilton, Charlene Ryan, VirginiaScribner, JoMay Modesto, Celeste Hughes, Mike Connelly, Willie Pink, Chris Sandoval, Ray Reeder, and Ernest Siva.

FIESTA DAY

of the

Mission Indian Federation

at Council Grounds, 181 E. Prospect Avenue
RIVERSIDE, CALIFORNIA

Thursday, October 17

Begining Promptly at 10:30 in the Morning

A Splendid Program of Speaking, Music and Singing

BARBECUE
from 12 to 2 P. M.

Cafe and Refreshment
Booth on Grounds

Indian Hand-work
For Sale

conducted by
Indian Women

October 19 – Dedication of Indian Collection at Pomona

A DELEGATION OF INDIANS
will come from Northern California Grand President

EVERYBODY IS INVITED

Mission Indian Federation flyer from the Evans Collection,
Archives, Riverside Metropolitan Museum, Riverside, California

INTRODUCTION

In 1851, Cupeño Indian resistance leader Antonio Garra wrote to a potential ally that the fight for justice, sovereignty and equal rights for Southern California Indians was a "war for a whole life."[1] For more than 250 years, Indians of Southern California have waged a constant battle to secure their lands, natural resources, and respect for themselves and their way of life. It is a war fought for the rights guaranteed them through treaties callously discarded by disreputable federal and state governments eager to advance their own imperialistic designs over the fertile lands of California.

The war has taken many shapes. Resistance in Southern California ranged from escape when possible to violence and assassination when forced. Acts of civil disobedience ranged from blocking roads to blocking legislation. They have waged war with guns and law books but they have never surrendered their beliefs or their homes easily to the Euro-American invaders of their land. Throughout this struggle there were leaders who stepped forward to give voice to the needs of their people. These men, and later women, sprang from the hereditary leadership clans of Southern California Indians and accepted the responsibilities of their traditional roles despite acrimony and hostility from the growing Anglo world around them. Their story, like the story of the people they led, was one of adaptability to the changing trials of their lives. These leaders such as Juan Antonio, Olegario Calac, William Pablo, Leonicio Lugo and Adam Castillo provided stability and a consistent link to the traditions that had sustained the people of the area for thousands of years.

This work follows the path of leadership, resistance and adaptation that provided direction during times of confusion, showed strength when outside forces seemed overwhelming, and inspired hope when days seemed darkest. The names and actions of these individuals are unknown to most but their actions were as heroic, determined and selfless as any in the history of this continent's first nations. Their stories are not about the joys of success but dedication to the ways of their ancestors and commitment to the lives of the people who remained. It was not the moments of victory that marked their lives but instead the heroic attempts to do what was right because it was right, regardless of the consequences.

Early California history was not kind to its native people. Writers often labeled California Indians as dull, docile victims—mere casualties to the avaricious greed of Euro-Americans.

That is an inaccurate and simplistic assessment. From the mission revolts of the eighteenth and nineteenth centuries to the political activism of the Mission Indian Federation in the twentieth century, Southern California Indians, despite unrelenting hardship, neglect, and abuse, survived, produced leaders of dynamic worth and character, and tenaciously protected their cultures. They also were highly pragmatic people who often conformed to the new realities they faced. Much was lost but much was hidden from the insidious view of outside invaders. This book examines the pattern of resistance among Southern California Indians and the leaders who emerged to continue the struggle, challenging those who would be their oppressors. It is a story worth telling.

The final chapters of this work center on a native political organization which unified the tribes of Southern California in 1919 and went on to be a force for activism and native civil rights throughout the Southwest and across the nation. The Mission Indian Federation was built on a legacy of sacrifice of earlier Kumeyaay, Cupeño, Luiseño, Cahuilla, and Serrano resistance leaders who organized, fought, and died for the rights of their race and culture. Federation leadership also emerged from those families whose ancestors had borne that hereditary responsibility.

The Federation wove the numerous tribelets of Southern California into a viable political entity. At the height of its operation, particularly in the 1930s, the Federation operated as an independent native government, often in opposition to the federal hierarchy which sought to control reservations by rigid control of native practices and leadership. Openly defying the Bureau of Indian Affairs, the Federation appointed its own captains and judges to reservations throughout Southern California, and created its own police force as protection from oppressive federal officers, white and Indian. Under the long tenure of Federation Grand President Adam Castillo, the organization became an unshakeable voice for acknowledgement of the abrogated 1852 treaties and fair compensation for the broken promises of those treaties.

From the burning of the San Diego mission in 1775 to the killing of Indian Agent William Stanley in 1912 and the Campo Shootings of 1927 and beyond, Indians of Southern California have consistently resisted assaults on their way of life. They steadfastly followed traditional leaders of skill and courage even when threatened with punishment. From initial contact through violent conflict, segregated reservations, discarded treaties and broken promises, allotment of tribal lands and hostile government policies, Native Americans of Southern California remained true to their culture, their religion and their understanding of the world. They killed when necessary, compromised when forced and fled when other options failed. But, always, they maintained their connection to the native world of their fathers and those leaders who rose from this traditional world, accepting the inherited burden that came with leadership. As loss, death and disruption brought alterations to the traditional world of some patriarchal native cultures, women stepped forward to fill a political and spiritual void.

Indian culture remains the bridge to understanding the native world. It is a spiritual construction of the universe; it is a way to maintain balance in a world where center is sometimes hard to find. Songs, dances, stories, art, religious ritual, and a sense of place all combine to define Indian people. Native Americans never left their homelands looking for a New World. The invaders of their homes were the foreigners.

The fight of those who came before was not lost on Mission Indian Federation President Adam Castillo. As late as 1951, Castillo invoked the spirit and sacrifice of Olegario Calac in a petition to the Secretary of the Interior, when he wrote that Calac was "an enthusiastic defender of his people and disposed to take advanced grounds on questions of their rights." Their rights and the war they waged to secure them was for a whole life.

Notes: _____

[1] Indian Department agent, John G. Ames, August 1873 as quoted by Benjamin David Wilson, "Observation on Early Days in California and New Mexico," annual publication of the *Quarterly of the Historical Society of Southern California*, (1934), 138; Arthur Woodward, "The Garra Revolt of 1851," *Westerners Brand Book* (Los Angeles Corral, 1947), 115.

THIS WAR

IS

FOR

A WHOLE LIFE

The Culture of Resistance Among

Southern California Indians, 1850–1966

1 Strangers in Their Own Land

*The priests can not hurt me—I am a medicine man...
If they shoot at me water will come out of the cannon;
if they shoot at me, the bullet will not enter my flesh.*[1]

—*Chumash informant Maria Solares, expressed during Chumash revolt, 1824.*

Rafael Solares, a Santa Inez
Chumash man, 1878. Rafael
was the father-in-law of
Maria Solares. Hayward
& Muzzall, photographic
artists, Santa Barbara, CA

Courtesy of Bancroft
Library, University of
California, Berkeley,
Online Archive of CA

Clara Sitales was a young girl in 1841—perhaps 15 years old. She was also known as Clara Tecupa, being a direct descendant of the Acjachemem Chief Tecupero. Her mother also was named Clara and her father, Diego, was a neophyte of the Mission at San Juan Capistrano. Clara's world was that of the missions and the padres who operated them. Instruction, labor, and discipline as defined by the Franciscans ruled that world, and there was no room for compromise. Neophytes such as her father toiled long hours to build, expand, and repair the mission buildings, plant nearby fields, and tend to the Mission's livestock. Any remaining hours were filled with learning the dogmatic lessons of the Christian faith. Girls such as Clara were often separated from their parents and other tribal members to prevent them from being defiled by latent pagan practices, or by the ever-present Spanish soldiers.[2]

The missionaries and their soldiers first came to the San Juan area in the fall of 1775. The Spaniards needed an area of rest and safety when making the journey from San Diego de Alcalá to Mission San Gabriel Arcángel. Franciscan Priest Junípero Serra, the father of California's mission system and President of the 1769 "Sacred Expedition,"[3] led them. They erected the cross of Christ and began work on a chapel. An insurrection by Kumeyaay Indians near San Diego, however, put a quick halt to all activity and the Spaniards returned to the safety of the San Diego Presidio. A year later Serra and the Spaniards came again and renewed their construction with the help of the "Juaneño," as they called the Acjachemem because of their affiliation with the Mission. Spanish priests successfully founded Mission San Juan Capistrano on November 1, 1776.[4]

Nearby were Juaneño Indian villages with names like Sejat, Putuidem, Ahachmai, Piwiva, Humai, and Clara's village of Alona, north of the mission and nestled in one of the lush canyons of the Santa Ana Mountains. Her people believed it a safe place. Villagers had mixed feelings about these new white men, including the priests. Some listened to the teachings of the padres and prayed to the man on the cross. Others clung to their lives as they had been and the stories that told of their arrival at this place given them by their God, Wiyot, and later Chingichngish. Still others combined elements of old and new, creating religious hybrids in which they found understanding.

Fray Junipero Serra of the Franciscan Order was the father of the California mission system, which had twenty-one missions and various cattle outposts such as San Bernardino.
Courtesy of Agua Caliente Cultural Museum, Palm Springs, CA. Historic Postcards Collection 1900-2000, Online Archive of California.

If the Juaneños lost some control of their lives with the arrival of the Spanish and suffered through efforts to make them conform, they suffered again when political conditions changed in the 1820s. Mexico won its independence and broke away from the colonial authority of Spain. California became Mexican territory. New administrators arrived who resented the grip that the Franciscans had on the life of Californians and the vast tracts of lands they administered. For the civilian and military authorities of Mexico, breaking the domination of the friars became a priority. In 1826, California Governor José María Echeandía began the gradual emancipation of Indian neophytes.

His decree curtailed the control of the padres over those Indians near the missions. It began the de-secularization of the missions throughout California and removed Church control of California land. Governor José Figueroa ended mission activities at Capistrano in 1833 and declared that much of the land would be held as a pueblo for the free Indians of the area and their livestock. This ideal, however, had to be carried out by men of good will and honest hearts. Such men were a minority in California in the 1830s.[5]

For Indian people in particular, Figueroa's emancipation was ill-defined. The government plan did not specify exactly which lands belonged to the Juaneño and which could be settled by Mexican colonists. Many Juaneño resisted the plan, or did not want to move from traditional sites to lands proposed by the authorities. Many simply returned or stayed at the village sites known to their ancestors and left the mission to the politics and machinations of the padres and their new masters, the Mexican administrators. The number of Juaneño near the mission dwindled as neophyte deserters joined their gentile brothers and sisters. Figueroa came under increasing pressure from what one author termed a "covetous young California crowd" of opportunists pushing him to distribute the land to the many Mexican speculators who clamored for possession and wealth.[6]

Figueroa appointed administrators to control the situation and appropriate the mission holdings. In 1841 California Governor Juan Bautista Alvarado gave Santiago Argüello a grant to Rancho Trabuco and the canyons that included the Alona village site, the home of Clara Sitales. She once recalled when the vaqueros came. They said the land kept for centuries by the Juaneño belonged now to Mexican rancheros—land they needed for their cattle. Village elders refused. This was their land as promised by the padres. They were emancipated Indians now and could live as they wished. The vaqueros returned, however. This time they told the villagers that there was a big fiesta at the Mission and all had to attend. Some Juaneños went willingly but others were suspicious and refused to leave their village. Those who refused were hunted down by the mounted vaqueros who herded them like cattle toward the mission, even lassoing the ones that made trouble, dragging them down the road to their fiesta.[7]

The Juaneño were forced to remain around the mission for days. During this time, Clara and others saw plumes of black smoke billowing up from the distant canyon that held Alona. Finally, when Clara and her people returned to their village site, they found only the charred remains of what had once been their homes. Their possessions, clothing, everything they owned was destroyed as well. Their animals were gone. The people were in a state of confusion. Many Juaneño just began drifting from the area, going north to the pueblo of Los Angeles or inland to their Luiseño cousins. Some stayed in the San Juan area, living in modest thatched shelters along the small creek bed that runs to the sea.[8]

Clara's family took refuge in the outskirts of Los Angeles. It was a place known today as North Broadway—a ghetto where other Indians lived and called "Dogtown." There, Indians crowded into dilapidated shacks where poverty and hunger were constant companions. Clara became a medicine woman like her mother. She married José María Uribez and bore him children but continued her doctoring ways. Her descendants speak of a mystical quality that was Clara's. She knew the power of herbs and healed with them. Age and distance prevented her from gathering the herbs herself but she directed others to those sites where the needed plants flourished, even though she had never seen the areas. Her reputation spread and Indians came from far around to visit her and gain from her knowledge. She died in Los Angeles in 1912, an honored elder and healer among a forgotten people.[9]

Clara's story is similar to those of many Southern California Indians following their encounter with Europeans. From the moment in 1769 when the expedition of Gaspar de Portolá made contact with the tribes of the region, their lives and lifestyles came under attack and would never be the same. As described by some authors, "they were fugitives, displaced groups, and literally strangers in their own land."[10]

This work will examine resistance, from the lone native lifting a fist in defiance of his tormentors to that of pan-tribal cooperation in the nineteenth century, and the sophisticated efforts of pan-tribal political organizations of the twentieth century. It is a story common to the plight of Native Americans across the United States. The initial curiosity exhibited by intruders who invaded Indian territory quickly turned to disdain, abuse, and neglect by members of these encroaching cultures, whether Spaniard, Mexican, British, or American. In Southern California, the lack of large-scale warfare created an image of Indians in the region as dull-witted, frightened, and docile victims of larger and more dominant cultures. It is a false image. As with the slander toward the black slaves of America's southeast, it is a rationalization and justification that white European and later American Christians chose to accept and promulgate to soften the stark reality of a society which could condone the genocidal practices enacted by a reportedly civilized nation. It is a legacy of shame.

The response of Southern California native peoples to the invaders ranged from curiosity and bewilderment to fear and anger. These probably are the same reactions that all human beings, whatever their race or ethnicity, anywhere in the world have felt when awakening one day to the presence of well-armed and menacing foreigners in their midst. Perhaps, that is why initial impressions of the priests who accompanied the soldiers were more favorable, because they seemed less threatening. The priests spoke kindly and carried the man on the cross who, at least in the beginning, meant them no harm.

Southern California Indians were not prepared for the onslaught of coercion, physical, emotional, and spiritual. They had dealt with enemies but had experienced nothing to prepare them to endure under these new invaders. These were not the nomadic tribes of the Great Plains with their warrior societies, but small political and social organizations contained within larger tribal units. These were democracies in the true sense of the word where consensus ruled. War generally was resorted to as a means to resolve an insult, or a breach of promise, or an abduction, or a retaliation for some manner of sorcery or violations of tribal territories or resources. It was not, as Europeans understood it, a mechanism to conquer territory, subjugate other peoples, or a means to force others to believe and think as they did.[11] The brutality of the Europeans, however, forced Southern California Indians

North Broadway area, Los Angeles, 1873.
Courtesy of Los Angeles Public Library Photo Collection

to understand aggression on a different level. These naturally peaceful people learned compromise, flight, deception, and violent resistance as a way of survival.

A sense of place defined the tribes of Southern California. Their environment certainly contributed to the social interaction of tribes throughout the region. They moved with the seasons within traditional territories. At various temporary village sites they hunted, fished, and gathered food from the area's abundance. They traded prolifically. Neighbors and cousins to the Juaneño were The Kumivit or Gabrieleño people. They lived north of San Juan in what is today the Los Angeles Basin. Their name later derived from their association with the Mission at San Gabriel. The extensive networking by Indian groups such as the Gabrieleño later proved invaluable for the survival of these and other Southern California Indians. Flight from the European aggressors was often the most expedient choice by enslaved Indians.[12]

Gabrieleño village sites, either permanent or temporary, extended to areas around the present-day inland cities of Riverside, San Bernardino, Redlands, Crafton, and Corona, where they actively exchanged trade goods and interacted culturally with the Serrano, Cahuilla and Luiseño nations. Shells, shell beads, and steatite from the coastal plain and offshore islands were customarily used as means of exchange, making their way across the desert to the Mohave Indians to the east and the Ipai-Tipai to the south. Ideas passed as easily as trade goods among these people. Belief in the God Chingichngish began among the Gabrieleño and quickly spread with little variation to the Luiseño, Juaneño, Cupeño and Ipai-Tipai.[13]

Old Graveyard, San Gabriel Mission, nd.
Courtesy of Agua Caliente Cultural Museum, Palms Springs, CA.
Historic Postcards Collection 1900-2000, Online Archive of California.

One can easily imagine that the generally positive reception given the Spaniards by California Indians might be expected. While these foreigners looked and acted strangely, they would have afforded the prospect of new trading partners. While cautiously curious, it is doubtful that many Southern California Indians initially suspected that these oddly dressed, white-skinned people would be intent on taking their lands, raping their women, denigrating their culture and religion, and enslaving the general Indian population for the imagined needs of the newcomers. Indians soon learned these harsh realities.

Within the forced enslavement of the mission system, harsh treatment, confined living space, and disease took its toll on the Indian population. Their Spanish jailers, primarily soldiers, lost even guarded respect for their prisoners. Shifting opinions reflect the deteriorating physical conditions that plagued Southern California Indians who were forcibly removed from their homes. In 1769, both soldier and priest found positive receptions among the Indians. Miguel Costansó, Portolá's engineer, wrote that "the whole country is inhabited by a large number of Indians...They are very docile and tractable, especially from San Diego onward."[14] Father Juan Crespi also accompanied the Portolá expedition. He wrote that the Chumash "are of good figure and disposition, active, industrious, and inventive. They have surprising skill and ability in the construction of their canoes."[15] French ship Captain Auguste Duhaut-Cilly offered a more jaundiced interpretation of the Indians of Alta California during his voyage along the coast of California in the latter 1820s as the mission system was coming to an end. He viewed the Indians as disassociated, unable to form a nation. "Even their languages exhibit great variation over small distances," he wrote.

"This race of Indians is one of the dirtiest in the world," Duhaut-Cilly said. Physically, "while athletically formed, they have neither grace nor beauty," and, "the ensemble of their crudely fashioned features is a sign of stupidity, an overall characteristic of their appearance."[16] Yet, Duhaut-Cilly highly praised the artistry and skill that Indians showed in making their clothing, baskets, and even their arrows. However, the French mariner was acutely aware of the debilitating effects on Indians from the loss of freedom. He wrote that the high mortality rate among Indians "lies entirely in slavery, which withers the faculties and weakens the body." [17] According to some accounts, Native Americans in Baja succumbed quickly to the Spanish invaders. That would not prove to be the case in Alta California where opposition to conversion and abuse by authorities was readily apparent.[18]

Resistance to the injustices imposed upon the original inhabitants of California took many forms. At times, individuals acted alone attacking their oppressors where and when possible. When the opportunity arose, groups of Indians, like inmates of a prison camp, would secretly organize and make plans to rise and expel or kill the invaders of their land. But, as with Clara Sitales and countless other Native Americans since the European discovery, the most expedient means of resistance was escape. Duhaut-Cilly understood that when he wrote that "some [Indians] put a great value on freedom and seek to get it by fleeing… these men have only exercised the most natural of rights."[19]

Escape—flight from oppression—became commonplace among all Indians including those in Southern California. The success of many who chose this path to survival is due to the networks of trade and familial relationships that typified Southern California tribes, whether their traditional homes were along the coast or the Colorado River. Historian Douglas Hurt wrote that "flight from the missions, or fugitivism, became the most widespread form of active resistance."[20] It was not uncommon for many of these fugitives to find refuge among the villages of gentile or unchristianized Indians in California's interior. When fur trapper and American adventurer Jedediah Smith explored the Colorado River valley in 1826, he was guided by "two Indians who had escaped from Mission San Gabriel."[21]

California Indians resisted repeated attempts to erase any sign of their existence from the land stolen from them. However, their tactics of resistance were marginalized by later historians and chroniclers of the events that shaped the state of California. Occasional outbursts of violent conflict occurred but as with native counterparts on the East Coast, they were on the front lines of the Euro-American invasion. Much of the resistance of Southern California Indians was characterized by a quiet war: a war of obstruction, sabotage and assassination. Often their silence when dealing with Anglos obscured the heroic actions of their ancestors. Early writers of the mission system became propagandists of a distorted image of Southern California Indians. In 1907 William Smythe, in his history of San Diego, wrote that the Indians of Southern Alta California were "covetous, thievish and sneaking creature[s]" who were held in contempt by all except the missionaries. He continued that they had very few brave men and "ran like so many curs before the snap of a whip the moment their enemy obtained a momentary advantage." They had only a "vague, instinctive belief in a supreme being," Smythe said.[22]

One hundred years later, many historians still view California Indians as irrelevant and hapless victims. Author and historian Larry McMurtry wrote that "when it came to near total obscurity, the California Indians were in a class by themselves;" swept away "with brutal efficiency.…To this day, for that matter, the California Indians have contributed almost nothing to the popular iconography of the West," with the exception of the "noble [Modoc] Captain Jack" who led an uprising against federal troops in the early 1870s in Northern California.[23]

Ironically, Spanish law provided safeguards against the exploitation and abuse of indigenous peoples overseen by the Crown, including the *Ordenanzas sobre descubrimientos* of 1573, and the *Recopilacion de leyes de las Indias* of 1681. Historian Van H. Garner wrote that, "by 1769, when Spaniards moved into California, they carried with them a tradition of humane missionary expansion into frontier areas and their laws not only guaranteed Indian rights of citizenship, but also protected Indian rights to the land they occupied." This protection by the rule of law continued under the Mexican government, said Garner, although he acknowledged that such laws were not always "totally effective."[24] Stories such as that of Clara Sitales and the work of historians such as Edward Castillo, Robert Jackson, Clifford Trafzer, George Phillips, James Sandos and Florence Shipek speak to the gross understatement of Garner's assessment. Rape of Indian women was all too commonplace and the perpetrators included not only the leather-jacketed Spanish soldiers but the priest protectors of the missions. Despite the announced intentions of the Franciscan fathers and the Spanish civilian and military authorities, the missions became the equivalent of forced labor camps where religious instruction was punctuated by brutality and depravation. Although Spain had outlawed Indian slavery, defacto slavery existed in the missions. Castillo called the missions "coercive authoritarian institutions."[25]

Resistance to this oppressive rule did not often take the forms of large pitched battles as seen in the eastern United States and the Great Plains, but in California, Indians resisted "piecemeal," wrote author Yolanda Montijo. "It is defiance, up front, often face to face, with guns, or knives, or stones, or hands. Yet, it is also about the idea of having to finally choose, in one way or another, action over words, and violence over non-violence, in order to protect and preserve what which is deemed most important—so important that you would give your very life. And many, many did."[26] That defiance, especially in the nineteenth century under American rule, would also find a new sophistication in the form of legal challenges and wider pan-Indian organization. It could be as intricate as a lawsuit and as simple as blocking a roadway or tearing down a fence.

Castillo, Montijo, and others have documented the numerous acts of resistance during the mission period. These include the burning of the San Diego Mission on November 5, 1775, and the killing of Friar Luís Jayme by a large group of Kumeyaay. The attack, according to

Statue of an unidentified Gabrieleño woman, San Gabriel Mission, San Gabriel, CA.
Courtesy of the author.

Father Vicente Fuster, included both gentiles and "Christian" Indians that he estimated as "more than six hundred."[27] Fuster recounted how Indians surrounded their rancheria and set it afire. He remembered "so many arrows that you could not possibly count them."[28] By morning the attackers had dispersed, leaving a destroyed mission complex. Marie Beebe and Robert M. Senkewicz wrote that despite being rebuilt, San Diego mission never attracted large numbers of native people, and Spanish and Mexican control of the area east and south of San Diego "always remained very tenuous."[29]

In July 1781 Quechan Indians along the Colorado River killed an estimated fifty Spaniards and took other prisoners to reclaim lands wrongly usurped by the invaders. Five years later, Kumivit (Gabrieleño) and Serrano Indians under the leadership of a neophyte named Nicholas José and female shaman Toypurina united six villages in a revolt against the San Gabriel mission. Spaniards, however, discovered the plot, and Spanish authorities exiled Nicholas José and Toypurina to distant corners of the mission system.[30]

During the Spanish period, perhaps the largest revolt occurred in 1824 at Mission La Purisma among the Chumash near today's Lompoc. An estimated two thousand Indians enraged by abuse and mistreatment destroyed many of the mission buildings. Several hundred barricaded themselves in a church and held out against Spanish military for almost a month before being overwhelmed.[31] Leaders of the revolt were either executed or condemned to a chain gang. At least two Chumash leaders escaped.[32] There are also cases of neophytes poisoning priests; Father Andrés Quintana, a priest known for his barbarity, was murdered by the Indians at Mission Santa Cruz in 1812.[33]

Mission outposts also existed under constant threat of destruction. The estancia located in today's Redlands was destroyed in 1834 after two separate attacks. Initial attacks by Paiute Indians raiding through Cajon Pass from the Mojave Desert destroyed buildings and ran off livestock in 1831. The Paiutes returned in October 1834 and succeeded in forcing defenders of the outpost to retreat toward San Gabriel. Intense fighting finally held sway against the Paiutes, stopping a suspected attack on Mission San Gabriel itself.[34]   Two renegade neophyte chiefs, who had previously escaped from Mission San Gabriel, planned a similar attack against that mission in December 1834. An estimated two hundred Indians, possibly Cahuilla, stopped to lay siege to the cattle outpost in San Bernardino Valley. The estancia was captured, laid to waste, and burned. The Indians took Padre Tómas Estenaga prisoner and held him for ransom. With secularization of the mission system under way, Church authorities at San Gabriel decided to abandon the San Bernardino estancia.[35]

When all else failed, when escape was futile and physical intimidation prevailed, silence became a weapon of protection and preservation. "Indians…purposefully withheld information, a trait often interpreted negatively by whites as a sign of Indian passivity and dullness."[36] In 1872 observer Stephen Powers, who had traveled extensively among the Northern California peoples, characterized them as a "shy, foxy, secretive, close-mouthed race."[37] He conceded, however, that "this singular secretiveness has kept the great body of the whites in profound ignorance of their ideas."[38]

In Southern California, Native Americans adhered to the new beliefs of the padres but did not surrender their faith in the religions of their ancestors. California Indians folded traditional ceremony into the ritualistic practices of Roman Catholic holy days. This was no contradiction but indicative of the flexibility incorporated within their religious cosmology. In 1900 an observation by anthropologist Constance Dubois interestingly showed the convergence of traditional practice and adopted Catholic beliefs during a visit to Mesa Grande Reservation in San Diego County. Food vendors had gathered for the first day of the fiesta. "An air of expectancy and preparation pervaded the scene,"[39] Dubois noted.

Mistakenly christened an asistencia, the building provided a romanticized version of the San Bernardino estancia (cattle outpost). It was reconstructed from ruins by the WPA in 1937 and the San Bernardino County Historical Society.
Courtesy of the National Archives and Records Administration.

Special preparations were made for the visiting priest and the Bishop, "whose rare presence at this fiesta lent it an especial sanctity."[40] Not surprisingly "religious worship" was the "most important feature of the day," Dubois reported. However, "upon the return to the fiesta ground the secular pleasures of the day began in earnest," although Indian dances were not to be performed, since, "Father Antonio [had] long discouraged these reminders of barbarism." Other white visitors, however, offered the dancers a monetary bribe to disregard the prohibition, which Dubois said was done "with enthusiasm."[41]

Whether initiated by war parties such as the one that destroyed the San Bernardino estancia or the actions of lone assassins who slowly and silently stole the lives of their persecutors, California Indians actively plotted and worked for their freedom and the protection of their way of life. Many historians have denigrated the efforts of Southern California Indians or overlooked the complexity of human action that drove them to fight for their cultural and literal life. If the so-called "Digger Indians" were as devoid of human agency as promulgated by some authors, they surely would have disappeared from the political, social and cultural landscapes of California. Past observers and historians have misrepresented their history.

Southern California Indians learned, adapted and survived within a world hostile to their very existence. They survived and survive today because of the astute forms of resistance which they utilized. It is a cultural tenacity worthy of respect.

In Southern California Native American cultures, datura or jimson weed was an important medicine plant and was used in rituals. Courtesy of Pat Murkland.

Notes:

[1] Maria Solares as quoted by Ed Castillo in, "Blood Came from their Mouths: Tongva and Chumash Responses to the Pandemic of 1801," *American Indian Culture and Research Journal*, Vol. 23, No. 3 (1999), 54.

[2] Information about Clara Sitales (Clara Tecupa) comes from transcripts of interviews done with Manuel Machado, the great-great-grandson of Clara Sitales. The transcripts were provided the writer by Manuel Machado's cousin Dorothy Machado Mathews and represent the oral tradition of the family. Manuel Machado's mother, Juanita Rossetti Ortega, lived with her grandmother from an early age until the death of Clara when Juanita was 16. Under the 1928 Indian Jurisdictional Act, Juanita brought her children to Pala Reservation in Riverside County, California, where they were enrolled as Juaneño/Gabrieleño Indians.

It is doubtful that the expulsion of the Juaneño from Trabuco Canyon took place in 1820 or 1825 as remembered by Manuel Machado. A more plausible time period would be between 1834 (when secularization of the missions took effect) and specifically 1841 when Captain Santiago Argüello was given the grant to Rancho Trabuco. California Governor José Figueroa issued his decree of confiscation in August 1834. Father Zephyrin Engelhardt in his 1922 book on the San Juan Capistrano Mission details the actions of competitive Mexican land speculators who vied for the rights to the extensive Mission properties in the ensuing years. By December 1840, Agustin Janssens was made acting mayordomo by authorities. "Janssens had been living for a time at Trabuco as representative of Captain Argüello who was soliciting a grant of the rancho." See Fr. Zephyrin Engelhardt, *San Juan Capistrano Mission* (Los Angeles, Cal.: The Standard Printing Co., 1922), 114, 129. Argüello was a former administrator of the mission properties in San Juan. Author Lisbeth Haas, wrote that the Juaneños had sought and been denied legal right to their properties after the decree of confiscation; they formally protested the encroachment by Mexican elite. "In 1841 the still-resident missionary stated, 'The Indian community came and informed me that efforts had been made to deprive them of Trabuco, Mission Vieja and Yuguilli.'" See Lisbeth Haas, *Conquests and Historical Identities in California, 1769-1936* (Berkeley and Los Angeles, California: University of California Press, 1995), 39.

[3] Clifford Trafzer in, *As Long As the Grass Shall Grow And Rivers Flow, A History of Native Americans* (Belmont, CA: Wadsworth Group, 2000), 33.

[4] Hubert Howe Bancroft, *The History of California*, vol. 1, 1542-1800, (San Francisco: A.L. Bancroft & Company, 1885), 298-303.

[5] Bancroft, *The History of California*, vol. 3, 1825-1840, 102-108, 336.

[6] Engelhardt, *San Juan Capistrano Mission*, 111-115.

[7] Ibid., 120-121; Oral history of Manuel Machado.

[8] Ibid., Machado.

[9] Ibid.

[10] James R. Young, Dennis Moristo, G. David Tenebaum, *American Indian Treaties Publications Series: An Inventory of the Mission Indian Agency Records* (Los Angeles: American Indian Studies Center, UCLA, 1976), 2.

[11] Lowell John Bean and Charles R. Smith, "Gabrielino," in *Handbook of North American Indians*, William C. Sturtevant, ed., v. 8, California, Robert Heizer, ed. (Washington, D.C.: Smithsonian Institution, 1978), 546-548.

[12] Ibid. The spelling of Gabrielino is used commonly by most historians. However, the Spanish spelling of Gabrieleño continues to be used by some descendants of these people in Southern California.

[13] Ibid., Bean and Smith; Bernice Johnston, *California's Gabrielino Indians* (Los Angeles, California: Southwest Museum, 1962), 16; William Duncan Strong, *Aboriginal Society in Southern California* (Banning, California: Malki Museum Press, 1972), 8. A. L. Kroeber wrote that San Bernardino Valley was primarily inhabited by the Serrano people. However, Strong using both Serrano and Cahuilla informants in the 1920s found that there was common knowledge of Gabrielino sites in San Bernardino, Redlands and Crafton. His informants said that these sites "had originally been occupied by people who spoke the San Gabriel

language. The original owners had been succeeded by the Mountain Cahuilla who were brought down to the San Bernardino mission about 1846." The site mentioned in San Bernardino is most certainly what became known as Politana and was the home village for Cahuilla leader Juan Antonio when he and his people protected the ranchos of the Lugo family from marauding Paiutes. This is corroborated by G. Hazen Shinn as told him by Serrano and Cahuilla friends in 1885. Johnston quotes Shinn's informants as identifying the "pre-historic Gabrieliño village of Homhoa." Johnston states that Homhoa "existed at a spot between the present Colton Avenue and the Southern Pacific railroad tracks east of the Santa Ana River on lands that were taken over by the San Gabriel Mission fathers in 1810, now in Colton." While this 1810 date has now been refuted, the location of the Homhoa village site is consistent with the site of warm springs in a canyon near today's city of Loma Linda.

[14] Miguel Costansó, "1769: A Beachhead at San Diego, Miguel Costansó," in, *Lands of Promise and Despair: Chronicles of Early California, 1535 – 1846*, Rose Marie Beebe and Robert M. Senkewicz, eds. (Berkeley, CA: Heyday Books (Santa Clara University, 2001), 117.

[15] Johnston, *California's Gabrielino Indians*,7.

[16] Auguste Duhaut-Cilly in *A Voyage to California, the Sandwich Islands, & Around the World in the Years 1826-1829*, August Frugé and Neal Harlow, eds. (San Francisco: The Book Club of California, 1997), 164-166.

[17] Ibid., 118.

[18] Bruce Harley, "Did Mission San Gabriel have two Asistencias? The Case of Rancho San Bernardino," *San Bernardino County Museum Association Quarterly*, (Winter, 1989), 9.

[19] Duhaut-Cilly, *A Voyage to California*, 96.

[20] Douglas Hurt, *The Indian Frontier, 1763-1846* (Albuquerque: University of New Mexico Press, 2002), 63.

[21] *Lands of Promise and Despair*, Beebe and Senkewicz, eds., 357.

[22] William Ellsworth Smythe, *History of San Diego, 1542-1907: An Account of the Rise and Progress of the Pioneer Settlement on the Pacific Coast of the United States*, (San Diego: San Diego History Co., 1907), 48-59.

[23] Larry McMurtry, *Oh, What A Slaughter: Massacres in the American West, 1846-1890* (New York: Simon & Shuster, 2005) 47-48. The Modoc war erupted in the early 1870s when the Modocs left the Klamath Reservation in Northern California for their traditional lands near Tule Lake. The Modocs had suffered from years of persecution in which the United States government supported Anglo claims against their lands. They were forced to live with the more numerous Klamath peoples with whom they had a long history of enmity. In 1873 they held out against attacks by federal troops from their stronghold in the lava beds of the area. During a peace negotiation in April 1873, Modoc leader Captain Jack killed General Edward R. S. Canby. The Modocs surrendered in June 1873. Captain Jack and five others were hanged for Canby's murder in October 1873 and the remaining members of the Modoc tribe were forcibly relocated to Quapaw land in Indian Territory.

[24] Van H. Garner, *The Broken Ring: The Destruction of the California Indian* (Tucson, Arizona: Westernlore Press, 1982), 54-56.

[25] Edward Castillo, as quoted by Clifford Trafzer in, *As Long As the Grass Shall Grow And Rivers Flow, A History of Native Americans* (Belmont, CA: Wadsworth Group, 2000), 54.

[26] Yolanda Montijo, "The Other History," *News From Native California: An Inside View of the California Indian World*, (Spring 1993), 5.

[27] Vicente Fuster, "1775: Rebellion at San Diego," *Lands of Promise and Despair*, 186-192.

[28] Ibid.

[29] *Lands of Promise and Despair*, Beebe and Senkewicz, eds., 186-192.

[30] Montijo, "The Other History," 5-6; Edward Castillo, "Gender Status Decline, Resistance, and Accomodation among Female Neophytes in the Missions of California: A San Gabriel Case Study," *American Indian Culture and Research Journal*, (1994), 67-93. Early work has identified Nicholas Jose and Toypurina as

Gabrieleño. However, a 2004 report by archaelogist and ethnographer Dr. Chester King presents evidence that they were actually Serrano. See Chester King, "Ethnographic Overview of the Angeles National Forest: Tataviam and San Gabriel Mountain Serrano Ethnohistory," prepared for the U.S. Department of Agriculture, Southern California Province, February 6, 2004, 19-20.

[31] Montijo, "The Other History," 5-6.

[32] Bancroft, *History of California*, vol. 2, 536-538.

[33] "Communications, California Mission Indians: Two Perspectives," *California History*, vol. 70, no. 2 (Summer 1991), 207-238. In this article the editors examine the debate over the death of Father Quintana between Professor Edward Castillo and Professor Doyce Nunis.

[34] J.M. Guinn, *A History of California and an Extended History of Its Southern Coast Counties*, v. 1 (Los Angeles, Cal.: Historic Record Company, 1907), 434; Rev. Father Juan Caballeria, *History of the San Bernardino Valley From the Padres To The Pioneers, 1810-1851*, (San Bernardino: Times-Index Press, 1902), 74-77.

[35] Ibid.

[36] Brady, Crome & Reese, "Resist! Survival Tactics of Indian Women," *California History*, (Spring 1984), 146.

[37] Ibid.

[38] Stephen Powers as quoted by Brady, Crome & Reese in "Resist! Survival Tactics of Indian Women," 146.

[39] Constance G. Dubois, in *Some Last Century Accounts of the Indians of Southern California*, Robert F. Heizer, ed., (Ramona, California: Ballena Press, 1976), 54, 57.

[40] Ibid.

[41] Ibid.

2 THE UPRISING OF 1851: THE RIVALRY OF JUAN ANTONIO AND ANTONIO GARRA

"Lifting his eyes with a smile denoting contempt, he said in a loud and clear tone, devoid of all tremor, "Gentlemen, I ask your pardon for all my offenses and expect yours in return."[1] —Antonio Garra at his execution, 1852

Gravesite of
Antonio Garra,
Old Town San Diego
Courtesy of author

For Indians of Southern California, the transitional period from the days of Mexican control to that of the new American authority was one of suspicion and confusion. The American invasion of California in 1846 challenged existing power relationships in the state among Southern California Indians.

Chief Juan Antonio and his Mountain Cahuilla already were aligned with the powerful colonial family of António María Lugo. They were employed to protect the Lugos' property in San Bernardino Valley from Indian raiders. Their influence ranged from there south to Anza Valley of today's Riverside County. Juan Antonio maintained his strong ties to the Lugo family during the initial confrontations that marked the American incursion of California in 1846.

Others, such as the Luiseño and Cupeño of San Diego County, initially supported the new American forces or at least attempted to incur favor. The charismatic leader of many of these people was Antonio Garra. Garra was an educated man, having received his instruction at San Luis Rey Mission. "He was a man of wealth and influence," wrote Millard Hudson, "and well fitted for leadership."[2] The *Los Angeles Star* called Antonio Garra "one of the principal chiefs," whose "power and influence over the Indians is almost unbounded." That influence with the lower Colorado River tribes was very likely based on blood as well. While historians refer to Garra as a Cupeño, some contemporaries believed him to be a Quechan by birth.[3]

With the arrival of an American army in California late in 1846, Juan Antonio and Antonio Garra found themselves pitted against each other. In December of that year Californios, led by General Andres Pico, defeated General Stephen Watts Kearny and a small army of American dragoons at the Battle of San Pasqual. After the battle, a band of "renegade" Indians, from the followers of Garra, captured eleven of the Californios at nearby Pauma. Allegedly, upon the advice of an unscrupulous American named Bill Marshall, Garra's men killed their Hispanic captives, thinking to impress the Americans and garner leverage. In retaliation, a force led by José del Carmen Lugo, and aided by Juan Antonio and his Cahuilla, later ambushed Garra's men. Many of the Luiseño and Cupeño perpetrators of the massacre of Californios were, in turn, massacred while captives of Juan Antonio.[4]

The American spear point at San Pasqual had been blunted and Juan Antonio reaffirmed his commitment to the Lugo alliance by exacting punishment from the Luiseño/Cupeño perpetrators of the Pauma massacre. The killings at Pauma and Temecula strained relations between Juan Antonio and Garra. They remained suspicious rivals competing for the loyalty of the area's various tribes. This rivalry would have significant repercussions six years later.

Juan Antonio was a calculating politician. His acceptance in 1844 of an alliance with the influential family of Lugos was a way of strengthening his political position with not only the European invaders but with other tribal leaders. The Spanish and later the Mexicans controlled much of the traditional Indian territories along California's coast. The Cahuilla, however, still maintained a good deal of autonomy by their location in Inland Southern California's valleys, mountains, and desert. The real strength of the Cahuilla nation, however, lay in the tight-fisted leadership of Juan Antonio.

Juan Antonio was born in approximately 1783 in Anza Valley in the shadow of the San Jacinto Mountains. Physically, he was described as "thick, stout and wiry," a man who "looked very much like an African lion about his eyes and forehead."[5] Nothing is really known of his early life or his initial rise to power within his band of Mountain Cahuilla. Author Tom Hughes wrote that Juan Antonio's father and brother were traditional leaders from the San Gorgonio Pass area named Cabezon (the elder often referred to as "Old" as in "Old Cabezon"). These leaders ruled the Desert Cahuilla into the latter nineteenth century. Their sphere of influence extended from San Gorgonio Pass to what is now the Salton Sea. Sometime in the 1820s Juan Antonio became leader over the Cahuilla to the west, including San Timoteo Canyon and the western side of the San Jacinto and Santa Rosa mountain ranges.[6] Of the two brothers, Juan Antonio was the more warlike, Hughes said. The Serrano people called him Yámpooche, meaning, "Quick mad." Juan Antonio may have had some Spanish blood, according to Hughes, and he was known for a brutal administration of justice to his people. Juan Antonio enjoyed the absolute respect of his people, in part, due to his iron-fisted administration. Accounts of Juan Antonio burying alive an accused murderer with the corpse of his victim, or cutting off the ears of Cahuilla boys caught stealing, often find their way into stories of the famed leader.[7]

The 1850s were a time of widespread lawlessness and violence in Southern California. The new El Pueblo de La Reina de Los Angeles was largely unprotected from the gangs of cutthroats traveling to and from the northern gold fields. The closest federal troops were stationed in San Diego. Beatings, shootings and lynchings became commonplace in what one resident called a "carnival of murder."[8] The primary victims of this violence were Latinos and Indians.

Governor Juan B. Alvarado granted the Lugo family nearly 38,000 acres in the valley of San Bernardino in 1839. The family's patriarch, Don António María Lugo, gave the valley to his three sons and a nephew, Diego Sepulveda. The vast grasslands of the valley, stretching

The Lugo Ranch circa 1888. Courtesy of San Bernardino County Museum, Redlands, California.

from today's Rancho Cucamonga to Yucaipa Valley, became home to herds of horses and cattle—surplus from the Lugos' great Los Angeles rancho.[9]

Soon, however, marauding bands of High Desert Paiutes and Chemehuevis, or eastern Utes, slipped down Cajon Pass and found targets of opportunity in the vast herds of the Lugo family. Initially, the Lugos turned for protection to a newly arrived group of immigrants from New Mexico, many of them Hispanicized Indians called genízaros led by John Rowland and William Workman. Several of the genízaro families, headed by Lorenzo Trujillo, agreed to settle in San Bernardino Valley and defend the area against attacks by the "wild Indians."[10]

The genízaros, however, were soon enticed farther south to the rancho of Don Juan Bandini by the promise of several hundred acres of land, forcing the Lugos to search again for allies to defend their property. Juan Antonio and his people were invited to a large barbecue and council where "a defensive alliance formed against the wild marauders of the desert."[11] The Cahuilla inhabited an old village site near modern-day Colton adjacent to the Santa Ana River called Politana. The relationship between the Lugos and Juan Antonio's Cahuilla appears to have been beneficial for both groups and one based on mutual respect.

In May of 1851, after resisting an extortion attempt, the Lugos became the targets of a particularly brutal band of thugs under a former cavalry captain, John "Red" Irving.[12]

Irving was a former Texas Ranger who came to California looking for easy money. He led a group of outlaws, many of them Australians, who, disappointed by their failure in northern gold fields, had drifted to Los Angeles.

Irving and these so-called "Sydney Ducks" "had become the terror of the citizens of Los Angeles; they defied the laws; they robbed citizens in open day and with utter impunity," according to a local newspaper.[13] Irving demanded thousands of dollars from António María Lugo and his attorney, Joseph Lancaster Brent, in exchange for breaking Lugo's grandsons, Chico and Menito, out of jail. The young men had been arrested and charged with killing Irishman Patrick McSwiggen and a Creek Indian named Sam in Cajon Pass in January 1851. Trial testimony said the killings occurred after the Lugos and a party of vaqueros were led into an ambush while chasing Indian marauders.[14]

António Lugo and Brent rejected the attempted blackmail and Irving swore revenge. The sudden arrival of fifty United States dragoons from San Diego thwarted a plan to assassinate the Lugo grandsons when they were released from jail on bond. Soon afterward, however, Irving and his gang sought their revenge by raiding the Lugo rancho in San Bernardino Valley. Discovered by its Cahuilla defenders, the raid changed quickly into a running battle between Irving and his handful of men and several hundred Cahuilla. The Indians launched showers of arrows at the retreating outlaws. The outnumbered but well-armed Anglos rode east into the Yucaipa area, where they mistakenly turned into today's Live Oak Canyon in hopes of escaping. Trapped in the area where Live Oak Canyon spills into San Timoteo Canyon, Irving and his men were exterminated; their bodies stripped and mutilated. A posse composed of Anglo gamblers and Hispanic Californios arrived on the bloody scene shortly after the skirmish's conclusion.[15]

The relief that Anglo and Hispanic posse members felt over the elimination of the Irving menace soon changed to anger by many who believed it a worse evil that white men, even outlaws, were killed by Indians in this manner. Another potentially bloodier battle was barely averted by the arrival and intervention of local militia under command of Joshua Bean. Fearing an attack upon his Cahuilla, Juan Antonio took his people to the mountains until assured that they faced no repercussions. A coroner's inquest exonerated Juan Antonio and his people from any wrongdoing in the killings of Irving and his gang.[16] The Cahuilla remained at this time the most powerful threat to Anglo imperialism in Southern California but Juan Antonio knew that adaptation, compromise, and finally deception were the only real weapons at his command. He would exercise all of those in the months and years ahead to ensure the survival of his people.

Two months later an incident occurred that Juan Antonio, in all likelihood, staged for political purposes. In August 1851, Juan Antonio and fifty of his armed warriors rode into Los Angeles, allegedly on a rescue mission after hearing that "bad men" again threatened the city.[17] There had been no bad men this time but the Cahuilla remained in the city for three days.

In a strange turn of events, the local newspaper reported that the Cahuilla deposed Juan Antonio in a ceremony before the county judge and elected a new leader. The local newspaper reported that the Cahuilla considered Juan Antonio "too headstrong."[18] It is odd that this mission to save the city quickly turned into a political realignment of the tribe's leadership with the formalities performed so visibly with Anglo participation in Los Angeles. This was likely a ploy by Juan Antonio to deflect attention from himself and distract his enemies.

Game ca 1890.
Courtesy of Special Collections & Archives at the University of California, Riverside.

Regardless of his intentions, two months later Juan Antonio was once again firmly in command of his band of Cahuilla. One night in late October 1851 a popular game of Indian gambling called peon was played in Los Angeles, with violent results. A melee between Cahuilla people and a contingent of Californios ended with several people killed and many of the surviving Indians in jail. The next day, Juan Antonio, "with a party of his warriors," arrived in Los Angeles to "investigate" the incident. The chief was "rigged out in epaulets, and other paraphanalia of military chieftans [sic]," and conducted himself with a "martial bearing."[19] Juan Antonio's prestige was sufficient for him to liberate the members of his tribe from the town jail and return to Politana. Clearly, Juan Antonio believed that maintaining a strong profile with the Anglo community of Los Angeles lessened the potential for misunderstandings and hostile rumors to circulate.

The circumstances surrounding the killing of Irving and his men, however, foreshadowed a change for the Lugos. They nervously viewed the growing hostility of the Anglo population and sold the valley to a party of immigrant Mormons in the fall of 1851. Juan Antonio must have felt, as well, that the new American control would force a change for his people. The Mormons no longer needed the military services of Juan Antonio and the Cahuilla. The Cahuilla moved from Politana to a village they called Sahatapa in San Timoteo Canyon located to the southeast near today's city of Beaumont.[20]

Juan Antonio now realized that former alliances forged with the Lugos were meaningless in this new political climate. It would take all his political cunning and maneuvering to reposition himself under the hostile scrutiny of yet another invader, the Americans.

For Antonio Garra and the native people of San Diego County, American occupation brought immediate problems. Indians in San Diego County, with no rights of citizenship, were enraged by a tax imposed on them by the County Sheriff. The unfair taxation of Indian peoples imposed by the Sheriff of San Diego County stirred Garra to act with what was ironically a tax revolt.

Sheriff Agostin Haraszthy stated that "there is no doubt that the possessions, real and personal, of Christianized Indians, are taxable."[21] Those facing taxation were primarily members of the Luiseño, Diegueño (Kumeyaay), and Cupeño tribes. These Indians faced losing their land or livestock unless able to pay the taxes, despite the absence of any representation in California's state or county governments. This was identical to the offense that began the American Revolution against Great Britain. With no elected official to turn to, Garra saw resistance as the only option available. He sent runners to solicit help from tribes as far away as California's Central Valley, the Tulares in San Joaquin Valley, the Colorado River and Baja California. He asked them to join him in a war to expel or kill the whites between Santa Barbara and San Diego.[22]

News of Garra's plans soon swept the major Anglo centers of Los Angeles and San Diego. Local militias were organized and equipped to defend against any attacks. All the tribes including the non-Christianized, but well-armed, Cahuilla were now considered as hostiles. Duff Weaver, and his famous mountain-man brother, Paulino, had a ranch in San Gorgonio Pass near Juan Antonio's village. Duff Weaver reportedly delivered a note to the *Los Angeles Star*, allegedly written by Garra, taunting the "coward" Americans. One author suggested that a "riled" Paulino Weaver outfitted the Cahuilla and persuaded Juan Antonio to "go after" Garra.[23]

Garra's effort had limited success. In October 1851 the Quechan attacked Fort Yuma on the lower Colorado River and forced the evacuation of a small force of American soldiers. Perhaps emboldened by news of the attack on Fort Yuma, Garra, on November 23, 1851, with a force of Luiseños and Cupeños, attacked Warner's Ranch near today's Warner Hot Springs (then called Agua Caliente). The attackers killed four Americans. Other tribes, however, including Diegueño (Kumeyaay) and most Luiseños, rejected Garra's call for revolt. Tribes of the San Joaquin Valley refused to violate a peace treaty recently signed with federal authorities.[24]

Juan Antonio had no intention of joining the uprising. He did not, however, send that word to Garra. Instead, he made plans to deliver Garra to his enemies. It is likely that the Cahuilla chief believed he could form an alliance with the Americans as he had with the Lugos before them. Cahuilla traditional lands were still largely unmolested and American negotiators were moving through the state proposing a treaty of peace. It is also probable that the rivalry which marked the relationship between Juan Antonio and Garra at the time of the Pauma massacre guided Juan Antonio's decision. Without the regional pan-tribal alliance, Garra's dream of driving out the whites was hopeless.

Still, news of the attack on Fort Yuma and the deaths at Warner's Ranch combined to send the city of San Diego into a panic. Refugees with overloaded wagons of belongings crowded the streets. Word spread that Garra had three thousand warriors with him. Military authorities declared martial law, posted sentries, and formed a militia company, the Fitzgerald Volunteers, after Major E. F. Fitzgerald.[25]

In December 1851, as troops moved into the mountains near Agua Caliente to attack Garra's Los Coyotes Canyon village, Garra received a message to meet Juan Antonio and his captains (including Cabezon and Juan Bautista) at the Razon rancheria in Coachella Valley. Paulino Weaver accompanied the Cahuilla. During the meeting, the Cahuilla seized Garra and stripped him of his clothing. Juan Antonio declared that Garra was "the devil that is always playing tricks and at last I have caught you."[26] Garra was taken to the Weaver ranch and later transferred to the state militia under General Bean. He sent for his son Antonino Garra and other rebellion leaders, who also surrendered to Bean.[27]

Hearing of Garra's capture, his warriors took refuge in Los Coyotes Canyon just north of today's Borrego Valley. Troops under Major Samuel Heintzelman and Major John B. Magruder divided their forces to surround the camp. Indian Agent Oliver M. Wozencraft later reported that the Indians showed great courage in attacking the soldiers and attributed this to Garra's guarantees that he "would charm the bullets of the white men so that they would not hurt them [the Indians] any more than water."[28] The skirmish was brief, with a shower of reed arrows repulsed by musket fire of the troops; they killed an unknown number of Indians. Most then escaped except for four ringleaders, who were tried by a court-martial and shot on Christmas Day 1851.[29]

On December 26, 1851, Garra's son Antonino and three others were tried before a military court at Rancho del Chino. The verdict was simply a formality, according to one writer. At daybreak on December 27 the four men were executed by firing squad.[30] The senior Garra was transferred to Los Angeles and then to San Diego, where in early January he was tried before a military court-martial. At the end of the two-day trial the court found Garra guilty of murder and robbery. On January 10, 1852, Garra was led to his gravesite. Along the way, Garra had refused the priest's insistent urging that he pray for forgiveness. Finally succumbing to the pleas, Garra began a prayer and according to one writer, "we found that Garra knew more Latin than the priest did." As the firing squad readied itself, Garra "lifted his eyes and said, calmly and with a contemptuous smile: 'Gentlemen, I ask your pardon for all my offenses, and expect yours in return.'" With that the command to "fire" was given and "with a laugh actually upon his lips, Antonio Garra sank into his grave."[31]

The Anglo community of Southern California credited Paulino Weaver's influence with Juan Antonio for Garra's capture and quashing the Indian rebellion. Far from praising Juan Antonio, The *Los Angeles Star* noted his "remarkable cunning" and dishonesty, and attributed his participation in Garra's demise "to his judgement in choosing between two enemies rather than from any good feeling towards the Americans."[32]

Juan Antonio may have courted both sides of the conflict in an attempt to ensure his tribe's dominance, regardless of the outcome. There certainly were bad feelings between the two leaders. At Weaver's ranch, following Garra's capture, Juan Antonio continued to taunt the younger Antonino Garra until the prisoner grabbed a knife and stabbed Juan Antonio in the left arm and side, saying, "I am your prisoner but I will not permit you to insult me."[33] Another writer suggested that Juan Antonio was swayed by the lure of the $300 reward for Garra. Ironically the story of Garra's capture, probably more than any other event, established Juan Antonio's place in history as the protector of Southern California's Anglo community.[34]

What was Juan Antonio's true involvement in the rebellion? On November 21, 1851, Garra wrote Don José Estudillo (a potential ally, he hoped) that "it is possible that the San Bernardinos are now rising."[35] Yet, by the time of his meeting with Juan Antonio he apparently suspected that the Cahuilla were not with him. He had not wanted to meet with Juan Antonio, a tribal member testified, but his captains insisted that he go.[36]

With Garra's removal, Juan Antonio asserted his control as a politically powerful leader among Southern California Indians. However, the decision of the formidable Lugo

Warners Hot Springs, San Diego County, Cal.

Postcard of Warners Hot Springs, San Diego County, CA.
Courtesy of Agua Caliente Cultural Museum, Palms Springs, CA.
Historic Postcards Collection 1900-2000 Online Archive of California.

family to sell their inland valley holdings deprived Juan Antonio of his closest ally. His relationship with the new American authorities was still uncertain when Commissioner Oliver Wozencraft ordered all local tribes to meet him at Temecula to discuss a treaty in early January 1852. Juan Antonio at first declined. Wozencraft reported to Commissioner of Indian Affairs Luke Lea that the Cahuilla chief was "fully inflated with self-sufficiency" and informed Lea that "he had taken charge of the government of Indian Affairs."[37] Juan Antonio and his people finally conceded to attend the Temecula treaty conference only after Wozencraft threatened to send troops to forcibly bring them in if necessary.[38] Thus, on January 4, 1852, an indignant Juan Antonio joined with the other headmen and captains of the Serrano and Luiseño who gathered near and around the home of Pablo Apis at Temecula, California, to meet with American authorities who promised treaties of friendship that would secure the future of the southern tribes.

So, as the Cahuilla rode into Luiseño territory that January day in 1852, they were suspicious, brooding and ready for a fight. They had a very "warlike appearance as they rode up to Apis' Ranch," reported the *San Diego Herald*. The Cahuilla and Juan Antonio were suspicious of the Luiseño.[39] The rivalry between the two tribes during the American invasion in 1846 and the mutual losses inflicted at Pauma and Temecula were still keen in their memories.[40]

The Cahuilla/Luiseño rivalry created an opportunity for the Americans. Long-standing animosity and Juan Antonio's personal ambitions ensured that Garra's hope of a pan-tribal

Oliver M. Wozencraft ,1850s-1860s.
San Bernardino Public Library,
Online Archive of California

alliance was dormant for now. The Luiseño captains in San Diego County had, in fact, adopted a policy of compromise to co-exist with the Americans encroaching into their homeland.

Sixty-year-old Apis, along with Manuelito Cota, were captains of various Luiseño tribes in the area. Cota was reportedly of Diegueño and Spanish descent but gained prominence through favor with Rancho Guajome owner Cave Johnson Couts. Couts, a Tennessean who first came to California with the United States dragoons, was "a violent racist Southerner," and former slave owner with a history of cruelty, according to one writer.[41] Cota's influence grew when, after the Battle of San Pasqual in December 1846, he and Pablito Apis, stepson of the chief, cast their fate with the American invasion force and assisted in the slaughter of the eleven Californios at the Pauma Rancho. These Californios, who had participated in the attack on Kearny's dragoons, were captured while sleeping and then executed.[42] The tribes gathering at Pablo Apis' Temecula rancho had rejected Garra's recent call to form an alliance and drive Anglos from California. Pablo Apis took his people and cattle to Mission at San Luis Rey to avoid the conflict. Now, tribes and clans from all over Southern California gathered at his adobe for the ceremonial signing of a treaty of peace with American authorities.

Later on the evening of January 4, 1852, Commissioner Wozencraft called Juan Antonio to Apis' private room. Despite being credited with capturing Garra, Juan Antonio was accused of attempting to mount his own uprising. Juan Antonio assured Wozencraft that he was a "good Indian" and "a faithful guardian."[43] Wozencraft had evidence to the contrary, however. His emissary had earlier visited the tribes of the Tulare Valley and learned that Juan Antonio had sent runners to the Chowchillas and others, "asking them to join his tribe in the war."[44] Only their refusal had induced Juan Antonio, according to Wozencraft, "to be a good friend of the Americans." Caught in his treachery, Juan Antonio thought he was going to be killed, said Wozencraft, and "all his boasting arrogance departed."[45] Instead, Wozencraft bragged, Juan Antonio had been placed "in his proper position."[46]

Juan Antonio's bluff was called. He had delivered Garra and broken the back of the rebellion. Unlike the loyalty shown him by the Lugos, the Americans only demonstrated their contempt. His refusal to share power with Garra divided California Indians. His only choice now was to comply and wait for a better day to reassert himself as a leader for Indian sovereignty. After Wozencraft's reprimand, Juan Antonio offered no excuses and made no other demands at the proceedings. The next day, January 5, 1852, twenty-eight signatures, including those of the gathered tribal leaders, joined that of government negotiator Wozencraft on the document. The promises, both implied and abrogated by the treaty, set the stage for the continued mistrust and conflict between Southern California Indians and American authorities that continues today.[47] As Anglo betrayal became apparent in the years ahead, the anger of Southern California Indians turned again to action. They never surrendered their demands for cultural integrity, protection of their land resources and recognition of their rights as the area's first nations.

The Treaty of Temecula guaranteed to the signatory tribes large tracts of land stretching from San Diego County to the "eastern base of the Sierra Nevada," along with annuities and protection from white squatters attempting to force their way onto traditional ground. In return, the tribal representatives pledged their cooperation and acknowledgement of the governing power of the United States. It is important to note that the language in the treaty always referred to Southern California tribes as "nations." This distinction carried with it the implicit acknowledgement of the sovereignty of these "nations;" this point became critical to future generations of California Indians. Neither Pablo Apis nor Cota, however, signed the document. Instead, in keeping with traditional lines of leadership, they left that authority with the headmen of each of the various villages.[48]

As the various captains came forth to place their mark on the paper, they were unaware of the political forces aligned against them. While the lands they relinquished were worth millions, so was the property retained by California Indians. The new Anglo administrators of this coveted land were not about to permit California's "savages" to secure their land, even if legally mandated by the treaty.. Opposition by the California Congressional delegation and the governor were immediate. In the spring of 1852 a sympathetic United States Senate accepted California's denunciation of the treaties. With the Senate in secret session, little debate ensued before Senators rejected all eighteen treaties made with tribes throughout the state.[49]

The treaties the United States made with California tribes in Northern and Southern California were a sham of incompetence and deceit. Unlike the Spanish tradition of benignly recognizing Indian homelands, even if without formal title, the American solution to the Indian problem was to remove all tribes from California—a racial cleansing meant to steal valuable agricultural lands, timber and mineral resources, especially gold. Stealing land was easier than working it, however. Mexican rancho owners maintained and accepted Indian populations on their land as a controlled labor pool. Anglos who laid claim to lands of the former ranchos modified the system. They desired Indian labor but, as with slaves in America's South, preferred them segregated on generally useless land. These were the same people that the Treaty of Temecula promised to prevent from encroaching on Indian land.[50]

It is logical that many tribal captains accepted promises of concessions through the treaty process as preferable to Garra's violent alternative. Reinforcing the logic of that decision by their presence on January 5, 1852, was a force of United States soldiers commanded by Major Samuel P. Heintzelman, fresh from punishing renegade Garra supporters hiding in Los Coyotes Canyon.[51]

Incredibly, Garra's attempted uprising, according to popular thought among the Anglo community, was due to treating local Indians too well. The *Los Angeles Star* reported in December 1851 that "the too common mode when Indians have committed crimes…is to make a treaty with them, rig them out in red flannels and calico, and distribute liberal rations of beef. When they want more trinkets, they will wash their hands in the blood of some peaceable traveler or frontier settler, and make another treaty."[52] Whether it was through friendship, intimidation, or just dangerous political intrigue, Southern California chiefs cast their trust in the treaties. It was an ill-fated choice and perhaps one of the greatest lost opportunities in native California history.

The Treaty of Temecula set aside thousands of acres of land for the Cahuilla and Luiseño people and included most of the Santa Rosa and San Jacinto mountain ranges extending to the area of today's Redlands. While some fertile valleys were part of the established reservation, Wozencraft was "mindful not to rob Peter to pay Paul for I presume there is no white man that would be willing to live on these lands."[53] He could not have been more mistaken. With the Treaty of Temecula secretly shelved, along with the seventeen other treaties concluded with California tribes, whites encroached on Indian lands and promised annuities that were critically needed were never delivered.

Juan Antonio, however, quickly moved to reestablish his position as a dominant leader in the eyes of Southern California Indians and the American authorities. In late January 1852, Juan Antonio led a sizable force to Los Angeles, where he demanded compensation as guaranteed by the treaty. The proposed policy of annuities came under assault by Anglo critics. One writer to the *Los Angeles Star* said that "by affording sufficient provisions to the Indians to live upon without work, has created a grand 'fiesta.'" Supplying the Indians, complained the writer, "has crazed the heads of the leaders…induced pride, self-importance and clan-ships, which had almost ceased to exist."[54] In such an atmosphere it was soon evident that American authorities, however well-intentioned, would be unable to keep promises of securing livestock and other supplies for the Cahuilla. Food shortages for Southern California tribes became critical. Raids, especially by the Cahuilla, increased against local ranches, including that of the Weavers. The actions of Juan Antonio came under closer scrutiny and by the end of 1852 he stood accused of attempts to "stir up" tribes along the Colorado River. One writer referred to a "guerilla war" between primarily Cahuilla and whites that "lingered for a year in the wake of the Garra conspiracy."[55] The tribes of Southern California, treaty or no treaty, were a viable military force which when provoked took action to achieve what they knew was their right.

```
1126      PART IV.—TREATY WITH THE SAN LOUIS REY, ETC., 1852.

      by the United States for the period of five years, and as long thereafter as the Presi-
      dent shall deem advisable.  The United States will also erect suitable schoolhouses,
      shops and dwellings for the accommodation of the school-teachers, mechanics, agri-
      culturists and assistants above specified, and for the protection of the public property.
          In testimony whereof, the parties have hereunto signed their names and affixed
      their seals, this fifth day of January, in the year of our Lord one thousand eight hun-
      dred and fifty-two.                            O. M. WOZENCRAFT,  [SEAL.]
                                                       United States Indian Agent.
          For and in behalf of the San Louis Rey Indians:
      PEDRO, (Ka-wa-wish) of the Mission, his x mark.                     [SEAL.]
      CISTO, (Go-no-nish) of Las Flores, his x mark.                      [SEAL.]
      BICENTE, (Poo-clow) of Buena Vista, his x mark.                     [SEAL.]
      PABLINO, (Coo-hac-ish) of Pala, his x mark.                         [SEAL.]
      FRANCISCO, (Pah-hoo-vole) of Pauna, his x mark.                     [SEAL.]
      JOSE, (Cah-lac) of El Potrero, his x mark.                          [SEAL.]
      CALISTRO, (Chah-cwal-ish) of Yah-peet-cha, his x mark               [SEAL.]
      SANTIAGO, (Yu-loke) of La Joya, his x mark.                         [SEAL.]
      PEDRO, (Pal-e-gish) of La Puerta, his x mark.                       [SEAL.]
      BRUNO, (Cwah-si-cat) of Puerta Cruz, his x mark.                    [SEAL.]
      YSIDRO, (To-sho-vwul) of Tovin, his x mark.                         [SEAL.]
      CERVANTES, (Ca-hal) of Ahuanga, his x mark.                         [SEAL.]
      LAURIANO, (Cah-par-ah-pish) of Temecula, his x mark.               [SEAL.]
      JOSE NOCA, (Chan-gah-lang-ish) of Agua Caliente, his x mark.        [SEAL.]
      JOSE YGNACIO, (Tesh-mah-ken-ma-wish) of San Ysidro, his x mark.  [SEAL.]

          For and in behalf of the Kah-wé-as nation of Indians:
      JUAN ANTONIO, (Coos-woot-na) chief, his x mark.                     [SEAL.]
      LEONARDO, (Parlewit) of the people of Razon, his x mark.           [SEAL.]

          For and in behalf of the people of Too-va:
      FRANCISCO JAVIEL, (——) of Tierra Seca, his x mark.                 [SEAL.]
      JOSE, (Coos-pa-om-nu-it) of Pah-nuc-say, the country of Cabezon,
                                                  his x mark.             [SEAL.]
      JUAN, (Kah-we-a) of Pal-se-wish, his x mark.                        [SEAL.]
      GINIO, (——) of Wah-ne-pe-ah-pa, his x mark.                        [SEAL.]
      YLARIO, (Sahtoo) of Wah-kigh-na, his x mark.                        [SEAL.]
      TEODORO, (Chu-cal) alcalde of Juan Antonio and of Cah-be-nish,
                                      or Palma Seca, his x mark.          [SEAL.]
      YGNACIO, (Chin-gal) of the people of Toro of Pal-kay-witch-ish, or
                                      Agua Corta, his x mark.             [SEAL.]
      JUAN BAUTISTA, (Sah-at) of Pow-ky, his x mark.                      [SEAL.]
      GERONIMO, (——) of Co-ro-vang-ang, his x mark.                      [SEAL.]
      VICTORIANO, (Kwe-vish) of Sow-wah-wah, his x mark.                  [SEAL.]

          For and in behalf of the people or tribe of Cocom-cah-ras, alias Serranos:
      EHETERIO, (——) of Maronga, his x mark.                             [SEAL.]

          Signed, sealed and delivered, after being fully explained, in the presence of—
                      J. J. WARNER,
                      G. WILLIAMS,
                      L. D. VINSONHALER,
                      R. SACKETT,
                      J. HAMILTON, Secretary.

          ADDENDA.—In case the government of the United States and the actual pro-
      prietor of the Temecula grant cannot agree upon its purchase, the said government
      agrees to add some other portion of territory of equal extent to the above described
      Indian grant.                                  O. M. WOZENCRAFT,
                                                       United States Indian Agent.
          J. J. WARNER,    ⎫
          L. D. VINSONHALER, ⎬ Witnesses.
          G. WILLIAMS,     ⎪
          R. SACKETT,      ⎭
```

Treaty of Temecula, 1852

The exact motives behind Juan Antonio's actions remain unclear. He undoubtedly was angry over the unfulfilled needs of his people and the intransigence of American authorities. He may also have believed that the frustration of other tribes in a similar position opened the door for a new and successful alliance against the Americans. He was unfortunately wrong and nothing came of Juan Antonio's alleged efforts to unify the Indians of Central and Southern California. In the aftermath of Garra's uprising, American military operations against the Yumas and Mohaves along the lower Colorado River continued in 1852, hampering any participation by these fierce desert warriors in a new general revolt.[56]

Four years later, the Superintendent of Indian Affairs described the tribes in San Bernardino and San Diego Counties as having "suffered severely by their depredations."[57] Thomas Henley reported: "The Indians in and about the City of Los Angeles are in a miserable and degraded condition."[58]

Rumors of Indian disturbances had circulated with those Indians residing "in the vacinity of San Gorgonio" representing a great danger because of the inattention paid them by the government, Henley said.[59] During this time the army informed Henley that Juan Antonio had again been "visiting in a suspicious manner, not only the Yumas and Mohaves, but the Tejon, Kern and Kings River Tribes."[60] Henley responded that there was no serious danger of an Indian disturbance. Physical resistance against the growing American military presence added larger difficulties to a new pan-tribal alliance of the area's Indians.

An increased American presence along with the weakened positions of area tribes combined to make any serious threat of an uprising doubtful. Garra's old allies, the Quechans and Mohaves, were hesitant to join in another rebellion with Juan Antonio. After all, it had been Juan Antonio who conspired to capture Garra. The window of possibility for Southern California tribes to keep their native homelands had opened in 1851 but closed with Garra's execution. Juan Antonio had gambled for the Indian leadership of the area and lost. He vanquished Garra but he left the way open for his real rivals—the American conquerors.

Conditions worsened for the Cahuilla in the years ahead. Anglo squatters occupied Cahuilla land and ruined Indian crops by diverting scarce water resources. Politically, however, Juan Antonio remained the primary Cahuilla leader in Southern California. In 1863, Juan Antonio contracted the most insidious of Anglo weapons, disease. The old man became the victim of a smallpox epidemic that scourged the area. Duff Weaver hired a Mexican to carry provisions to the leader, who had been abandoned by his people. The nonChristianized Juan Antonio held fast to the traditional ways and followed a treatment of sweats to battle the disease. After his death it was rumored that dogs and wild hogs in the area mutilated his unburied body.[61] His band of Cahuilla left San Timoteo Canyon for Cabezon Valley where Chief Cabezon's tribe made their home, or made their way back to their traditional lands in Anza Valley of today's Riverside County.

In a last irony, it was Chief Cabezon whom an Indian agent later praised as a true friend of local whites. "He is a remarkable man, venerated by all of his people over whom he has long exercised a powerful influence and always in the interest of peace and good will towards the whites," John G. Ames said in 1873. "Through his efforts the tribe has been kept from allying itself with the tribes of the Colorado river for the purpose of making war upon the whites." Chief Cabezon's spurious reward is a desert site marked with his name while Juan Antonio has become an obscure historical footnote.

Juan Antonio, the great Cahuilla war leader, played a dangerous game of conciliation and intrigue. He was not a leader who could share power with Antonio Garra or anyone else. An alliance between Garra and Juan Antonio could have shaken the foundation of American influence in Southern California for many years.

In early December 1851 Garra wrote to Juan Antonio: "If we lose this war, all will be lost—the world if we gain this war; then it is forever; never will it stop; this war is for a whole life."[62] Garra's prophecy was all too accurate.

Alvino Siva of Los Coyotes Reservation stands in 1999 near what is believed to be the burial site of Cahuilla leader Juan Antonio near Sahatapa. Courtesy of The Press-Enterprise.

NOTES:

[1] *San Diego Herald* newspaper, January 17, 1852.

[2] Millard F. Hudson, "The Last Indian Campaign in the Southwest," *Pacific Monthly* (1907): 154.

[3] *Daily Alta California*, December 4, 1851; Benjamin Davis Wilson, *The Indians of Southern California in 1852: The B.D. Wilson Report*, ed. John Walton Caughey (San Marino: Huntington Library, 1952), 7-8.

[4] Leonard B. Waitman, "The Watchdogs of San Bernardino: Chief Juan Antonio and Lorenzo Trujillo," *San Bernardino Museum Quarterly*, Winter, 1970, 7.; Hudson, "The Last Indian Campaign", 158. Juan Antonio and his men supported his Lugo allies in punishing those Luiseños who had massacred eleven Californios at Pauma following the Battle of San Pasqual against the Americans. The Luiseños under Manuelito Cota and Pablito Apis hoped to incur American favor. An estimated thirty-eight to one hundred Luiseños were killed by the Cahuillas and Lugos near Temecula in December 1846. This has been called the Temecula Massacre.

[5] Wolcott, "The Lugos and Their Indian Ally," 23-24. The description of Juan Antonio comes from Judge Benjamin Hayes who met and knew the Cahuilla leader. See also John W. Robinson and Bruce D. Risher, *The San Jacintos: The Mountain Country from Banning to Borrego Valley* (Arcadia, California: Big Santa Anita Historical Society, 1993), 101.

[6] Tom Hughes, *History of Banning and San Gorgonio Pass in Two Parts* (Banning, CA: Banning Record Press, 1938), 106-107. Contemporaries and historians refer to Cabezon the elder as Old, Old Cabezon and his son as merely Old Cabezon. The name, which also applied to physical territory of the desert Cahuilla in the lower Coachella Valley, means "big-headed in Spanish and denoted the large head of Old, Old Cabezon. Reportedly, his Cahuilla name was Pal-se-ta, meaning "Alkali Water," and he belonged to the *Kauwicpameauitcem* clan of Cahilla. After the mid-1840s it appears that Old, Old Cabezon controlled matters east of the San Gorgonio Pass while Juan Antonio commanded Cahuilla to the west. Juan Antonio died during a smallpox epidemic in February 1863 at his village in San Timeteo Canyon called Sahatapa. Old, Old Cabezon was reported to be 140 years years of age when he died in 1883. His son, Old Cabezon (also known as Hervasio or Jervasio Cabezon) died in December 1906. According to a reservation census, he was 87 years old. See Jane Davies Gunther, *Riverside County, California, Place Names: Their Origins and Their Stories*, (Riverside, CA: Rubidoux Printing Co., 1984), 81-83; *Sacramento Daily Union*, May 31, 1884.

[7] Ibid, Hughes.

[8] Joseph Lancaster Brent, *The Lugo Case: A Personal Experience* (New Orleans: Searcy & Pfaff, LTD., 1926), 7.

[9] Wolcott, "The Lugos and Their Indian Ally," 22.

[10] Richard A. Hanks, "Vicissitudes of Justice: Massacre at San Timoteo Canyon," *Southern California Quarterly* (Fall 2000): 239-240; Wolcott, "The Lugos and Their Indian Ally," 23. Ute chief Walkara is often cited as the primary leader of the "wild Indians" and responsible for the raids upon the Lugo rancho.

[11] Ibid., Wolcott.

[12] Ibid., Brent; Hanks, "Vicissitudes of Justice," 233-256.

[13] Ibid., Hanks, 244.

[14] Ibid.

[15] Ibid., 245-246.

[16] Ibid., 254-255. In October 1852 all charges against Menito and Chico Lugo were finally dismissed. The only member of Irving's band to survive the Cahuilla onslaught was George Evans who returned to the area and gave an interview to the *Los Angeles Star* in November 1851. The interview is only extant today in the scrapbooks of Judge Benjamin Hayes, Bancroft Library, University of California, Berkeley (hereafter cited as "Scraps").

[17] *Los Angeles Star*, August 2, 1851, August 9, 1851, in *Benjamin Hayes Scrapbooks*, v. 38.

[18] *Daily Alta California* newspaper, November 13, 1851.

[19] *Los Angeles Star*, November 1, 1851 in Hayes "Scraps," v. 38.

[20] George Harwood Phillips, *Chiefs and Challengers: Indian Resistance and Cooperation in Southern California* (Berkeley. Los Angeles: University of California Press, 1975), 59.

[21] Richard L. Carrico, *Strangers in a Stolen Land: American Indians in San Diego, 1850-1880* (Newcastle, California: Sierra Oaks Publishing Co., 1987), 46.

[22] Leland E. Bibb, "William Marshall 'The Wickedest Man in California:' A Reappraisal," *Journal of San Diego History*, (San Diego, Winter 1976), 17; Waitman, "The Watchdogs of San Bernardino Valley," 7.

[23] Arthur Woodward, "The Garra Revolt of 1851," *Westerners Brand Book* (Los Angeles Corral, 1947), 115.

[24] Hudson, "The Last Indian Campaign," 152-154; Carrico, *Strangers in a Stolen Land* , 46; Letter, Oliver M. Wozencraft to Luke Lea, January 9, 1852, *Letters Received by the Office of Indian Affairs*, California Superintendency, 1824-1881, (hereafter cited as *Letters Received*) Microcopy 234, Roll 32.

[25] Hudson, "The Last Indian Campaign," 153-154.

[26] Testimony of Jose Nocar in the trial of Bill Marshall as recorded in Hayes "Scraps," v. 39.

[27] Bibb, "William Marshall 'The Wickedest Man in California:' A Reappraisal," 18-19.

[28] Oliver M. Wozencraft statement to Hubert Bancroft, 1877, in Bancroft Papers, Bancroft Library, University of California, Berkeley, C-D 204.

[29] Hudson, "The Last Indian Campaign," 158.

[30] Woodward, "The Garra Revolt of 1851," 116. Captain Christopher Lovell, who commanded a detachment of the 2nd United States Infantry stationed at the Chino outpost, protested the proceedings.

[31] Hudson, "The Last Indian Campaign," 158-159.

[32] *Los Angeles Star* newspaper, January 24, 1852, as quoted in Phillips, *Chiefs and Challengers*, 118-119.

[33] Woodward, "The Garra Revolt of 1851," 116.

[34] Hudson, "The Last Indian Campaign," 158-159.

[35] Letter Antonio Garra to José Estudillo, printed in *Daily Alta California*, December 3, 1851. Despite the testimony of Bill Marshall and accusations of the *San Diego Herald*, the court-martial that convicted Garra found no evidence linking Latino leaders to the uprising. See Phillips, *Chiefs and Challengers*, 114-115.

[36] Testimony of José Nocar in Hayes "Scraps," v. 39.

[37] Wozencraft to Luke Lea, January 9, 1852, *Letters Received*, Microcopy 234, Roll 32.

[38] Wozencraft statement to Hubert Bancroft, 1877.

[39] *San Diego Herald* newspaper, January 10, 1852 as quoted in Leland E. Bibb, "Pablo Apis and Temecula," *Journal of San Diego History*, (Fall, 1991), 259.

[40] Edward Castillo, "The Impact of Euro-American Exploration and Settlement," *Handbook for North American Indians*, William C. Sturtevant, ed., v. 8, *California*, Robert Heizer, ed. (Washington, D.C.: Smithsonian Institution, 1978), 106.

[41] Michael Magliari, "Free Soil, Unfree Labor: Cave Johnson Couts and the Binding of Indian workers in California, 1850-1867," *Pacific Historical Review* (August 2004), 358. Couts took advantage of the 1850 Act for the Government and Protection of Indians passed by new legislature of California aimed at solving the Indian problem by labor codes meant to ensure an available work force through debt peonage and general suspicion of civil rights. Couts' power as a justice of the peace and militia member "helped transform Couts into a latter-day feudal lord," Magliari wrote. Couts was accused of child stealing and flogging to death at least two of his Indian workers.

[42] Anne J. Miller, "Maria Antonia Apis: A Young Luiseño Indian Woman," *Southern California Quarterly*, (Summer 2004), 117. See also Phillips, *Chiefs and Challengers,* 49.

[43] Statement of Oliver M. Wozencraft to George Bancroft, 1877 in the Bancroft Papers; Wozencraft to Luke Lea, January 9, 1852, *Letters Received.*

[44] Letter, Wozencraft to Luke Lea, January 9, 1852 in *Letters Received.*

[45] Ibid.

[46] Ibid.

[47] Bibb, "Pablo Apis and Temecula," 257-260. Isaac Williams, owner of Rancho Chino, son-in-law to the powerful Antonio Mariá Lugo, signed as a witness. Williams, a widower, had close ties to the family of Pablo Apis. Two of Apis' daughters bore him children in 1846.

[48] Ibid. The lands guaranteed by the American commissioners to Southern California Indians included those stretching from the Temecula area to the area around present-day Redlands, California. The treaty stated that "the said nations of Indians acknowledge themselves, jointly and severally, under the exclusive jurisdiction, authority and protection of the United States." It can be argued that sovereignty was implied in this treaty since American negotiators dealt with the Indian signatories as representatives of "nations" within the jurisdiction of the United States. This distinction, which the U.S. government ended in 1871, was a critical point to Southern California Indians who organized in the early 20th century. Future claims against the United States government emphasized this point despite the government's failure to ratify the treaties. Scholar Robert Heizer wrote that "one cannot imagine a more poorly conceived, more inaccurate, less informed, and less democratic process that the making of the 18 treaties in 1851-51 with the California Indians." See Heizer, *The Eighteen Unratified Treaties of 1851-1852 Between the California Indians and The United States Government* (Berkeley, CA: Department of Anthropology, University of California, Berkeley, 1972), 5.

[49] Kimberly Johnston-Dodds, *Early California Laws and Policies Related to California Indians, Prepared at the request of Senator John L. Burton, President Pro Tempore*, (Sacramento, CA: California Research Bureau, September 2002), 23-24.

[50] Harry Kelsey, "The California Indian Myth," *Southern California Quarterly*, (Fall 1973), 231. Kelsey wrote that "what Congress and the citizens of California really wanted was Indian removal without the need to negotiate for Indian land claims." See also, Florence Shipek, *Pushed Into the Rocks: Southern California Indian Land Tenure, 1769-1986*, (Lincoln and London: University of Nebraska Press, 1988), 35.

[51] Leland E. Bibb, "William Marshall 'The Wickedest Man in California:' A Reappraisal," 21.

[52] *Los Angeles Star* newspaper editorial, December 6, 1851 as quoted in William Rice, *The Los Angeles Star, 1851-1864: The Beginnings of Journalism in Southern California*, John Walton Caughey, ed. (Berkeley: University of California Press, 1947), 34.

[53] Ibid.

[54] *Los Angeles Star* newspaper, January 24, 1852 as cited in Phillips, *Chiefs and Challengers,* 130-131; *Los Angeles Star* newspaper, August 14, 1852.

[55] Burr Belden, "Celebrations to Mark Centennial for Butterfield," *San Bernardino Sun-Telegram* newspaper, July 15, 1956.

[56] Letter, Duff Weaver to Joshua Bean, February 12, 1852 in Hayes "Scraps," v. 39; *San Diego Herald* newspaper, January 28, 1852.

[57] Letter, Superintendent Thomas J. Henley to George W. Manypenny, Commissioner of Indian Affairs, December 18, 1855, *Letters Received*, Microcopy 234, Roll 35.

[58] Ibid.

[59] Ibid.

[60] Letter, Assistant Adjutant General, E. D. Townsend to Thomas J. Henley, December 27, 1855, *Letters Received*, Microcopy 234, Roll 33. Henley responded on December 31, 1855.

[61] *Los Angeles Star* newspaper, February 21, 1863 as cited by Judge Benjamin Hayes in *Pioneer Notes From the Diaries of Judge Benjamin Ignatius Hayes, 1849-1875* (Los Angeles: Privately printed, 1929), 281.

[62] Indian Department agent, John G. Ames, August 1873 as quoted by Benjamin David Wilson, "Observation on Early Days in California and New Mexico," *Quarterly of the Historical Society of Southern California*, (1934), 138; Woodward, "The Garra Revolt of 1851," 113. It is likely that Garra's letter to Juan Antonio was written in Spanish. Garra was an educated man, trained at a mission. His son, Antonino, wrote to Joshua Bean in Spanish before his surrender. See Woodward, "The Garra Revolt of 1851," 115.

3 Olegario's "Insurrection of 1871"[1]

Olegario is…"an enthusiastic defender of his people and disposed to take advanced grounds on questions of their rights. A more competent man altogether cannot be found in the tribe.[2] —Special Indian Agent John G. Ames 1874

OLIGARIO.

TEMICULA.

Olegario Calac

Photo BAE GN 01724A 06296100, National Anthropological Archives, Smithsonian Institution.

Native Californians entered the treaty councils of 1851-1852 in good faith but quickly became witnesses to aggressive encroachment on their lands by Anglo farmers and ranchers and a feudal labor system that bound Indians to the aggressors. Cave Couts is credited with promoting this system and greatly benefiting from it. Couts used the 1850 Act for the Government and Protection of Indians. These "red laws" mirrored the black codes found in the old Northwest before the Civil War that denied African Americans basic civil and legal rights. They were as effective in California after the Civil War as Jim Crow laws were in the creation of debt and wage slavery among freed blacks in America's southeast. The 1850 Act gave local justices of the peace power of interpretation and enforcement over Indians. County justices, such as Cave Couts, procured Native American labor for surrounding ranchos. They semantically side-stepped anti-slavery laws by calling these Indian workers "prisoners," "custodial wards," or "apprentices." A particularly heinous provision permitted employers to take custody of Indian children until they reached majority age. A clause requiring a parent's permission was often overlooked, facilitating a system of child stealing.[3]

Couts built his Rancho Guajome near Temecula through his abusive misuse of these labor codes. He ran his rancho like an antebellum plantation and often resorted to the whip incited by his quick and violent temper. Couts was indicted a handful of times for homicide or violent assault, including for the flogging death of a Luiseño captain named Urbano in July 1855.[4]

If Couts attempted to re-create the antebellum South with its "peculiar institution," in San Diego County, Manuel Cota was his overseer. Cota built an adobe at Pala where he farmed and raised horses and sheep. His own "need for workers made him a willing collaborator with rancheros who employed his services as an Indian labor recruiter and contractor," Michael Magliari wrote. It was, Magliari said, a splendid partnership for both men. "I have been comparatively unmolested in my authority and control over the San Luisenians," Couts wrote in 1855.[5] This cooperation by Cota was more the result of personal ambition than concern for his people but was not uncommon among enslaved people, whether southern blacks or Indians who viewed such compromise as necessary for survival.

Rancho Guajome, 1936. Photo courtesy of Library of Congress, LC-USZ62-13459

With the death of Pablo Apis shortly after the treaty signing, Couts, using his position as Indian sub-agent for the area, attempted to solidify his control over the Luiseño people by appointing Cota as Captain General in September 1853.[6] This set the stage for an important confrontation that pitted Anglo administrators such as Couts against the recognized will of the people. Cota's opposition came from a Luiseño leader named Olegario Calac.

Olegario Calac (or Manuel Olegario as he was also called) was born in approximately 1830 and worked for many years in Los Angeles until an outbreak of smallpox brought him back to northern San Diego County in 1869. Soon after his return, the Luiseño elected Olegario as general of twelve principal villages. Historian Richard Carrico wrote that the ouster of Cota by the Luiseño and Olegario's elevation to a position of leadership over so many "geographically disparate and autonomous villages" indicated "a political cohesion apparently not expressed previously" and was "a drastic departure from traditional leadership roles." While this "political cohesion" may have been an elevation of the traditional role, Olegario, by his familial connection, was an acknowledged leader among his people. Olegario was the nephew of José Calac, one of the original signers of the January 1852 treaty, who represented the Luiseño of El Potrero (now La Jolla).[7]

The Luiseño people had ousted Cota once before in 1862 and replaced him with Francisco, one of the signers of the Temecula treaty. In this way the Luiseño people asserted their tribal will against outside pressure represented by Anglos such as Couts and showed clear lines of resistance to maintain and protect their cultural, political, and social beliefs.

Judge Benjamin Hayes visited Temecula in May 1862 and found Francisco "favored" over Cota and the people "unwilling to submit to Cota's rule."[8] Couts, however, denounced Francisco to officials of the Office of Indian Affairs as a drunkard and thief. Francisco infuriated the bigot Couts through his unwillingness to recognize Couts' superiority. This subterfuge by Couts appeared to be successful since, in 1865, Indian Agent W. E. Lovett, removed Francisco and reinstated Cota under authority of the Office of Indian Affairs.

The rise of Olegario, according to Carrico, "set the stage for a pan-Indian self-determination movement."[9] The struggle, as it would be time and time again, was over land. Then, as in years to come, land represented sovereignty and survival. In January 1870 President Ulysses S. Grant signed an Executive Order authorizing more than 138,000 acres for the Diegueño and Luiseño peoples. Cota, probably responding to the desire of Couts and others, favored moving onto these new reservations. Olegario and his followers resisted, fearing a loss of control of their own affairs and a dangerous dependence on the government. Olegario insisted that before any migration, the new land titles had to be verified, reservation boundaries defined, and agencies established.[10] The Luiseño people saw Cota as a "reservationist." They again removed Cota from power and selected Olegario in his place. Native leaders sought to legitimize the selection by presenting their case before Judge Benjamin Hayes and San Diego County Judge Thomas H. Bush, and stood fast in their demands for their right to choose their own leadership and protection of their property rights.[11]

These actions by Olegario and the Luiseños demonstrated, Carrico wrote, that they had an understanding of the "American political-legal system" and sought to use that system to their advantage. Olegario argued to the government officials that his election was democratic and "in concert with American ideals."[12] He continued to lobby local officials for certification of native reservations. White squatters, however, moved to take advantage of lax enforcement of native rights by Indian Agent Augustus Greene and settled on Luiseño land. Local Anglos protested the creation of reservations to Greene. Greene and others such as Judge Benjamin Hayes and the Rev. Antonio Ubach, a Roman Catholic priest, openly expressed support for Cota.

Luiseño refusal to move onto ill-defined reservations was presented to Washington as proof that Grant's Executive Order was mistimed, so on February 13, 1871 Grant rescinded the order and the promised lands returned to public domain. This validated Olegario's worst fears that the government's order was tenuous and increased the erosion of support among local Luiseño for Cota. Despite this, Anglo officials continued to back Cota and called Olegario's election "an improper interference."[13]

Through the traditional leadership of Olegario, the Luiseño were active participants in their own fate. Through their actions, they gained respect for their leadership and integrity as a sovereign people even if unsuccessful in securing a defined land base. Despite setbacks, their willingness to sacrifice for the values inherent in their culture and established political systems speaks to the unity they maintained as a people even in the face of overwhelming adversity. The flaws of abandoning traditional homelands, as voiced by Olegario, became apparent when President Grant revoked his Executive Order. Carrico wrote that "had Olegario's people moved to reservations as Cota insisted, they would have become landless indigents without even the tenuous claims which they now held for traditional settlements."[14]

Tension grew between the shrinking Cota faction, supported by Agent Greene, and Olegario's followers until violence erupted in the summer of 1871 at the reservations of Pala and Potrero. Several people were injured, including Cota's sister Margarita. The woman was taken by Olegario supporters and hung by her wrists. The clash drove other Luiseño to abandon Cota ,with only a few Indians remaining loyal.

In August 1871, Olegario, accompanied by Manuel Largo of the Mountain Cahuilla, took their case against Cota to Justice Wagner of San Bernardino. Largo's support showed the concern existing among neighboring tribes over the problems of the Luiseño securing a protected land base. It is likely that Largo understood the threat to his own people from the insidious encroachment of white settlers onto Indian lands throughout Southern California. If efforts to preserve Luiseño land proved unsuccessful, Cahuilla land would be next.

It is also important to note that less than twenty years after the Temecula Treaty signing, traditional leadership of the Luiseño and Cahuilla had put aside their differences and joined to support each other against the greater threat to their lands and way of life. This reconciliation was certainly made easier by the death in 1855 of Pablo Apis and in 1863 of Juan Antonio, who were leaders during the Pauma and Temecula massacres.

Convincing Wagner of Cota's threat, Olegario was given a warrant for Cota's arrest. When word of the alliance of Olegario and Largo reached the white population of San Diego, fears immediately surfaced. Panicked whites feared another potential Indian uprising such as the one mounted by Antonio Garra. Exaggerated newspaper stories with wording such as "attack feared" and "Indian outbreak" aggravated emotions.[15] These fears fueled the hostility that whites already had directed toward local California Indians. The fears were used to justify efforts to destroy native-backed leadership.

Olegario enlisted the aid of a trusted white rancher, Daniel Sexton, and agreed to another election to allay the panic of local Anglos. Indian Superintendent Billington Whiting assured Cota that Olegario would not be recognized as the Luiseño captain or general. Cota's lack of support was evident, however, when Whiting met with Cahuilla and Luiseño tribal members in September 1871. Whiting therefore accepted the forced resignation of Cota but refused to recognize Olegario, instead appointing Cota's relative José Antonio as General-in-Chief.[16] Despite the intransigence shown by Whiting and others, the Luiseño continued to overwhelmingly support Olegario.   In July 1873, Special Agent John G. Ames reported that "by far the larger part of these Indians recognize Olegario as their

President Ulysses S. Grant, 1876. Courtesy of Library of Congress, Prints and Photographs Division. DID cwpbh.03890.

Chief and have done so from the time of José Antonio's appointment by Mr. Whiting."[17] The federal government, however, refused to officially recognize Olegario's leadership.

The Luiseño leader continued his fight to create a recognized and identifiable reservation for his people. He insisted that a complete survey of Indian holdings should be done but remained suspicious of San Diego County Surveyor James Pascoe's ability to render a fair evaluation. Olegario attempted to use the American legal system to define Southern California native land rights but with limited success. Legal standing in California courts was tenuous at best. Indian treaty rights remained unratified, citizenship rights were denied by the government, and laws such as the 1850 Act for the Government and Protection of Indians worked to devalue California Indians as a people in the eyes of the Anglo majority.[18]

Meanwhile, San Diego authorities continued evicting Luiseños from traditional homelands at the behest of white ranchers even while acknowledging that Indian rights were being violated. Whites feared the continued strife might precipitate new violence on the part of the Luiseño. In October 1875 this renewed the question of government reservations. In November Olegario traveled to Washington, where he had an interview with President Grant.

This may well have been the first time that a Southern California Indian captain gained a personal audience with a United States president. Carrico wrote that Olegario sought the interview through his attorney; that may have lent the request greater attention. Unlike bureaucratic reports, Olegario put a human face on the dire problems faced by the Luiseño. Olegario's appeal brought the desired results. Assured that lands would be set aside for his people, Olegario returned home where on December 27, 1875, Grant signed the Executive Order establishing nine reservations. These included reservations in Luiseño territory as well as the Potrero Ajenio near Banning, and Agua Caliente near Palm Springs.[19]

Cahuilla chief Manuel Largo fought his own battle to secure justice and a land base for his Mountain Cahuilla. Largo had been the loyal lieutenant of Juan Antonio. Largo took over as leader of the Cahuilla after Juan Antonio's death by smallpox in the winter of 1862-1863. Largo brought most of the Cahuilla back to the greater San Jacinto Valley. He struggled to preserve parts of Cahuilla traditional land from encroaching Anglo ranchers. The Estudillo family began selling off portions of their rancho, including lands traditionally owned by Cahuilla in Anza Valley, beginning in 1868.[20] By the early 1870s upwards of fifty settlers had purchased parts of the former Rancho San Jacinto Viejo that had been awarded to the Estudillo family in 1842.

White ranchers fenced off Indian land, restricting access to long-held water sources and food supplies. Indian people, pushed to desperation, fought back, taking cattle and other foodstuffs from Anglo ranchers. Inevitably, confrontations occurred between Indians and local whites, leading to several arrests of Indians. Not surprisingly, local newspapers leveled blame at Largo. The *San Diego Union* reported in July 1873 that Largo "considers himself the owner of the land occupied by his band, and declares that he means to hold possession."[21]

Two months later the same paper stated: "a large number of Indians have lived for many years" in San Jacinto Valley, "and they regard the land as their own, and already resist its settlement by a white population."[22]

Olegario's 1875 appeal can likely be credited for raising awareness with the federal administration of the specific problems facing Indians in Southern California. Special Agent Ames also recommended that the government purchase small tracts of land for Southern California Indians, to be held in trust for them by the government. That coupled with mounting reports of trouble between Indians and white settlers again prompted federal action. A presidential Executive Order in May 1876 enlarged the Potrero Ajenio (later Morongo Reservation) and Agua Caliente Reservation near Palm Springs and created six new ones in Cahuilla land, primarily in San Gorgonio Pass and lower desert areas, including Torres-Martinez and Cabazon. The Cahuilla Reservation in Anza Valley of Riverside County was the only land protected for Manuel Largo's Mountain Cahuilla. These lands, however, remained unsurveyed, permitting ongoing disputes about boundary lines and further encroachment by white farmers and ranchers.[23]

Olegario's victory to create a recognized Luiseño reservation was short-lived and the war to define Luiseño land and tribal rights continued. With legal recourse seemingly inadequate, Luiseño people again resorted to confrontation as a means of resisting injustice.

In June 1877, Olegario and his warriors blocked the access of cattleman Antonio Varela to the Cuca or Potrero Rancho (now La Jolla), which lay just west of Warner Hot Springs. Varela leased the land from rancho owner Margarita Trujillo. The grazing land lay outside the boundaries of federally designated reservations but within traditional Luiseño territory. Varela's herds threatened Luiseño food sources. Inaction meant suffering for the people. Indians react like any other people when denied reasonable discourse and compromise. Violence was never the first resort for Southern California Indian but neither was docility in the face of abuse. Although bloodshed was averted, several Luiseño were arrested and brought before Justice of the Peace Couts. Uncharacteristically, Couts, with a legacy of abusing local natives, declared he had no jurisdiction in the case and released the Indian prisoners.[24]

As victorious Luiseños sought the removal of proprietor Margarita Trujillo from Cuca, infuriated Anglos in San Diego demanded and received action. Deputy Sheriff Ed Bushyhead traveled to Cuca, intending to serve the Luiseño general with an arrest warrant and take Olegario into custody. In an act of bold defiance Olegario and his followers refused to recognize the authority of the warrant, leading to a nervous standoff between Deputy Bushyhead and the Luiseño. After several hours Bushyhead was granted safe passage back to San Diego, but without his prisoner. Olegario again went to the courts and argued that Cuca was traditional land, owned and worked by his people "since time began"—a fact recognized by earlier Mexican authorities. Judge Moses Luce promised an investigation but doubted that lands outside of those designated by the government could be considered owned by the Luiseño.[25]

Olegario used every means at his disposal to fight for the sovereign rights of the Luiseño people. He showed a sophistication often not acknowledged for native people of this time period. Olegario's continued visits to Los Angeles and Washington intensified resentment among whites, who saw an Indian wage war for his rights not with a spear or bow, but instead with a law book. Olegario opened a new chapter in the story of resistance by Southern California Indians.

Manuel Largo and unidentified Cahuilla men, ca. 1870.
Courtesy of Gerald Smith Collection, Unprocessed Material,
Archives, A.K. Smiley Library, Redlands, California

Olegario's leadership ended on July 31, 1877, when he died in his sleep. His followers suspected that either conspiring whites or Cota sympathizers had poisoned him. A coroner's inquest and autopsy ruled that no foul play was involved in Olegario's death. The justice in charge of the investigation was Cave Johnson Couts. Carrico noted that many Luiseño people today still believe their dynamic general was murdered. Manuel Cota ended his life poverty stricken and peddling grapes to pay his way. He died in 1895. Cota was dressed in a Mexican cavalry officer's uniform and buried at the old mission in Pala.[26]

With the death of Olegario, Carrico wrote that "self-determination as a political movement became dormant until well into the twentieth century."[27] The events surrounding the life and leadership of Olegario are certainly remarkable but the fight for self-determination did not go dormant. Leadership continued to emerge at the village level as well as regionally. The war continued, sometimes with less sound and fury but always with a determination to resist American aggression and regain what had been taken from Southern California Indians. Resistance ranged from simple obstruction to assassination, but local Indians remained ready to respond to the next Indian leader of passion and conviction.

Fifty-three years after the death of Olegario Calac, a new generation of California Indians invoked his name, remembered his sacrifice, and rallied to advance his struggle. As remembered by another iconic Indian activist in 1934: "Chief Oligario [sic] Calac was chosen by all the bands of the Mission Indians to proceed to Washington and lay before the officials the petition and plea of the Indians for protection and the return of their lands. …Chief Calac was given an American flag—with 37 stars—and also presented with an enlarged picture of himself by Washington officials as evidence of their further promise of justice."[28]

Olegario returned from Washington with that promise and the flag that symbolized it. His people met him at the Rincon Reservation where the Luiseño proudly raised the American flag as an expression of mutual allegiance and respect. Olegario "announced that soon there would be received papers confirming the verbal promises for justice to the Mission Indians." Unfortunately, as future leaders pointed out, for the Luiseño the "papers" did not prevent continued injustice as "more white settlers came to California and it was under the greatest handicap that the Indians were able to continue their reservation and district tribal relations." Despite adversity Olegario kept his people together, maintained the tribal integrity of their reservations, and represented the whole of the Luiseño nation with dignity and wisdom.[29]

Future generations of Indians remembered Olegario Calac's battle for fairness, truth and respect for the First People of California and revered him as a symbol of what could be accomplished by a people committed to achieving justice. Olegario Calac redefined the nature of resistance in Southern California by his use of the courts and well as confrontation. For many other Indians of the region, however, circumstances left very few options but to fight for survival.

Notes:

[1] Helen Hunt Jackson used this phrase in a letter to Secretary of the Interior Henry Teller in May 1883. Historian Valerie Mathes believed that Jackson referred to the violence at Pala between the followers of Cota and Olegario. Mathes wrote that Billington Whiting met with three hundred Indians and effectively "diffused the situation." See Mathes, *The Indian Reform Letters of Helen Hunt Jackson, 1879-1885* (Norman: University of Oklahoma Press, 1998), 259-260.

[2] United States Congress, House, Mission Indians of Southern California, "Report of John G. Ames," Executive Document 91, 43rd Congress, 1st Session, 1874, pp. 4-5, as quoted by Carrico, *Strangers in a Stolen Land*, 72.

[3] Magliari, "Free Soil, Unfree Labor," 352.

[4] Ibid., 373, 377.

[5] Ibid., 378, 380.

[6] Phillips, *Chiefs and Challengers*, 137-138. There is disagreement about the death date of Pablo Apis. Phillips placed Apis' death in 1855. Miller believed that there was a confusion concerning use of the names of Pablo Apis and his son or stepson Pablito Apis who participated in the Pauma massacre. Miller wrote that the elder Pablo died in 1852 after the signing of the treaty since only Pablito is listed in the October 1852 census as "chief" over all San Luis Indians. Bibb placed the elder Pablo's death as either late 1853 or early 1854 based on a land claim filed to validate the Mexican grant of the Little Temecula Rancho. The United States Land Commission rejected the claim in 1854. Subsequent appeals reversed that decision in 1872 when the Apis title was declared valid. Miller interpreted an October 1853 report of Apis' appearance in San Diego as that of Pablito Apis, not the elder. She wrote that Pablito died soon afterwards. It would seem logical given the reputation and political power of Pablo Apis senior that Couts would not have elevated Cota to captain general until after the death of the senior chief and that Miller's assertion about the confusion between accounts of Pablo senior and junior has validity. See Miller, "Maria Antonia Apis," 118-119; and Bibb, "Pablo Apis and Temecula," 262.

Phillips and Richard Carrico also disagree on when Cota was appointed as Captain-General of the Luiseños. Phillips has the date as September 1853. Carrico wrote that Couts made the appointment in 1851. Again, considering the potential clash with the elder Pablo Apis, the 1853 date seems more plausible. See Carrico, "The Struggle for Native American Self-Determination in San Diego County, *Journal of California and Great Basin Anthropology*, v. 2, no. 2 (Winter 1980): 201.

[7] Carrico, "Struggle for Native American Self Determination," 201; Statement of Adam Castillo to Congressional Committee, 1934. See *Hearings before the Committee on Indian Affairs, House of Representatives Seventy-third Congress, Second Session on H. R. 7902* (Washington, D.C.: United States Government Printing Office, 1934), 287-288. In that hearing, Castillo stated that "Chief Jose was an able leader and for many years continued his efforts to have the Government approve the treaties. There was present in 1852, at the time the treaties were signed by the Indians, another, but much younger leader, a nephew of the famous Chief Jose. This man was named Olegario Calac. At this time he was about 40 years of age. He had much ability and was called upon to explain to other Indians the conditions of the treaties." Here the Luiseño of the are continued to follow traditional leadership families ignoring attempts to have new leaders such as Cota imposed on them. While many historians are more familiar with the smallpox outbreak in the winter of 1862-1863, Carrico reported a similar "devastating" epidemic which swept through Los Angeles County in 1868-1869.

[8] Carrico, "Struggle for Native American Self Determination," 203.

[9] Ibid., 204.

[10] Ibid.

[11] Carrico, Ibid, 203-204.

[12] Ibid., 204, 206.

[13] Ibid., 206.

[14] Ibid.

[15] Ibid., 207.

[16] Ibid., 208.

[17] Ibid.

[18] Ibid., 208-209.

[19] Ibid., 209. Helen Hunt Jackson in a letter of May 1883, praised an attorney she refers to as "Mr. Wilson" who "has been a friend & councillor of the Indians in many difficulties." Jackson believed that Wilson might be able to prevent the forced removal of Indians from Soboba. Mathes identified this man as Christopher N. Wilson, born in Ohio in 1830. He practiced law in the east before moving to Los Angeles in the 1870s. It is highly probable that this Mr. Wilson is the same lawyer "Wilson" mentioned by Carrico as the attorney for Olegario in his fight to retain Indians lands. See Mathes, *The Indian Reform Letters*, 259-260.

[20] John W. Robinson and Bruce D. Risher, *The San Jacintos: The Mountain Country from Banning to Borrego Valley* (Arcadia, California: Big Santa Anita Historical Society, 1993), 104-106.

[21] Ibid., 105.

[22] Ibid., 106.

[23] Ibid., 106-107.

[24] Carrico, *Strangers in a Stolen Land*, 84, 86.

[25] Grant's 1875 executive order mistakenly grouped four rancherias, Rincon, Potrero, La Jolla and Ya Piche together under the name of Potrero. Rincon was the only one in a valley canyon and it was separated from the other mountainous rancherias by the Mexican grant of Cuca. The Trujillos were still living at Cuca in the late 19th century and forcibly removed the Luiseño from Potrero to Rincon at that time. See Shipek, *Pushed Into the Rocks*, 100 and Robin Paige Talley, *The Life History of a Luiseño Indian: James (Jim) Martinez*, Masters Thesis, San Diego State University, 1982, 60.

[26] *They Passed This Way, Biographical Sketches: Tales of Historic Temecula Valley at the Crossroads of California's Southern Immigrant Trail* (Temecula, California: Laguna House, 1970), 19.

[27] Carrico, "Struggle for Native American Self Determination," 206-209.

[28] Adam Castillo, statement to United States Congress, House, Committee on Indian Affairs, Hearings on H.R. 7902, *Readjustment of Indian Affairs*, 73rd Congress, 2nd Session, 1934. 288.

[29] Ibid.

4 A "Fight to the LastExtremity": The Paiute Wars of the 1860s

A hungry stomach makes a short prayer. —*Paiute proverb*

Indian Village, Redlands, CA, 1870s Courtesy of Archives, AK Smiley Library, Redlands, CA

Hundreds if not thousands of Indians in California were not approached by government agents, were not asked to participate in peace talks, did not sign one of the eighteen treaties and were left unaffected by the promises, even if unfulfilled, made by those treaties. In the southern part of the state those people were chiefly the nomads of the desert—the Chemehuevi people, a branch of southern Paiute. From the earliest days of Spanish occupation to United States control, these groups lived in the deserts near Southern California trade routes and posed a constant threat to immigrant trains and valley settlers.

For several decades starting in the 1840s, California's southern deserts were a dangerous place for non-Indians to be. In 1839 Mexican Governor Juan Alvarado granted the powerful Lugo family San Bernardino Valley from Rancho Cucamonga to Yucaipa. The Lugos formed an alliance with Juan Antonio's Cahuilla around 1844 to control the huge rancho and protect people and livestock from the mounting depravations by outlaws and hostile Indians.[1]

Anglo control of the area after 1846 did little to stop the Paiute raiding. Explorations and surveys of the area in the 1850s by the United States army opened roads from Albuquerque, New Mexico, through Yuma, Arizona, to San Diego, and, north to San Bernardino. A short-lived uprising by the Mohave Indians in 1858 along the Colorado River threatened wagon trains traveling west along the thirty-fifth parallel. This led to the United States army building additional forts along the trails to provide greater safety for the increasing flow of Euro-American immigrants. One such fort was Camp Cady located in the Mohave Desert, just to the east of present-day Barstow, California. More trouble developed as ranchers claimed larger and larger tracts of desert land for their cattle herds.[2]

Deadly clashes between Paiutes and cowboys began grabbing headlines in early 1860. "MORE MURDERS ON THE MOJAVE," screamed the *Los Angeles Star* in March 25, 1860, as it reported on the latest killings at Bitter Springs and demanded more military posts along the Salt Lake Road.[3] A second article on March 31, 1860, reflected a large anti-Mormon sentiment in the area. "A severe castigation should be dealt out to these Indians, and they be compelled to inform on those white men who instigate them the perpetration of these bloody deeds."[4] The newspaper concluded that "no mere Indian hate led to this murder and subsequent revolting exposure—personal and fanatical rage prompted the deed. There is no manner of doubt but that the murder is the result of Mormon counsel and Mormon policy."[5] Such stories sold newspapers as white immigrants moving into the area worried about those unlike themselves—the other—who might pose a threat to these intruders stealing their homes. These stories produced a near hysteria which sanctified ridding the land of Indian menaces and created popular support for government policies that denied America's first peoples equal justice.

Heavy rains and snow along with the disastrous flooding during the winter of 1861-1862 created great hardship for many people in California, especially among Native Americans.[6] Constant rains, swollen rivers and distended lakebeds made locating food even more difficult than usual in California's Owens Valley. Local natives saw the healthy cattle herds owned by Anglo encroachers as a means of warding off starvation. Killings of Indian poachers led to retaliatory murders by the Paiutes.[7]

A peace treaty signed by local whites on January 31, 1862, provided only a short respite. Paiutes, like any people, reacted to immediate needs such as hunger and continued to steal cattle. They felt no loyalty to the United States, the state of California, or the whites who now claimed their land. A large skirmish in early April 1862 along Bishop Creek in the Owens Valley resulted in three whites and possibly eleven Indians killed. The fight forced whites to abandon the area. In April 1862 Indian Agent Warren Wasson told a Nevada newspaper that the combatants were "mostly California diggers" (Chemehuevi) from the west and south and not the more peaceable inhabitants of the area.[8]

At nearly the same time federal troops under Lieutenant Colonel George S. Evans moved from Los Angeles and joined a local militia with had retreated from the Bishop Creek area. Wasson accompanied Evans but found little hope for peace among the local survivors of the fight who expressed a desire to exterminate the Indians once and for all.[9] Urged on by Nevada Governor James W. Nye, Wasson hoped to negotiate peace between the parties but within a couple of days of the fight at Bishop Creek there was a clash between federal soldiers and Paiutes at Round Valley just northwest of Bishop Creek. Although outnumbered, the Indians won the day and Colonel Evans and his troops were forced to retreat south to secure more supplies. A clearly sympathetic Agent Wasson wrote to Governor Nye that the Paiutes "have been repeatedly told by officers of the government that they should have exclusive possession of these lands, and they are now fighting to obtain that possession....Having taken up their abode along the Owens River as a place of last resort, they will fight to the last extremity in defense of their homes."[10] Author Willie Chalfant wrote that by May 1, 1862, the Indians were in "almost undisputed possession of the whole Owens Valley."[11]

Such control, however, was only temporary. General George Wright sent additional military expeditions to secure the valley. The discovery of gold in autumn 1862 also drew a flood of miners and squatters determined to grab their own share of the "new bonanza."[12] New Indian Agent J.H.P. Wentworth reported the discovery of precious metals in and around the borders of the Great Basin changed the unknown region to "a great thoroughfare; and the importance of averting at this time such a calamity as an Indian war is more pressing."[13] Wentworth also objected to the idea, then being considered by California Senator Milton Latham, to sell reservation lands in the southern part of California and move those Indian populations to Owens Valley.[14]

The year 1863 saw continued bloodshed in Owens Valley. Paiute raiders targeted isolated white travelers or settlers, and occasionally skirmished with government troops from ongoing military expeditions. The Indians suffered greatly through increased attacks by troops of the Second California Cavalry. Government troops waged a war of attrition. Native populations often found initial success in blunting invasion of their lands but could not sustain their victories. Immigrant trains of Euro-American settlers seemed never ending in the mid-nineteenth century and were assisted by well-armed and unsympathetic state and federal troops. Indian nations, such as that of the Paiutes, saw their food sources overrun and villages destroyed while they constantly moved to escape a relentless enemy.

As the bloodshed in Owens Valley began in earnest in 1862, Nevada Paiute leader Numaga, with great eloquence, appealed for peace, despite the injustices done his people: "The white men are like the stars over your heads. You have wrongs, great wrongs, that rise up like these mountains before you," he told his people. "But can you from the mountain tops reach up and blot out those stars?"[15] He argued that the enemies of the Paiutes were "like the sands in the beds of your rivers; when taken away they only give place for more to come and settle." Numaga warned that with continued warfare hunger would stalk the Paiute, "where you will see the women and old men starve, and listen to the cries of your children for food."[16] His were not the words of a "digger" Indian scorned by much of white society as a useless sub-human, but those of a proud leader and father to a proud people who desired that his people's name be remembered. "I love my people," he concluded, "let them live; and when their spirit shall be called to the great camp in the southern sky, let their bones rest where their fathers were buried."[17] Numaga's warning foreshadowed an agonizing truth for the Paiutes: that they could not gain final victory. On June 4, 1863, several hundred Paiutes surrendered to federal forces. Their leaders signed a new treaty a month later. On July 22, 1863, an estimated 850 members of California's Paiute nation were forced to their new home on the Fort Tejon Reservation. A few escaped in route and returned to hide and live in the mountains and grasslands of their Owens Valley.[18]

It is unlikely that many Chemehuevi, or southern Paiute, met the same fate as their northern cousins despite Agent Wasson's statement that these Chemehuevi had sent warriors to fight in Owens Valley. Their homelands were south of the Valley in the eastern wastelands of the Mojave Desert, stretching from the San Bernardino Mountains to the Colorado River. Throughout the 1860s, groups of Chemehuevi continued to defend traditional territory from the increasing number of white ranchers and speculators moving in from

San Bernardino Valley.   Historians note three bloody encounters occurring between 1866 and 1867 by Chemehuevi in Summit Valley of today's High Desert near Cajon Pass. This outbreak of violence may have been, in part, an extension of the hostilities further north. For the peaceful Serrano tribe of the San Bernardino Valley, however, the outcome of these confrontations would be dire.

According to one Anglo account, this eruption of killings began, as on other occasions, with a mindless act of barbarism by whites. In 1902, Albert Clyde, a rancher in San Bernardino, recounted the story of four Paiute youths around the age of 16 brought to San Bernardino in 1865 by a wagon train from Utah. It would be logical to assume that in light of the just concluded war, these boys were more captives or slaves than guests. Clyde wrote that the Paiutes were given out to various families in the area, including the James family.[19]

One Sunday the James boys and the Paiute youth were hunting rabbits in the Santa Ana wash when boys belonging to the Thomas family came upon them. Words were exchanged between John Thomas and the Indian boy. Both boys, white and Indian, carried shotguns and when he lost his temper, Thomas raised his weapon to threaten the Paiute youth who reacted with "direct action" and instantly shot John Thomas dead.[20] Amazingly, local authorities took no action against the Indian boy, ruling the killing a tragic mishap premised on self-defense. Clyde said that the Thomas family was furious and conspired to exact their revenge.[21]

"Some time later" in February of 1866 members of the Thomas clan and others mounted a trek to Utah and took the Paiute boys along ostensibly to deliver them back to their homes. While traveling through the heavily wooded Sawpit Canyon just east of today's Interstate 15 through Cajon Pass, one Paiute boy "got suspicious" and "made a quick getaway."[22] The other three Indian boys were not so lucky. Members of the Thomas family took the Paiute boys to the lower end of the Dunlap ranch (later the Las Flores Ranch) where the Thomases killed and decapitated the Indian boys. The severed heads were stuck on long poles as a warning to other Indians. The vigilantes then returned to San Bernardino Valley.[23]

Although Clyde had no direct proof, it was his belief that the surviving Paiute boy relayed his escape and fears for his friends to other Indians in the area. Pike and Clyde drew a direct link between this incident and the killing of three cowboys, Nephi Bemis, Ed Parrish and Pratt Whiteside, a month later in the same area where the Indian boys had been murdered. Bemis, Parrish and Whiteside were part of a crew set to drive a herd of cattle to Montana.[24] The herd was located on the Dunlap ranch just north of Lake Silverwood. J. W. Gillette, another young cowboy who signed on to assist in the cattle drive, left an account of the Chemehuevi attack in 1904: When the cowboys first arrived at the ranch on March 12, 1866, Gillette and a vaquero named Antonio "who was a native of the San Bernardino valley," (probably Serrano) were rounding up strays when they found a "soft trail full of moccasin tracks" which Antonio "laconically" identified as "Chimahueva," [sic].[25]

Los Flores Ranch Lands ca. 1900s (previously Dunlap Ranch) Courtesy of Gerald Smith Collection, Unprocessed Material, Archives, A.K. Smiley Library, Redlands, CA

When Gillette reported the activity, however, Parrish downplayed any possible danger from the Indians. Gillette then wrote that a man named Anderson, "a shiftless fellow" and "an arrant boaster" produced "the skulls of two Indians killed in one of the encounters, thereabouts," which Anderson fastened to the big posts of the ranch gates. Anderson offered no specific information about the skulls but said that he "better than any one else, . . . knew the why and wherefore of those skulls, and that any Indians prowling near him would meet the same fate." It seems very likely that the skulls which Anderson so cryptically produced belonged to two of the unfortunate Paiute boys murdered the month before.[26]

The next afternoon Gillette, Bemis, and Pratt rode out to check the herd and round up strays. The men decided that Gillette, mounted on a mule, would take ten stragglers back to the herd while Bemis and Parrish, joined by Whiteside, continued to patrol for strays. Later, Antonio rode to Gillette's location and mentioned a "peculiar discharge" in the distance. Within minutes of each other, two riderless horses ran wildly past them toward the ranch. Once caught, the horses revealed a violent encounter. Both saddles were covered in blood and one horse carried an "ounce ball in the hip…and the terror of the poor beast was infectious from its intensity," Gillette said.[27]

Left to Right: Bill Holcomb, John Brown Junior, John Brown Sr., George Miller and B.B. Harris. Courtesy of San Bernardino County Museum, Redlands, California.

Others at the ranch were alerted and the search began for the remaining horse and the men who rode them. A "queer acting coyote" led them to the nude bodies of Bemis and Whiteside. Whiteside's face had also been crushed with a great stone. The stripped body of Parrish would not be found until the next day. Gillette surmised that all three must have been pushing their way through a small ravine when the Indians, "from the left, in ambush, poured in the volley that had sounded to Anton as one shot, sending an ounce ball into the neck of each victim, not differing in location over three inches, so deliberate and perfect was their aim."[28]

Gillette and the remaining cowboys took the bodies to San Bernardino, where the slayings "sparked a campaign in which San Bernardino raised a ranger posse."[29] The *Los Angeles News* of April 13, 1866, reported that funeral services for the three young cowboys (none said to be older than 17) was the "most largely attended of any event recalled in the town."[30] During the funeral, however, word reached the town that the ranch had been attacked in their absence and the guards left behind chased down Cajon Pass. A posse reported that they "found all the improvements smoking ruins." Gillette never returned to the ranch.[31]

The Dunlap Ranch had not been the only target of the Indians. The Chemehuevis attacked a small sawmill in Little Bear Valley near the dam at today's Lake Arrowhead. George Miller remembered the attack and subsequent battle in a letter published in 1917. He believed that between 250 and 300 warriors were involved. "They were mostly Piutes, [sic] and a few Chimihueve [sic] and renegades," he wrote. Anglos in the area barricaded themselves near Blue Jay Camp at the mill owned in part by Frank Talmadge and Jonathan Richardson.[32] Indians ransacked and burned a house belonging to Bill Kane. The next morning a group of the lumber camp workers began tracking the Paiute raiders. Their task was made easier by the five to six inches of snow that had fallen the night before. Soon encountering a group of eight Indians, a skirmish erupted with the Indians firing a few shots before disappearing into the thick mantel of underbrush and forest. "The ground was uneven and well timbered, which, of course, gave the Indians great advantage, and well they knew how to take it," participant Bill Holcomb later wrote.[33] Two of the whites, Kane and John Welty, were wounded in the exchange. Miller noted that the marauders carried away their dead and wounded. "Those Indians that were killed," he wrote, "had their shoes, or sandals, tied to their belts and their feet in the snow. They all were barefooted, as their tracks showed in the snow."[34]

The mill workers sent word for reinforcements to San Bernardino, where the news created a frenzy of excitement. "Quite a number volunteered," Holcomb said, "and without delay took up such firearms as they were in possession of."[35] Merchants such as Dr. Ben Barton opened their stores, freely equipping the makeshift militia with provisions and ammunition. Two separate groups departed San Bernardino, one by way of Brown's Ranch in the upper reaches of the Cajon Pass, the other making its way to the lumber camp in Little Bear Valley.[36]

Tracks indicated the Chemehuevi had made their way down the mountainside to the desert floor, passing nearby the now-ruined buildings of the Dunlap Ranch. The ranch soon became a staging point as men and provisions arrived from San Bernardino and Little Bear Valley. This "army of the Mojave,"[37] as Miller dubbed it, divided into two groups with Preacher Stout selected as captain of the group that traveled northeast by way of a wagon road toward Rabbit Springs, which all the tracks indicated was the route taken by the Indians. The second group headed by John St. John and including Miller and Holcomb, traveled through rough terrain along the western flank, which slowed their progress. They started just after midnight and even years later Miller remembered the bitter cold—"the coldest weather that I had experienced in many a day. Men's moustaches froze from their breath."[38]

Stout and his men arrived at their destination on time. Not seeing Miller's group they fired off their weapons to mark their whereabouts—an action that also alerted the Indians.

Talmadge Mill, Little Bear Valley ca. 1878.
Courtesy of Archives, A.K. Smiley Library, Redlands, California

Hearing the shots St. John's group hurried forward. As they made their way up a steep grade, Miller and the men of his party saw the Indians scatter for the safety of the nearby rocks while his group stumbled through a rocky and difficult terrain. The Chemehuevi laid in wait for Stout's group, unaware that St. John and his men were preparing to surprise them from behind. Moving slowly but deliberately, Miller said that "we got right in their among them before they knew it. Then the guns began to crack and arrows began zipping about, and you could not see any distance for so many big rocks." The scene became very chaotic with the Indians yelling and darting through the rocks very close to their Anglo attackers.[39]

Suddenly, a Chemehuevi rose up from behind a rock "drew his bow and quick...sent an arrow with great force into the breast of brave Jonathan Richardson," Holcomb wrote.[40] Miller reported that most of the Indians made an escape through the rocky field. However, the militia captured five Chemehuevi, two women, an infant, a girl about ten and a fourteen years old boy.[41] Some of the white posse attempted to track the Indians over the next couple days, which resulted in another ambush by the Chemehuevi and near disaster for their Anglo pursuers, who then decided to break off the chase. Holcomb later reported that while attempting to parley with the Chemehuevi, the Indian prisoners "made a dash for their liberty " which "cost them their lives."[42]

Writer Burr Belden reported that the Chemehuevi raiders returned a year later in January 1867 and again attacked the Talmadge sawmill and nearby houses. If so, this was a last ditch attempt to protect the land of their ancestors—land that had been traditional hunting grounds for the Chemehuevi. Being pushed entirely into the vast desolation of the Mojave and denied access to the rich hunting fields of the local mountains jeopardized the life the Chemehuevi knew and would never know again. Reportedly the mill and lumber camp workers were again joined by vigilantes from San Bernardino bent on exacting a lasting revenge on Indians—any and all Indians. Again, chased to the desert floor, another skirmish occurred near the Rabbit Springs area at a landmark called Chimney Rock. Reportedly after a heated fight, most of the raiding Indians were "exterminated."[43]

The victory achieved over the Chemehuevi was not enough for the excited militia members who sought out other targets of opportunity. In a pattern repeated throughout the West, their next victims were guiltless of any violation. The Serrano were peaceful farmers and herders who lived in the hills northeast of San Bernardino. The attack on these people was purely malicious and fired by racial hatred. According to one historian, victims of this mindless killing included men, women and children. This genocidal attack, which most historians place in the year 1866, while premised on race, was also underscored by greed. Serrano leader Santos Manuel ended the attacks by moving his people from the mountains to the valley floor. The land and resources held by the Serrano were coveted by whites in the area and some used the galvanizing fear of the Indian attacks as a means to eradicate the Serrano and steal their property. Whether by fruitless treaties or overt murder, the intent and outcome was always the same for native peoples across the United States.[44]

Human action, however, is never as cut and dry as even some historians would like. The deserts of Southern California remained very dangerous for decades after the fight at Chimney Rock, even if the accounts of continued violence went largely unnoted.

The San Bernardino Daily Times wrote in March 1880 about a group of cowboys looking for Indians to punish for lost cattle. The cowboys stumbled into a hornet's nest of Kumeyaay Indians near Jacumbia Rancheria in the barren mountains east of San Diego. A two-hour battle described as a "hot fight"[45] ensued between gun-wielding Anglos and Indians armed with bows and spears. William McCain was found shot though the head and an unspecified number of Kumeyaay died in the battle. "Lieutenant Hayden" and troops left immediately for Campo. Authorities feared that this was the beginning of a "small border war."[46] The Colorado Desert, likewise, was still a dangerous place for whites to wander alone. A month after the Kumeyaay skirmish the same paper reported that "Chimehueva" [sic] killed George Lee, a "veteran prospector." Indians tied his corpse to a horse and sent it into the mountains. Single prospectors were warned not to travel in the area for peril of their lives.[47]

The Paiutes of Owens Valley and the Chemehuevi of the Mojave resisted the best way they could for as long as they could, emulating the actions of every Native American tribe from the very first contact with strange white invaders. The outcome, unfortunately, was always the same, whether the tribes were mighty and warlike like the Shawnee or Sioux or comfortably passive such as the Gabrieleño or Serrano.

NOTES:

[1] Hanks, "Vicissitudes of Justice: Massacre at San Timoteo Canyon," 237-240.

[2] Dennis G. Casebier in *Carleton's Pah-Ute Campaign* (Norco, California: Dennis G. Casebier, June 1972), 2-16.

[3] *Los Angeles Star* newspaper, March 25, as cited by Casebier, *Carleton's Pah-Ute Campaign,* 6-7.

[4] *Los Angeles Star,* newspaper, March 31, 1860, as cited by Casebier, *Carleton's Pah-Ute,* 7.

[5] Ibid.

[6] Willie A. Chalfant, *The Story of Inyo,* (Los Angeles: Privately Published, 1933), 147-148.

[7] Ibid., 149.

[8] Ibid., 156-159.

[9] Ibid., 163.

[10] Ibid., 166.

[11] Ibid., 167.

[12] Ibid., 170.

[13] Ibid., 172.

[14] Ibid., 171.

[15] Ibid., 155.

[16] Ibid.

[17] Ibid.

[18] Ibid., 194-195.

[19] Albert Clyde, "History of Pioneer Days," July 28, 1902, copy in unprocessed pamphlets, Gerald Smith Collection, Archives of A.K. Smiley Public Library, Redlands, California. Clyde received his information from a pioneer resident of San Bernardino Valley he identified as J. F. Pike, whom he said "was intimately acquainted with all of the parties involved." Clyde continued that the account was "written in the very firm belief that the information is authentically accurate and...was the active cause of the breaking out of the Piute [sic]war in March 1866." See also Clifford Trafzer, *The People of San Manuel* (Patton, California: San Manuel Band of Mission Indians, 2002), 66.

[20] Ibid.

[21] Ibid.

[22] Ibid.

[23] Ibid.

[24] Ibid.

[25] J. W. Gillette, "Some Indian Experiences," *Annual Publication of the Historical Society of Southern California and of the Pioneers of Los Angeles County, 1904,* 160. Early writers and historians often gave a phonetic interpretation of Indian names in print regardless of whether those names were derived from native or a European language such as Spanish. It is not uncommon to see variations of spellings for tribes such as the Chemehuevi and Cahuilla.

[26] Ibid., 161.

[27] Ibid.

[28] Ibid., 162.

[29] Burr Belden, "Indians v. Ranchers: History in Making," *San Bernardino Sun* newspaper, September 2, 1962.

[30] Belden, "Indian Raiders Kill Youths, Are Then Defeated," *San Bernardino Sun* newspaper, September 13, 1953.

[31] Gillette, "Some Indian Experiences," 164.

[32] Letter, George Miller to Byron Waters, July 18, 1916 as cited by Dr. H. W. Mills in "De Tal Palo Tal Astilla," *Annual Publications Historical Society of Southern California*, 1917, 160.

[33] Bill Holcomb, *History of San Bernardino and Riverside Counties*, John Brown, Jr. and James Boyd, eds., vol. I (Madison, Wis.: The Western Historical Association, 1922), 23.

[34] Letter, George Miller to Byron Waters, in "De Tal Palo Tal Astilla," 161.

[35] Holcomb, *History of San Bernardino and Riverside Counties*, 23.

[36] Ibid.

[37] Letter, George Miller to Byron Waters, in "De Tal Palo Tal Astilla," 161.

[38] Ibid., 162. The leader of one of the groups, Miller only knew by his last name of Stout. Bill Holcomb called the man "Preacher Stout." This man could be William Stout, who appears in federal census records for San Bernardino County in 1860. William Stout had a ranch near San Salvador township, which was the home of the "genízaros" from the Rowland-Workman party who settled there in 1844. His son joined William Stout on the vigilante group and records show 24-year-old H. J. Parker Stout at the same ranch in 1860.

[39] Letter, George Miller to Byron Waters, in "De Tal Palo Tal Astilla," 162-163.

[40] Holcomb, *History of San Bernardino and Riverside Counties*, 24.

[41] Letter, George Miller to Byron Waters, in "De Tal Palo Tal Astilla," 163.

[42] Holcomb, *History of San Bernardino and Riverside Counties*, 24.

[43] Belden, "Indian Raiders Kill Youths." *San Bernardino Sun*, September 13, 1953.

[44] Trafzer, *The People of San Manuel*, 66, 68.

[45] *San Bernardino Daily Times* newspaper, March 2, 1880.

[46] Ibid.

[47] *San Bernardino Daily Times* newspaper, April 6, 1880.

5 Brothers of the Same Spring: The Battle for the Leadership of Potrero

It is to be ardently hoped that the Indian will never feel that his reliance on Washington as the abode of justice has been misplaced. —*John Hamilton Gilmour, 1892*

Will Pablo Postcard
Photo courtesy
of Palm Springs
Historical Society

Near the present-day city of Loma Linda is a canyon known by the Cahuilla Indians as Homuba or Jumuba, containing three mineral springs. William Pablo, shaman, captain and police officer of the Cahuilla, told the following story of three Indian children, who one day disappeared. Their frantic parents consulted a "witch-doctor" who took them to the springs where he said the children now lived. As he stood in the middle spring, he said: "Listen to the Great Father who is above us, the Creator of the World. He has taken your boy and put him in the spring, so that this spring will bring health to you and to others."[1] Then, according to Pablo's story, the Indian doctor called to the children and a voice arose from the spring:

> I am here with my two sisters. We were placed here by our Lord, the Creator of the world. He has given me the power to bring new life to those who are sick. You may come and visit me and my sisters whenever you wise.…We are all three in this one place, and if you will live together and honor the great Lord, when you are sick if you will use these life springs, we will help you get back your health. These springs shall be know as the 'Two Sisters and Brother Life Springs.'
>
> And the people listened. Therefore the Indians went up there and held a great ceremony and from then on they used these springs for medical purposes. Then, the Catholic missionaries came to this country and established the missions. They took the Indian children by force and made them Catholics. And these Christians also went up to the springs and used them for many years.
>
> Later on the United States Government came to this country and took these lands and gave the Indians reservations for their use. And the Indians had to leave the springs, which originally belonged to them.
>
> When the mission was first built at San Gabriel the priest asked an Indian: 'Why do you Indians take your children, when they are sick, to those springs, instead of taking them to a doctor?'
>
> And the Indian answered:
>
> 'Father, the springs at Homuba Canyon can cure any sickness. That is why we take our children there when they are sick, and they are healed. Our ancestors used those springs and became healed.'

Then the priest went to the springs to examine the water, and took some of the water and made the Indian carry it to the chapel, and he blessed the water, and held Mass with it and used it to cure the sick. And finally the priest moved the mission from San Gabriel to San Bernardino, Old San Bernardino now known as Redlands. And from there the priest used to send the Indians to bring the waters to the mission, using it as medicine. And he cured many sick Indians. Now there were two Indians villages nearby, and they fought over possession of the springs. They went on the warpath over the Two Sisters and Brother Life Springs. So the mission went away and settled elsewhere, and the priest also went away.

Then our white neighbors came, as I said, and drove the Indians from our sacred springs. That is why the Indians are dying out in Southern California, became we must live on worthless lands far away from those springs.

Our white neighbors may think we Indians have no religion, but that is not so. We do believe in God who is the Creator of the World, and of the firmament, of Indians as well as white people…therefore we are brothers in God, as we are created by God.

I often hear white people say they are Americans in America, and we are Indians. I say we are the native sons of America. We are good to our country and to our white neighbors, and do not trouble them. When the mission first came to this country the Indians were numerous and the country well inhabited by the Indians. Then the Indians did not know that the country was going to be filled with intoxicating liquor. If they had known that, they would never have allowed the missionaries to establish any missions in this country. For a great number of Indians died of intoxicating liquor.

However, the United States Government made a law prohibiting the sale of intoxicating liquor to the American Indians. But by that time it was too late. The American Indians are nearly all gone. But maybe a few will be saved.

It was in 1908 that special officers suppressed the liquor traffic among the mission Indians in Southern California. The chief of these special officers came to me and asked: 'Why is it that you are always fighting the whites?'

'Because they are all liars, thieves, and whisky peddlers,' I answered.

He looked at me and said:

'Am I a liar and a whisky peddler?'

'No,' I answered. 'You do not look like one. I think you are on the square.'

So he said to me:

'I want you to work with me on the same job.'

'What job do you mean?' said I.

'To suppress the liquor traffic among the mission Indians,' he said.

So I was deputized as Special Officer since then, and I became Chief of Police in the Indian Service for nine Indian reservations under the United State[s]

Government, to protect the Indians, to make transactions for the Indians, and to help them become sober, improve their morals, and become civilized. In 1847 if the United States Government had sent us a man like Mr. C.T. Coggeshall, who is the superintendent of the nine Indian reservations, the Indians would never have lost the Two Sisters and Brother Life Springs. Mr. Coggeshall is a man with large experience and he had done a lot of good for the Indians under his jurisdiction.
Chief William Als Pablo[2]

William Pablo was a Wanikik Cahuilla born at the Potrero village site near present-day Banning around 1861. He was a shaman, herbalist, and hereditary leader of his clan, like his father. Pablo was a close ally and relative of Cabezon, the son of the respected leader by the same name who died in 1883. The younger Cabezon was a hereditary leader of the Pass Cahuilla and well-respected among his people.[3]

Pablo's story of the Two Sisters and Brother Life Springs reflected on a life dedicated to the struggle of preserving the culture, land base and resources of Southern California Indians in and around San Gorgonio Pass and his home village of Potrero. Like Olegario Calac, Pablo became adept at using all available means to continue the fight, whether against zealous Indian agents or rival Native Americans.

One of Pablo's first tests concerned preserving the Potrero village site and the critical water resources that made the land so valuable and coveted by local Anglo ranchers and farmers. Pablo testified in the government's case in 1889 when it brought suit against whites who claimed ownership of the disputed property. The focus of the court fight were those parcels of land which contained water, many of which were claimed illegally by white poachers. The court ruled against the Native Americans but a government commission later settled the dispute to the satisfaction of all involved.[4]

The war of survival for Southern California Indians, however, had many fronts. Besides physical assault on their land and water rights, they faced the insidious attack of government agents determined to eradicate Indian culture from the American landscape.

If Cave Couts represented the vicious child of manifest destiny who perceived Indians as so much chattel to be used, abused, and discarded by a superior race, Indian Agent Samuel S. Lawson viewed Native Americans as unruly children in need of discipline and constant oversight to wean them from their pagan and nonChristian ways. Neither man offered Indians in Southern California the answer to their plight: to have their culture respected, their land protected, and the freedom to make their lives their own.

Lawson was appointed Special Agent to Mission Indians in August 1878 and moved the agency office from Los Angeles to San Bernardino. He was the Reverend Lawson and an Evangelical Lutheran from an Illinois church. The government initiated a policy of assigning different Christian denominations to the reservations with Lutherans receiving Southern California for a time.[5]

The Grant administration replaced isolation and extermination of Native Americans as a national policy with an effort to peacefully deal with Indians. In 1867 the Grant administration formed a Peace Commission which "endeavored to conquer by kindness" native tribes.[6] Not surprisingly, Commission members and other associated government officials bore names that just a few years earlier were synonymous with the abolitionist movement to end black slavery during the Civil War. Men such as Samuel Tappan, John Brooks Henderson, Zachariah Chandler and Carl Shurz now tackled the question of "what do we do with the Indian." The Commission's findings criticized government policy as being "uniformly unjust"[7] toward Native Americans and an Indian bureau riddled by inefficiency and corruption. In an effort to counter the problem and oversee disbursement of funds, in 1869 the Congress authorized the creation of a civilian advisory group, the Board of Indian Commissioners, which was composed primarily of Protestant laymen such as Quaker and educator Albert Smiley.[8]

The Grant administration and later Hayes government dismissed the issue of sovereignty; reservations became a place to isolate, Christianize, and civilize the Native American.   The storm troopers for this crusade were reformers, such as Lawson, armed with Christian zealotry of the conservative religious movement. The Catholic Church was not represented on the Board of Indian Commissioners and began losing ground on the number of reservations assigned to its care. In 1874 the Catholic Church created the Bureau of Catholic Indian Missions, which lobbied the government for equal consideration.[9] Their efforts proved successful when, in 1881, Secretary of the Interior Schurz declared that reservations were open to all denominations unless the rivalry threatened peace and order.[10] That is exactly what happened a few years later on the Potrero reservation when, fueled by Christian denominational conflict, an internal battle for leadership of the area often turned violent.

Temperance was a basic tenet of the Calvinist belief system brought by agents, such as Lawson, to the reservations. Redlands, California, farmer Myron Crafts shared the belief in the dangers of alcohol, and sought to reform or at least control the use of it by Indian laborers on his farm. Crafts was a staunch Unionist from New England who moved into the Redlands area in 1861 as the nation went to war against itself. At that time the greater San Bernardino area was a breeding ground for secessionist activity, and Crafts was often the focus of death threats. His orchards and vineyards flourished but, being personally temperate, he refused to let his grapes be used for wine and instead dried them into raisins.[11]

Crafts' initial attitude toward the Native Americans in and around San Bernardino Valley was cautious and sensitive of the injustice done the area's native peoples. "The Indians had rights," Craft wrote to his brother George in 1873. "Every foot of land we occupy is theirs.

And should we continue the crime as well as folly of robbing them? And better stop when we are sure they try to take the reins of justice into their own hands. We cannot afford to fight the Indian only as a last resort." Crafts was aware, however, of the underlying threat that could materialize any time. "We flatter ourselves whilst the Indians are quiet now—that they will continue to be so—But we have learned how unwise it is to cherish such expectations. The Kowas or Cowhilles [Cahuillas] could keep our entire national force at bay in their fortresses in the mountains over their vast extent of territory. What have not 60 Modocs cost us on life and treasure."[12]

His views on alcohol governed his treatment of his Indian laborers who lived in a village on his ranch in the hills above Redlands. He paid them only in goods from his store instead of money to prevent wages being used to purchase liquor. One historian acknowledged that this system "invited the suspicion that so often attaches to company stores" but regarded it as best for the laborers.[13]

While alcohol was certainly a tool used by many whites to control and demoralize native populations, the system of serfdom imposed by Crafts was just as controlling. Crafts' intentions may have been more benign than most white settlers but were just as manipulative and ultimately demeaning to Native Americans.

Ironically, despite Lawson's evangelical background, he opposed Crafts' system of feudalism. Lawson listened to the Indians on Potrero (now Morongo) Reservation near Banning, who complained that Crafts cheated them out of their money. Lawson and Crafts engaged in a public war of words for a time. Lawson accused Crafts of forcing his Indian laborers to purchase poor quality goods from Crafts' own store for their work on his farm. Local Cahuilla and Serrano Indians saw a chance to exploit the situation and openly criticized both Lawson and Crafts, pitting one evil against another. This was a clever way of resisting by encouraging a contest between their oppressors. An 1879 newspaper reporter wrote that "San Bernardino Indians" were seriously dissatisfied with Lawson who, they said, collected their wages from Crafts and only distributed part to the native wage earners.[14] The report continued that armed Indians refused efforts to force them onto a reservation and during one visit, attacked Lawson. The account credited Lawson's Indian interpreter, Serrano John Morongo, with saving the agent.[15] A few days later Lawson said the trouble was "a trumped-up affair" created by a few Indians prevented from buying liquor through the vigilance of Morongo.[16]

Historian Helen Pruitt Beattie, however, wrote that the "Indian excitement" of 1879 was very real for residents of Lugonia, a small township created a few years before today's city of Redlands along the Santa Ana River wash. Many local Indians considered this part of San Bernardino Valley their home and saw no reason to leave because some white men desired to continue their land theft without bothering the original owners. Beattie quoted Lugonia school teacher "Mrs. Brink" who reported that "one day about a dozen bucks came galloping, shouting, and flourishing weapons." These "husky Indians" clearly made their

John Morongo, undated.
Courtesy of Weinland Collection,
Huntington Library, San Marino, CA

point about the potential of solving their problems by physical action. [17]

It is ironic that at around the same time, in September 1879, Crafts was arrested for inciting insurrection among the Indians. It seems likely that Agent Lawson instigated this action as a way of neutralizing an enemy and distracting attention away from his own troubles with local Indians. The charges against Crafts were dismissed after a late September hearing in Los Angeles before a commissioner of the United States District Court. Two unidentified Indians, however, spent a week in the federal prison at Alcatraz before being exonerated of the charges.[18]

The show of force by Serrano and Cahuilla people of San Bernardino Valley jolted white settlers of the area but could not prevent the government's effort to relocate natives to the Potrero near Banning. Lawson, of course, promised the usual enticements, including land, seeds, housing, and goods that came with every forced removal from traditional Indian lands. Mrs. Brink, the Lugonia schoolteacher, remembered being present at the council between Agent Lawson (she thought) and Old Chief Cabezon where the largely one-sided agreement was reached. In words which emulated the eloquence of Paiute Chief Numaga, Cabezon pointed to the great mountains that rose above the gathering and reminded the audience of whites and Indians that "all this…was once theirs to ride, to hunt, to live as they chose." That changed, Cabezon said, with the coming of the white man, who said, "'Give me a little for my own,' so we move little way, not hunt there, then some more come, and say 'move more,' and we move again. So many times! Now we are a small people, we have little place; but they say move to new place . . . go from our home valley." [19]

This was a bitter pill for Chief Cabezon, whose history with Lawson was uneasy. Former Indian Agent Captain J. Stanley, in a government report of 1884, wrote of his visit to Cabezon and his people. They complained that Lawson never had visited their villages nor had shown "any interest in their welfare; that he had allowed his interpreter Juan Morengo [sic], to take the advantage of them." They accused John Morongo of contracting with a San

Bernardino man to cut wood needed for the railroad "on land claimed by the Indians" and that Morongo took the "lion's share" of the money for his own.[20]

Such internal politics worked to the advantage of government agents. Dissension worked to undermine efforts at unifying native peoples for a stronger voice when dealing with government officials. John Morongo was much more valuable to agents such as Lawson than simply an interpreter. He provided an option—a choice for native people other than leadership chosen along lines of traditional inheritance and clanship. Accepting Morongo meant accepting federal control since Morongo worked for Lawson. The rivalry that developed between Morongo and Will Pablo would be specifically about that choice.

John Morongo may be seen as an accommodationist by some, but according to Morongo Tribal Historian Ernest Siva, Serrano oral history tells that John was following a Serrano prophecy that foretold the coming of whites and the need to work with them and teach the "little brothers" despite the hardships which accompanied their arrival.

Agent Lawson's problems increased with the visit in May 1883 of Helen Hunt Jackson. Jackson, accompanied by friend Abbott Kinney, journeyed through Southern California on a fact-finding mission, evaluating the plight of local Indians. Jackson urged the dismissal of Pala schoolteacher Arthur Golsh who was within Lawson's jurisdiction. In letters to Lawson, Jackson accused Golsh of having sexual relations with two of his pupils at Pala and Pauma and impregnating the Pala girl. Lawson was reportedly sympathetic to Golsh.[21] Whether it was the clash with Jackson or poor relations with the Indian population, Lawson resigned his position in August 1883.

John Guthrie McCallum replaced Lawson despite lobbying efforts by Jackson and Kinney for activist Horatio Rust. McCallum's tenure was brief, however, as he resigned on August 22, 1885. McCallum dedicated his time to securing sections of land from Indian owners in Coachella Valley around today's Palm Springs.[22]

Kinney's enthusiasm for Rust's abilities undoubtedly swayed Helen Jackson to solicit Rust's appointment. Rust was also a member of the Los Angeles branch of the Indian Rights Association. As with Jackson and even Lawson, Rust represented the growing paternalism toward Indians and people of color generally. Based on a staunch orthodox Christian foundation, these activists, though well-meaning, sought to break the "pagan" traditionalism of Native Americans through a process that stressed acceptance of Christian values and assimilation into Anglo culture and the Jeffersonian ideal of democracy through development of yeoman farmers.[23] Jackson's support of Rust was rewarded when Rust was formally appointed in 1889 as agent over twenty-two reservations from Hoopa Valley in Northern California to the Mexican border. When appointed, Rust was the secretary of the Los Angeles chapter of the Indian Rights Association.[24]

Horatio Nelson Rust was another New Englander, born in Amherst, Massachusetts, in 1828. While a druggist in Connecticut he met the famed radical abolitionist John Brown

Several Indian Leaders of Southern California.
Front row, from left to right: Captain Habiel, Captain
Will Pablo, Captain Hervasio Cabezon, Captain Manuel,
Captain Jose Maria.
Back row, left to right: Captain Ramon, Captain Jim,
Captain Lastro.
Courtesy of Gerald Smith Collection,
Archives, A.K. Smiley Public Library, Redlands, CA

and became an ardent supporter of the zealot, raising money for the cause. He secured the contract for the manufacture of a thousand pikes which Brown had made for his failed slave insurrection of 1859. After the Civil War, Rust continued his support of causes such as the Chicago Relief Association, which assisted the emigration of freed blacks to Kansas. Rust's passion, however, was archaeology and he pursued his interests by visiting Indian sites in the Midwest and collecting or purchasing native artifacts. [25] Seeking a better climate, Rust moved to Pasadena, California, in 1881 at the age of 53. He became involved in efforts to build the Pasadena Free Library, where he met fellow member Abbott Kinney. [26]

Agent Rust, as with Lawson before him, maintained the services of John Morongo and imposed Morongo on the Indians of Potrero as their captain. Morongo and his people were accepted by the Cahuilla because of "marriage alliances," with the condition that the authority of the traditional leaders would be recognized by the Serranos. This situation was very similar to the confrontation between Manuel Cota and Olegario Calac thirty years earlier. For the first time, anthropologist Lowell Bean wrote, "the self-determination of the people at Morongo to elect leaders by the traditional process was seriously challenged."[27] Will Pablo refused to accept this intrusion into the lives of his people. Regardless of his relationship with John Morongo, Pablo asserted his right as a hereditary leader of his clan and tribe. Pablo's personal challenge was to creatively develop forms of resistance that would obstruct and derail Rust's program for the Potrero.

Southern California leaders: Front row, from left, Santos Manuel (with top hat),
possibly Francisco Morongo, Chief Cabezon (arms folded), possibly Pedro Chino;
second row: Juan Ramon, unknown, Will Pablo (leaning).
Courtesy of Weinland Collection, Huntington Library, San Marino, CA

Indian Agent Rust, following the policies of his predecessor Lawson, leased native agricultural and grazing lands to area whites but maintained control of the rents, supposedly for future irrigation expenses. Pablo, along with the younger Chief Cabezon, son of Old Cabezon who led his people to the Potrero area, opposed Rust's efforts to curtail their influence and control tribal leadership. Rust retaliated by denigrating their character in reports to Commissioner of Indian Affairs Thomas J. Morgan; Rust sought the arrest of the Indian leaders.[28] He excited opponents of Cabezon into having an election, in which Cabezon was replaced by an Indian named Bill Williams.

In the battle for leadership of the Potrero, Pablo secured the services of an attorney, John Brown Jr. of San Bernardino. Pablo, like Olegario, gained an understanding of the arenas of American government. American ideas of justice often differed from concepts of justice within a traditional Indian tribal environment. Pablo, however, learned, adapted, and realized the strength in forming political alliances with other tribes and white supporters. Pablo took the offensive and challenged American authority in the very halls of American power—the courtroom and corridors of legislative influence. Lawyers Wilson for Olegario and Brown for Pablo provided conduits to those Americans who could make decisions. For Indians, or any people unschooled in the arts of the democratic process, this is a savvy accomplishment, exposing an understanding of the outside world that most Americans of the time period would have thought impossible.

Rust wrote to Thomas J. Morgan, Commissioner of Indian Affairs in February 1891 complaining of the "shyster" Brown and Pablo's interference. He wrote that Brown had "been accustomed to advise these Indians for several years (his wife being part Indian)," and complained that Pablo was "constantly fomenting trouble, inciting lawsuits, and hindering those who desire to work." [29] Pablo and Brown organized a petition demanding Rust's removal. Morgan, of course, approved and supported Rust's actions. When told of Pablo's election as captain, Rust responded that Potrero Indians "would not have any captain" until they "elect a good man and obey him and me." [30]

It was not just the leadership of Potrero that Rust intended to control but religious beliefs as well. Rust's appointment to the Mission Indian Agency came at the same time as Thomas Morgan's appointment by President Benjamin Harrison to the post of Commissioner of Indian Affairs. Scholar Francis Paul Prucha accused Morgan of a strong anti-Catholic bias during a time when organizations such as the Indian Rights Association were in conflict with the Bureau of Catholic Indian Missions for religious control of the government-run reservations. Morgan also firmly believed that the way to break the hold of native tribalism was by curtailing reservation contract schools and creating off-reservation boarding schools that under his tenure expanded from seven to nineteen. [31]

Rust was obviously a disciple of Morgan's philosophy and looked to inhibit Roman Catholic influence on the Potrero by supporting the missionary work of Moravian Minister William Weinland. Reportedly, this was also encouraged by John Morongo and Protestant schoolteacher Sarah Morris. Weinland's personal attitude toward Catholicism was reportedly anything but Christian. Mesa Grande schoolteacher Mary Watkins wrote of being disturbed at a Los Angeles assembly of teachers meeting where the position of "drop the Indians and let them die" prevailed. "Mr. Weinland who is a Moravian missionary," she continued, "hates Catholics with a bitterness that poisons his own better judgement. He had not been successful in converting the Indians from that mode of worship and so says 'Let them die. They have had their chance, now drop them.'" [32]

Southern California reservations were a natural battleground for the test of ecumenical wills between advocates of the Protestant and Roman Catholic faiths. Catholics had controlled the religious frontier in California for over a hundred years. Grant's peace policy gave Protestant clergy the moral responsibility for saving Indian souls on America's reservations. For Native Americans such as Will Pablo, the denominational rivalry was another opportunity to undermine government control. Pablo, like most on the Potrero, was a Catholic. He also was a respected Cahuilla shaman like his father before him. California Indians, since the first invasion by the Spaniards, accepted many tenets of the Christian

Right to Left: Will Pablo, John Hyde & unidentified man.
Photo courtesy of Gerald Smith Collection,
Archives, A.K. Smiley Public Library, Redlands, California

faith without rejecting the traditional religion of their ancestors. Adaptation for Southern California Indians was not just political but religious as well.

While many Cahuilla initially attended the services conducted by Weinland, many left to continue their practice that combined traditional Indian beliefs with Catholicism.[33]

The Roman Catholic schools in San Diego and nearby St. Boniface in Banning, which opened in September 1890, each received a federal government subsidy for the attendance of each Indian student. Pablo was a "policeman" at St. Boniface. Resistance to Rust's administration included opposition to Rust's zealous attempt to convert tribal members to the Moravian Church. As an act of defiance, Pablo encouraged Potrero Indians to send their children to St. Boniface instead of the Protestant day school. Morgan downplayed Pablo's influence in an explanation to the Secretary of the Interior in July 1891, and said he represented only a "faction " at Potrero. Pablo's efforts, however did result in the closure for a short time of Weinland's school. [34]

In the correspondence, Morgan accused Pablo of "using his influence to deplete the [government] school," of controlling people by practicing as a medicine man, and of threatening the life of John Morongo. Morgan supported Rust's request for "a jail for the confinement of obstreperous Indians." In lieu of a jail, Morgan suggested that the military arrest Pablo and confine him at some "place remote from the agency." [35]

Ironically, Rust discovered evidence that the former agent in the area, Samuel Lawson, had conspired against him. In November 1890 Rust intercepted a letter between Lawson and Captain John Morongo asking, "how are you getting along in the 'Rust business?'" Lawson continued, "if you mean to get rid of Rust, and want my help—we can do it. Only keep this to yourself—If you are in earnest I would like to make a fight for appointment—provided you would be willing to come into the service with me as before. …But, whether I get it or not, I would fire him if I were in your place."[36]

Rust wrote to Morgan that Pablo "has joined hands" with Cabezon, Brown, "and Lawson, a disgraced Indian agent, of Colton, to drive me out as agent." By early December 1891, Rust still had not received a satisfactory answer from local military authorities about incarcerating Pablo. He wrote to Morgan of his commitment to John Morongo and accused Pablo and "a lieutenant named Segundo" of torching Morongo's property and attempting to injure or murder Morongo and Reverend Weinland.[37]

As a respected shaman, Pablo knew the power he had with the Indians of Potrero. Religion as used by Rust could divide and create controversy but Pablo knew the strength of religion could also generate unity of purpose and action. A year prior to Rust's complaining letters to Morgan, Lakota in South Dakota paid dearly for embracing the Ghost Dance vision of Paiute holy man Wovoka. The vision, which spread like a prairie fire across the West, promised a new age for native peoples where the white race would disappear—a cleansing of traditional lands and a return of cherished relatives. The panic of an inexperienced agent brought a military occupation of the reservations and directly led to the murder of mystic leader Sitting Bull and the slaughter of Chief Big Foot's band of Miniconjou Sioux in December 1890.

Six months later Rust accused Pablo of invoking the Paiute vision to unite his people and excite resistance to Rust's policies. Pablo did not seek a violent uprising through use of the Ghost Dance, only a method of galvanizing support in his war with Rust. Pablo also demonstrated his control over the actions of the Indians of Potrero, which undoubtedly unnerved Rust. On July 4, 1891, Rust wrote that Pablo's influence "has led many to believe that the Messiah will come about July 4 and white men will be destroyed." Rust continued that "now about fifty families are camped high up on San Jacinto Mountain on [the] west side of the desert, expecting their Messiah will run down the whites, and the overflow of the Colorado into the desert basin around Salton gives the medicine men hope and the Indians great fear."[38]

Rust was concerned enough about the Ghost Dance influence on the Potrero that he included it in his Annual Report in 1891. "The Messiah craze reached us, and a few were influenced by the statements of the medicine men, who said that the white man would be destroyed and that they would possess the land. Only a small number believed this until the Colorado River began to fill up the Salton Sea, when runners visited several villages telling wild stories of the waters to come which so frightened many good faithful Indians that they fled to the mountains in wild haste; but a few days of fasting reassured them and they returned disappointed. The medicine man told that the most progressive Indian of the tribe, John Morongo, must be driven out or die. Constant threats are made, and his haystack of 10 tons of hay was burned."[39]

It is less of a coincidence that it first appears that Rust described the attacks upon the property of John Morongo at the conclusion of his report on the effects of the "Messiah craze." Historian Florence Shipek noted that Pablo combined the mystical appeal of the Ghost Dance to form the "core of his oppositional organization."[40] Pablo turned the strength of traditional religious conviction into political resistance.

Pablo's adaptation to new tools of resistance took a different shape in early 1892 when he made a connection with reporter John Hamilton Gilmour of the *San Francisco Chronicle*. Pablo took his case for his people to the court of popular opinion aided by Gilmour's supportive reporting. Gilmour's article in March 1892 praised the efforts of Pablo, calling him "a remarkably able Indian…who has shown great political ability in this fight." Gilmour's analysis of Rust was far less flattering, accusing the agent of creating discord among the Cahuilla.[41]

Rust wrote to Morgan about meeting Gilmour on March 13, 1892. Rust said he was cautious and polite in his talk with the reporter, and "very careful not to speak of breaking up tribal relations." He complained, however, that "Gilmour incites them" (the Cahuilla) through his article on Pablo.[42]

The positive media attention had a chilling effect on the government's threats to arrest Pablo, but in May 1892 Rust still was suggesting arrest to Morgan, perhaps because Pablo's defiance was undeterred. Pablo enhanced his "oppositional organization" by issuing what Rust reported were "twenty commissions" to "his captains," and "lieutenants in different villages, assuming authority and defying mine."[43] His reputation and power growing, Pablo and his followers undertook acts of civil disobedience. "They have plowed and closed old roads long used by the public," Rust complained, and Pablo "allots lands and locates his friends in a most unreasonable manner."[44]

Gilmour wrote another article that appeared in the *Chronicle* on May 15, 1892, in which he described Pablo as a leader who held the respect of Indians and whites. "Captain William Pablo is certainly a remarkable Indian, and has a perfect mania for writing letters and issuing manifestoes [sic], either on his own account or that of entire villages. Some of the letters are unique in language and sentiment, and he so deluges the various settlements with his orders and instructions that the majority of the Indians believe he has some mysterious connection with the President, and his words have weight in the councils of the State."[45] The Cahuilla captain was a prolific letter writer, Gilmour said. "He pours out his soul in English."[46] Gilmour also printed one of the manifestos delivered to him by Augustine Chapo, appointed by the people of Rincon as their attorney. The declaration

Federal Indian Agent Horatio Rust & unidentified Indian.
Courtesy of Gerald Smith Collection,
Archives, A.K. Smiley Public Library, Redlands, CA

showed, Gilmour said, "that William Pablo and the Rincon Indians have quite an idea what constitutes Indian domain." It read in part:

"We the Mission Indians of San Diego County…Present this Notice for our Claim upon our homes in which our fathers and grandfathers lived, died and were buried…we have places where our horses go to Range and to pasture and also we go to get wood or seed. The land was cultivated by our fathers and grandfathers."

The statement threatened arrest for those violating tribal boundaries or resources and the punishment of anyone trying to bring liquor onto the Rincon reservation.[47]

Gilmour praised the loyalty and patience of Native Americans. "I cannot but admire the good sense of these people who so calmly separate the individual acts of individual officers, and who so firmly believe that the head of the Government is pure and that unworthy acts by unworthy officers will be promptly punished when their evil deeds are known to those in authority," he wrote.[48]

Pablo succeeded in creating an alliance among Southern California Indians and whites concerned with the plight of the area's native peoples. His network stretched at least as far south as the Rincon and probably farther. Pablo knew that such an alliance provided a dynamic strength necessary to better resist attacks on the traditional ways of the Cahuilla. Olegario's success had been premised on his unifying the various Luiseño villages. Pablo took that a step further, creating a pan-tribal network of Indian leaders in Southern California. He used whites friendly to the cause of California Indians, such as Brown and Gilmour, to relay the Indian voice to the greater public and to government authority. As Pablo built on the example of Olegario, the next generation of Southern California Indian leaders would borrow from him. Groups such as the Mission Indian Federation, which emerged after World War I, sought first to knit together local tribes and then to create a Pan-Indian political activism across the United States. Native Americans were learning how to make their own keys to the locked doors of American democracy.

A combination of Gilmour's acerbic criticisms and Pablo's manifestos apparently made their desired impact. The Indian Bureau sent an inspector to investigate the troubles at Potrero after the United States Senate asked for a reason for the problems with the Cahuilla. Gilmour kept the heat on in an August 27, 1892, article. Critical of the way Inspector Arthur M. Tinker was conducting his investigation, Gilmour launched into a direct attack on Rust. He denounced Rust's "unfriendly attitude toward the St. Boniface Catholic school and added that Rust had "never so much as paid a visit to the institution."[49] Gilmour was also critical of Rust's "peculiar methods" of using his office to make "extensive collections of curios, which he has sold for many thousands of dollars." According to Gilmour, much of Rust's time as an agent was spent in pursuit of "the handiwork of these industrious people."[50] Rust often took items from Indian homes without consent of their owners, Gilmour alleged. If the Cahuilla heard in advance of a visit by Rust to a reservation, they would bury valuables to protect them from Rust's looting. The official report by Tinker reasoned that Rust was "honest" and of "good moral character" but just lacked qualifications to be a successful Indian agent. Rust resigned in 1893.[51]

Pablo's influence at organizing resistance to government policy on Potrero and throughout Southern California cannot be overstated. His hereditary leadership position, respect

Henry Mathews (left) and Will Pablo, 1916.
Courtesy of Banning Public Library District, Banning, CA

as a shaman, and force of personality helped him galvanize support among all groups of Native Americans in the region. It was, as author Shipek called it, a "new interband and interreservation organization"[52] that worked to preserve native land and culture. The organization fought and successfully halted the allotment of Indian lands in the area between the years 1896 and 1920 (with the exception of Pala). The centers of this opposition to allotment, Shipek said, were at "Morongo, Santa Ysabel, Mesa Grande, and the other mountain Kumeyaay reservations," showing its pan-tribal influence.[53]

Pablo's efforts were transitional and set the stage for a new rise of pan-tribal and Pan-Indian cooperative organizations such as the Mission Indian Federation, one of the most significant "oppositional organizations" of the twentieth century. Land rights and compensation for the unratified treaties of 1851 and 1852, coupled with the question of sovereignty in defining who decided these critical issues, continued to drive the conflict. Renewal of the government's allotment plan for Southern California reservations in 1917 provided the new spark of action. Pablo and the lessons learned on the Potrero and throughout the region by his unnamed organization gave shape to the next resistance movement among Southern California Indians.

Will Pablo (on the right) & unidentified man.
Courtesy of Gerald Smith Collection,
Archives, A.K. Smiley Public Library, Redlands, CA

Notes:

[1] William Pablo, "The Legend of Console Mineral Springs near Homuba Canyon" as quoted by John Bruno Romero in *The Botanical Lore of the California Indians with Side Lights on Historical Incidents in California* (New York: Vantage Press, Inc., 1954), 72-73.

[2] Ibid., 73-75.

[3] Lowell Bean, "Morongo Indian Reservation: A Century of Adaptive Strategies," in *American Indian Economic Development, World Anthropology,* Sam Stanley, ed. (The Hague: Mouton Publishers, 1978), 170-171.

[4] Over several years, the Indian lands in the San Gorgonio Pass area became disputed property with confusion over the various regulations and treaty rights. Southern Pacific Railroad was rewarded with odd-numbered sections of land for laying tracks through the area which could then be sold to settlers. Other sections were guaranteed for local Indians by Presidential edict. The central point of the case concerned properties controlled by John North, son of Riverside's founder, and Richard Gird, owner of the Chino Rancho. They had purchased property from Southern Pacific and planted orchards above the Potrero Village. Pablo, John Morongo and others testified that the area had been Indian land as long as they could remember with Pablo stating that his father had always lived there. The court, however, ruled that the Indians occupied the area after the signing of the Treaty of Guadalupe Hidalgo and therefore had no rights to the land under treaty. The situation was finally resolved in 1892 when with the assistance of rancher C.O. Barker, the Smiley Commission developed a plan for consolidation of lands in the area which, through exchange and purchase, satisfied the concerns of both local Indians and white settlers. See Louis Munson, "A Picture Sketch of Our President," taken from the *Banning Herald* newspaper of November 7, 1891 in the C.O. Barker Collection, Archives of A.K. Smiley Public Library; *Banning Herald* newspaper, April 13, 20, 1889.

[5] Helen Pruitt Beattie, "Indians of San Bernardino Valley and Vicinity," *Historical Society of Southern California Quarterly* (September 1953), 242-243.

[6] Francis Paul Prucha, *American Indian Policy in Crisis: Christian Reformers and the Indian, 1865-1900* (Norman, OK: University of Oklahoma Press, 1976), 19.

[7] Ibid., 20.

[8] Prucha, *American Indian Policy in Crisis*, 33; Francis Paul Prucha, *The Churches and the Indian Schools, 1888-1912* (Lincoln and London: University of Nebraska Press, 1979), 4. Smiley was appointed to the Board of Indian Commissioners in 1879 at the age of 51. See Clyde A. Milner and Floyd A. O'Neil, *Churchmen and the Western Indians, 1820-1920,* (Norman and London: University of Oklahoma Press, 1985), 144.

[9] Prucha, *The Churches and the Indian Schools*, 1-2.

[10] Prucha, *American Indian Policy in Crisis*, 57.

[11] Beattie, "Indians of San Bernardino Valley and Vicinity," 241-242.

[12] Letter (partial), Myron Crafts to George Crafts, ca. 1873 in Crafts Collection, Box 1, Archives, A.K. Smiley Public Library, Redlands, CA. Crafts referred to the recent uprising by Modocs in northeast California under their Chief Captain Jack, who held off federal troops using the natural defenses of the harsh terrain provided by the lava beds near Tule Lake. The army attempted to force the Modocs from their traditional lands back to the Klamath Reservation where they said they were mistreated. In April 1873, Captain Jack, bowing to pressure from his own people, attacked members of a Peace Commission, and murdered General E.R.S. Canby. After continued fighting, Captain Jack and his Modocs were overrun and surrendered in June 1873. He and five others were hanged for killing Canby and his people were removed to the Quapaw Reservation in Indian Territory.

[13] Beattie, "Indians of San Bernardino Valley and Vicinity," 242.

[14] Beattie, "Indians of San Bernardino Valley and Vicinity," 245; *Riverside Press*, September 13, 1879 as cited by Beattie, 252.

[15] Ibid., 252.

16 Ibid., 253.

17 Ibid., 254.

18 Ibid, 245-246.

19 Ibid., 258-259. Morongo Reservation near Banning was originally known as Potrero; the name meaning "grassy spot," according to Beattie and referring to a canyon where wells supplied the water needs of local Cahuilla. A village site nearby was named Malki which also was used for the reservation name area until finally changed to Morongo, a derivative of Marranga. Marra is the Serrano place of origin.

20 Letter J. G. (probably J. Q. A.) Stanley to Helen Hunt Jackson in *Message from the President of the United States, A communcation of the 11th instant, from the Secretary of the Interior, submitting a draft of bill "for the relief of the Mission Indians in the State of California,* (Washington, January 14, 1884), 48th Congress, 1st Session, Senate Exec. Doc, No. 19, 34.

21 In addition, Jackson accused Golsh of forcing Indians off their lands and filing his own patents on their property. Jackson forced the issue by sending an affidavit on the alleged land theft to Commissioner of Indian Affairs Hiram Price, compelling Lawson to dismiss Golsh. Jackson complained to Price that Lawson had mounted a campaign to discredit her and noted newspaper articles which pictured her as Interior Secretary Henry Teller's "pet appointee" and a "busy body." See, Letter, Jackson to Mary Sheriff, March 19, 1883 and March 20, 1883, 253-255, Letter, Jackson to Hiram Price, July 27, 1883, 286-287 in Mathes, *Indian Reform Letters.*

Jackson also received credit for helping save the lands of the Soboba Band of Indians in San Jacinto Valley. She advised sub-chief José Jesus Castillo to file on the property under the Indian Homestead Act and even brought him a copy of the Act. Castillo and the Soboba band of Indians were successful in keeping their land. E. Bouton in a letter to the *Los Angeles Times* in 1888 wrote that the California Supreme Court decided the "celebrated" case by acknowledging the Indians' right to the land in San Jacinto Valley. "These Indians and their ancestors had been in peaceful possession of this land for 150 years when the [Mexican] grant was made, in 1842 or thereabouts. Their rights and possessions were recognized by the Mexican authorities, and they were named in the grant. The United States patent which I procured was subject to their claims. …In this case the equities are on the side of the Indians, and I think the decision is a just one." See *Los Angeles Times,* February 12, 1888 in Ralph E. Shaffer, *Letters From The People: The Los Angeles Times Letters Column, 1881-1889,* (Electronic book: http://www.intranet.csupomona.edu/~reshaffer/copyrtx.htm, 1999), 21.

22 Van H. Garner, *The Broken Ring: The Destruction of the California Indians* (Tucson, Arizona: Westernlore Press, 1982), 122-123. McCallum's resignation came just ten days after the death of Helen Hunt Jackson at her Colorado home.

23 Apostol, "Horatio Nelson Rust," 309-310.

24 Jane Apostol, "Horatio Nelson Rust: abolitionist, archaeologist, indian agent," *California History,* (Winter 1979/80), 309.

25 Ibid., 305-306.

26 Apostol, "Horatio Nelson Rust," 306; Mathes, *The Indian Reform Letters,* 252.

27 Lowell Bean, "Morongo Indian Reservation: A Century of Adaptive Strategies," 170-171; Apostol, "Horatio Nelson Rust," 311. Rust wrote to Morgan on December 20, 1890 where he derided the Potrero chief as a "drunkard" whom he would not recognize. The elder chief two days before had brought his son, Will Pablo, to Rust and announced that Pablo was chosen captain by the people. Rust considered the younger Pablo a "hard case." Rust asked Morgan to allow him to only deal with individuals in the tribe and no longer recognize captains. See letter, Rust to Morgan, December 20, 1890, *Letter From the Secretary of the Interior… ,* (Washington, 1892) 52 Cong., I Sess., Senate Ex. Doc, No. 108, 14-15, copy in the Gerald Smith Collection, A.K. Smiley Public Library, Redlands, CA.

28 Letter, Horatio Rust to Thomas J. Morgan, December 20, 1890 in The Letter From the Secretary of the Interior Transmitting In response to the resolution of the Senate of the 26th ultimo, information as to whether instructions have been sent to the Indian agent for the Coahuilla Reservation in California to

remove Cabezon and to place one Williams as chief of the tribe, etc., June 6, 1892, Senate Ex. Doc, No. 108, 14-15, copy in the Gerald Smith Collection, A.K. Smiley Public Library, Redlands, California (herafter cited as *Letter From the Secretary of the Interior.*)

[29] Letter, Rust to Morgan, February 4, 1891, December 2, 1891 in *Letter From the Secretary of the Interior,* 7, 14. The lawyer assisting Pablo whom Rust referred to is John Brown, Jr., who was the son of the mountain man and 49er of the same name. The family settled in San Bernardino in 1852 and later the Yucaipe [sic] Valley. Brown, Jr. was a school teacher and county superintendent before entering the legal profession. A 1904 history of the area written by Luther Ingersoll, said that "even the hapless, expatriated red man finds in him a tireless and faithful champion." Brown, Jr., is credited with assisting the Cupeño Indians when they were forced from their home at Warner's Ranch. "Mr. Brown and Washington friend, [Inspector Jenkins] accompanied the sorrowful procession of victims of heartless greed to their new home, which was reached without the loss of a single life, our subject aiding the deserving Indians to comfortably settle down at Pala," wrote Ingersoll. Brown's wife was Mattie Ellen Hinman. See, *Century Annals of San Bernardino County, 1769-1904* (Los Angeles: L.A. Ingersoll, 1904), 651-653.

[30] Letter, Rust to Morgan, December 20, 1890, *Letter From the Secretary of the Interior,* 14-15.

[31] Prucha, *The Churches and the Indian Schools*, xi, 6-16.

[32] Letter, Mary Watkins to Constance DuBois, March 7, 1900 in Constance Goddard DuBois Papers, Reel 1, Huntington Free Library, Cornell University

[33] Bean, "Morongo Indian Reservation: A Century of Adaptive Strategies," 171; Apostol, "Horatio Nelson Rust," 310-311; Letter, Rust to Morgan December 2, 1891, in *Letter From the Secretary of the Interior*, 8-9.

[34] Letter, Morgan to Secretary of the Interior, July 29, 1891 in *Letter From the Secretary of the Interior*, 11-12.

[35] Ibid.

[36] Samuel Lawson to John Morongo, November 22, 1890 in Horatio Nelson Rust Papers, RU 439, Huntington Library, San Marino, California. How Rust comes into possession of the letter from Lawson to Morongo is unknown. Either John Morongo voluntarily turned it over to Rust, or was discovered engaging in bit of political intrigue in an attempt to strengthen his position.

[37] Letters, Rust to Morgan, July 4, 1891, December 2, 1891 in *Letter From the Secretary of the Interior,* 13. Rust told Morgan that "Segundo" was in jail in Los Angles following the attempts against Morongo and Weinland. This Segundo is possibly Segundo Chino, later a constable on the Morongo Reservation. Chino was a close associate of Indian agent Clara True and was a member of the posse in 1909 which tracked Willie Boy down for murder. After 1919, Chino was also an officer in the Mission Indian Federation, an Indian political activist organization formed in Southern California after World War I. Both Chino and Will Pablo later became deputies under Special Agent Ben DeCrevecoueur.

[38] Rust to Morgan, July 4, 1891, in *Letter From the Secretary of the Interior*, 13. It is interesting that the Salton Sea's overflow, similar to the flood of the Old Testament, is incorporated in a potential cleansing of the land. The *Citrograph* newspaper of Redlands, California, reported on the Colorado River overflow on exactly the same day Rust penned his report. "As soon as the appearance of the water was known to the Indians they began leaving for the mountains. It is said one of their medicine men warned them there would be a flood on the Fourth, and as their tribes have a tradition that all this country except Grayback was once flooded, they are prepared for the worst." It is certainly ironic that the newspaper reported that "they [the Indians] are even leaving Banning, 3000 feet above the sea, for higher ground, and even so intelligent a man as Chief Morongo is among the refugees." See *Redlands Citrograph*, July 4, 1891. Re: the Salton "Sea"—The term "sea" was not widely used for this area of overflow by the Colorado River until the body of water currently known as Salton Sea began forming in approximately 1905. See Gunther, *Riverside County, California, Place Names*, 449-452.

[39] Horatio Rust, "Report of Mission Agency," *Sixth Annual Report of the Commissioner of Indian Affairs to the Secretary of the Interior 1891* (Washington: Government Printing Office, 1891), 223.

[40] Shipek, *Pushed Into The Rocks:* 50. Shipek received her information concerning Pablo's involvement with the Ghost Dance from personal communication with Anthropologist Lowell Bean. Professor Bean corroborated this information during conversations with this writer. Christopher Cardozo and Joseph D. Horse Capture

wrote that "it is not mere coincidence then that the great Ghost Dance religion of the 1880s found ready acceptance among California Indians. The Ghost Dance was the most significant and widespread of the Native American revitalization movements that emerged in the eighteenth and nineteenth centuries, and the all-pervasive devastation the California tribes suffered played a crucial role in the importance of the Ghost Dance in the region." Cardozo and Horse Capture noted that Wovoka traveled extensively preaching and performing miracles and disseminated his visions through messengers and apostles. These beliefs lingered among the people for some time, the writers noted. "Memories of the Ghost Dance were still fresh at the time [photographer Edward S.] Curtis visited the California Indians in the early 1900s." Christopher Cardozo and Joseph D. Horse Capture, *Sacred Legacy: Edward S. Curtis and the North American Indian* (New York: Simon & Schuster, 2000), 70-71.

[41] Apostol, "Horatio Nelson Rust," 311.

[42] Letter, Rust to Morgan, March 30, 1892, in *Letter From the Secretary of the Interior,* 6.

[43] Letter, Rust to Morgan, May 13, 1892, in *Letter From the Secretary of the Interior,* 5-6. In the letter of May 13, Rust wrote that "Old Cabazon was confined once by a former agent and kept quiet for some time, but prevented his men from accepting good from the Government." Rust's tactics were not new. The resistance of leaders such as Cabazon [sic] even when confined gives some idea of the will and tenacity of the Cahuilla people, or any people held prisoner, to conduct their own affairs.

[44] Ibid.

[45] John Hamilton Gilmour, "Indian Politicians," *San Francisco Chronicle*, May 15, 1892 in *Some Last Century Accounts of the Indians of Southern California*, Robert F. Heizer, ed. (Ramona, California: Ballena Press, 1976), 9.

[46] Ibid., 11

[47] Ibid., 10.

[48] Ibid., 11.

[49] Gilmour, "Thrifty Agent Rust," *San Francisco Chronicle*, August 27, 1892, in *Some Last Century Accounts,* 28.

[50] Ibid., 26-27.

[51] Scott E. Rupp, "Horatio N. Rust: A Founding Father of Both South Pasadena and Pasadena," *The Quarterly Magazine* (South Pasadena: South Pasadena Publishing Co., Spring 2003), 60.

[52] Shipek, *Pushed Into The Rocks*, 49.

[53] Ibid., 50.

6 The "Vanishing Policy"

Kill the Indian and save the man![1] —*Richard Pratt*

Lt. Richard Henry Pratt, Founder and Superintendent of Carlisle Indian School, in Military Uniform and With Sword, 1879. Photo Lot 81-12 06828100, National Anthropological Archives, Smithsonian Institution.

The Redlands *Citrograph* published the following story on June 28, 1902. It appeared originally in the Flagstaff, Arizona, *Sun*:

A Supai Indian Boy's Love of Home

Sheriff Johnson returned Tuesday from Cataract Cañon where he had gone to investigate the reported killing of an Indian boy of the Supai Tribe. The tragedy occurred and was reported that the youth had been assassinated, but such was not the case.

The son of Indian George, with a companion, had been ordered by the teacher in charge of the school at Supai to go to the Truxton Indian school. To this the boy objected but on the insistence of the teacher the boys started. On reaching the Hilltop house the son of Indian George fell behind. The other boy heard a shot and returned, to find his companion dying.

The boy had laid down on his back and placed his Winchester in such a position as to bring the muzzle of the gun under his chin, and pulled the trigger, the ball going through his head.

The cause of the suicide was that the boy, who was but 16 years old, did not want to go to the Truxton school, and preferred death to leaving his home and friends.

The Supai Indians are satisfied with the Supai school, and are willing to send their children to their home school, but do not want them sent away to other schools, which the government compels them to do. The Supais are considerable wrought up over the affair and now object to compulsory education of their children more than ever.[2]

This Supai boy's act of suicide was an act of resistance. He was driven to escape his situation, albeit tragically, rather than confront a world he did not want nor understand. Government officials forced their decision on the son of Indian George, but the young man through this ultimate act of defiance, made his will known. Most Native Americans did not choose such an extreme escape as suicide, but evasion remained a viable option of resistance. It was an option increasingly used by the victims of a controversial system that pitted advocates of reservation (home) day schools against proponents of off-site boarding schools in the debate over the best means of educating and civilizing the American Indian.

In 1879 Captain Richard Pratt opened his landmark Carlisle Indian Industrial School in Pennsylvania and set the precedent for removing Indians from their natural and cultural homes to Christianize and civilize the body of Native Americans and euthanize their spirit.[3] The former cavalry officer championed the idea of these "substitute homes" for Indian children where their environment would be controlled and their image of themselves re-created. Pratt's view, according to historian Prucha, was the "complete integration of the Indians into white society…We are not born with language, nor are we born with ideas of either civilization or savagery."[4] For Pratt, immersing Indians in the deep pool of civilization by controlling their speech, dress, and conduct would drown the savage within and baptize them as Americans. Pratt practiced his exorcisms at Carlisle with a firm hand. America was making a great mistake, Pratt said, "in feeding our civilization to the Indians, instead of feeding the Indians to our civilization."[5]

For Native Americans, forced removal of their children to boarding schools became just another battlefield in their fight to be released from government rule and given the respect and freedom to make their own decisions and live their lives as all other Americans did. Individual Indians reacted differently to the confinement of the boarding schools. Some withdrew within themselves, hiding their Indianness from the disapproving eyes of teachers and administrators. Others ran when given the opportunity, stole food when hungry, and responded with dulled indifference when offered no other choice. For some, the schools were a haven from the hardship of the reservation and these Indians learned the lessons of white society to break from reservation life—and often their indigenous culture. This, of course, was the intent of men such as Pratt, who sought to sever the connection of the Indian to his past, to create the Indian that white society wanted.

Pratt was bitterly opposed to contract day schools on or near reservations, such as St. Boniface Catholic school in Banning, California, and the Rev. William Weinland's Moravian school on Morongo Reservation near Banning. Commissioner Morgan, while expanding off-reservation boarding schools, still supported reservation day schools as a practical measure.[6] In 1893, a new law mandated that Indian students complete three years of study at agency schools before going anywhere else. Pratt saw this as a complete contradiction to the avowed policies of total assimilation of the Indian into white society.

The idea of creating an off-reservation school in Southern California was apparently Rust's idea alone. In 1890, Morgan instructed Rust "to select a site for a training school upon a reservation." Rust "felt sure it would be better to locate near some thrifty settlement, where the pupils would come in constant contact with civilization rather than their home influences." Rust "urged the landholders in different places to give land to induce the Government to locate near them, but an Indian school was not popular with the California land-owner."[7] While personal initiative governed his actions, Rust's efforts were not out of line with Morgan's thinking. At a Lake Mohonk conference in 1892, Morgan said that in cases where parents, without good reason, refuse to educate their children, "we believe the government is justified, as a last resort, in using power to compel attendance. We do not think it desirable to rear another generation of savages."[8]

Rust wrote that upon finally finding a man in Perris, California, who knew of Carlisle, he was able to secure 80 acres of "choice land" near the town. This "manual training school" for Indians was built in 1892.[9] The school continued in operation until 1901 when students began being transferred to a new facility, the Sherman Indian Institute in Riverside. For Native Americans in the area, Rust's legacy with the Perris school would outlive his tenure with the Indian Bureau.[10]

During his time in office, Rust stressed education through "practical training" with "the higher, the esthetic education" left for future generations of more capable Indians.[11] Rust's attitude was completely in line with the prevailing policy as pushed by the Bureau of Indian Commissioners and independent groups such as the Indian Rights Association.

Three years after its founding, the school received a glowing report from Albert Smiley during one of his excursions through Southern California. The Redlands *Citrograph* of February 2, 1895, reported that Smiley escorted eight ladies and gentlemen to the Perris institution. "The school was found to be in a flourishing condition, with 130 pupils in attendance and a corps of eleven instructors. The Industrial department is one of the most successful features of the school. The pupils seem perfectly happy, with no inclination to return to their native element," the paper reported.[12]

Smiley's Quaker background certainly gave him a particular view of Indian culture and the supposed benefits offered by the Perris school. The community of "Friends" still viewed themselves as distinctive within "the mainstream of American Protestant society," according to historians Clyde Milner and Floyd O'Neil. Yet Smiley advocated "the transculturation of American Indians," which favored "the harder road of imposed assimilation," and the subsequent loss of distinct Indian culture.[13] Not surprisingly, although Smiley headed the three-man commission that in 1891 helped create several small reservations in Southern California, he remained opposed to the concept of reservations. "I am opposed on principle to the reservation system, which is productive of much harm," he told a Banning newspaper reporter during one of his trips through the area in April 1889.[14]

Smiley's biased optimism concerning the operation of the Perris Indian School belied the underlying problems the school faced in an area where necessary resources were at a premium. Supplying water to the Perris school was always a concern. The water was to come from Big Bear Lake in the local mountains and negotiations had begun with that

Water District. However, agencies in the Redlands area soon took the bulk of the precious supply. As a result, agricultural fields in the Perris Valley dried up and were abandoned, and the hopes of Rust's Indian school also became dust.[15]

In 1897 Harwood Hall, who later ran Sherman Indian Institute, became Superintendent of the Perris facility and concluded that insufficient water supplies impeded any possible success of agricultural instruction at Perris. He declared the school "inadequate and the site inappropriate"[16] and lobbied for its removal to Riverside, which occurred in 1902 despite Rust's admonitions against the move. More than just water availability had changed at Perris since the visit of Smiley. Hall wrote Commissioner of Indian Affairs William Jones in June 1897 that, "the pupils of the school are in a most deplorable condition as regards health. There is hardly a sound pupil here. Scrofulous and other contagious sores. The double bed system fosters the trouble. In fact, until each child has his own bed, the present state of affairs will continue."[17]

Almost immediately operation of the Perris school was embroiled in controversy. Rust complained about its first superintendent, who, he said, "disgraced the school, robbed the government of several thousand dollars, and ran away."[18] Reported problems at the Perris Indian school played a key role in a deadly outbreak of violence on the Pechanga Reservation in 1894. Most of these Indians were the people of Pablo Apis who were forced from their homes in 1875 and relocated to the waterless canyon.[19] Life was difficult for the Luiseño people of Pechanga with increasing white encroachment and restricted water resources. A Riverside newspaper reported that the Luiseño were "greatly demoralized by their proximity to the whites."[20] This hardship and lingering factionalism, as a result of the violence in 1871 between the followers of Manuel Cota and Olegario Calac, created a volatile environment for Indians as well as for whites on the reservation.

Rust wrote that the widow Mrs. Mary J. Platt took the position of day-school teacher at Pechanga in 1889, "under most unfavorable circumstances." Whiskey, poverty, "worthless land" with no water and what Rust deemed "low whites had done their worst."[21] Platt, however, reportedly had changed the habits of the people for the better, according to Rust. Superintendent Rust's appraisal was obviously exaggerated considering an incident that occurred in July 1890 during his visit to Pechanga. He "found that Mrs. Platt and the school had gone to a cañon near by to spend the day in picnic. I followed and found them, young and old, a very happy people. Within half an hour a messenger came saying the schoolhouse was burning; and it was entirely consumed, with all Mrs. Platt's effects, for she had made this her home, and now family keepsakes, books, clothing, all were gone."[22]

Arson could not be proved but many people might see this incident as a message that the government intrusion onto the reservation was unwanted. Sabotage as a form of resistance was not unusual. Whether government officials such as Rust and Platt viewed the fire as arson is unknown, but unlikely. The school was rebuilt but the building would burn again four years later with the outcome far worse for Mrs. Platt.

Perris Indian School, ca. 1900.
Courtesy of Archives, Riverside Metropolitan Museum, Riverside, California.

On September 21, 1894, sheriffs and the Riverside County Coroner "Dr. Ruby" were called to the Pechanga after receiving news that the schoolhouse again was consumed by flames but, this time, along with Mrs. Platt as well. Riverside County Sheriff investigators considered the incident a homicide and a Coroner's Inquest was convened. The jury quickly determined that Mrs. Platt had been the victim of a murder. Within four days of the killing, news reports asserted that Platt was killed in connection to alleged abuse of Indian children at the Perris school.[23] The *Riverside Enterprise* reported that Indians at Pechanga were "greatly worked up" over "false" stories that children at Perris were not being fed properly and threatened Mrs. Platt after she denied Indian parents the required money and permits to go to the school and find the truth.[24]

Federal marshals arrested Mateo Pa, a captain of the Pechanga Luiseño, and 25-year-old Francisco Guavish, the young man who reportedly ran away from the Perris facility and spread the stories of the poor treatment of students at the school. A federal grand jury convened to hear evidence in the case. News reports said that Guavish accused Pa of murdering Platt, but testimony of Riverside County Sheriff investigators discredited Guavish. Guavish was personally jealous of Pa, according to sheriff's deputies, and desired to replace Pa as chief.[25] Pa was accused of attacking Platt in a fit of anger "for espousing the cause of some inimical Indian and for treating another with severity."[26]

Concerned by Guavish's allegations of poor treatment of the Perris students, Pa reportedly visited and demanded money and Platt's assistance to travel to the Perris facility. He wished

Mary Platt at the Pechanga schoolhouse with her students, ca. 1894.
Courtesy of Huntington Library, San Marino, CA.

to see for himself the conditions at the school and report to his people. Platt refused, angering the captain who threatened to have her school closed.[27] Captain Mateo Pa and Platt reportedly had a good relationship. He was described as a "surly fellow," whom Mrs. Platt greatly admired for his virtues according to one newspaper account.[28] In the end, the grand jury found insufficient evidence to hold both men on the charges. Riverside County sheriff officers, however, believed Guavish knew more than he was telling and pursued the case.[29]

On December 28, 1895, a San Jacinto Justice of the Peace issued a warrant for Guavish, who by this time had other legal problems pending, including accusations of committing highway robberies in the Los Angeles and Santa Monica areas.[30] By February, however, Riverside County law officials had found another key witness who reportedly confessed to the killing.[31] Thirty-nine year-old Ventura Molido laid out a story of robbery, rape and murder that ran counter to the initial reports of Platt's death. Participants in the heinous crime, said Molido, were himself, Guavish and Francisco Rodriguez.[32] Another defendant, Decco Trujillo, was later arrested on suspicion of being an accomplice to the murder. Molido said Mateo Pa instigated the crime but did not participate.[33] Later, Molido changed his story and said that Pa had only covered up the facts after Platt's murder. Molido then laid out a depraved tale for the jury of a Riverside County Superior Court.[34]

According to Molido, Guavish had asked the schoolteacher for money to spend at a fiesta and been denied.[35] On the night of September 20, 1894, Molido, Guavish, Trujillo, and

Rodriguez returned to the school. As Platt opened the door, she was grabbed by Guavish, Molido said, and dragged roughly 200 yards from the building, where each of the four men raped Platt.[36] According to Molido, Guavish then choked the woman to death, as Molido held her hands.[37] They brought her body back to the house where it was placed next to the iron stove in the kitchen. The Indians reportedly arranged a pile of oak logs and old clothing "into a funeral pyre…the whole being saturated with coal-oil."[38] After the murderers searched the house for money, Molido said, the body and the building were set ablaze. Platt shared living quarters in the rear of the school with her 10-year-old niece Hattie Leslie. Leslie reportedly heard nothing of the murder and only awakened as flames began to engulf her room. She escaped unharmed. The heat from the fire was so intense that the iron stove melted, leaving only the woman's bones to survive the flames. Identification of Platt relied on the burnt frames of her eyeglasses and remaining corset stays.[39]

Molido's story changed from day to day and from interpreter to interpreter. By the end of February, news accounts gave the exasperated report that Molido recanted his confession during a preliminary hearing. Later, Molido said his retraction sprang from fear that other Indians in the courtroom would later kill him.[40] If Molido's concerns for his life were, in fact, true, it points to anger in the tribe that a member was betraying other Indians. It also casts doubt on Molido's contention that Platt's murder was an act of robbery and rape and suggests a different motive for the killing such as the general fear for the welfare of Luiseño children at the Perris school.

In another blow to the prosecution, Molido entered a plea of "not guilty" in late March in Los Angeles and asked that the court appoint him an attorney.[41] The not-guilty plea was short-lived, however, since Molido delivered the desired plea in the court's afternoon session. Molido blamed the delay, at least according to news accounts, on being confused by the court's interpreter. In the meantime, the trial for Guavish, Rodriguez and Trujillo began in May 1896.[42]

The cultural diversity which made up the population of Los Angeles in 1896 was mirrored in the crowded Los Angeles courtroom. Anglos, blacks and Indians maneuvered for available space to hear the testimony in this highly charged case. Defense attorneys Lawrence Middlecoff and W. M. Peck attacked the character and veracity of Molido.[43] Peck regularly objected that an Indian interpreter was not utilized by the court and was consistently overruled by the judge. Peck also objected that he had been denied access to speak to Molido by Detective Martin Aguirre and asked the court to so order. The request was denied. Peck then moved that all charges be dismissed against his clients since the court did not have jurisdiction. Peck argued that the alleged crime was "committed on an Indian reservation, that the person alleged to have been killed was in the employ of the U.S. government, that these defendants were living upon the U. S. reservation and supported by the government," and that there was no proof that the alleged offense was committed in Riverside County.[44] The prosecution countered by placing Agency Doctor C.C. Wainwright on the stand, who testified that the schoolhouse was at least a quarter of a mile inside the county. Since the exact location of the murder could not be determined, Judge J. S. Noyes overruled Peck's motion.[45] The evidence against Guavish, Rodriguez and Trujillo was circumstantial. A Temecula store clerk testified, for example, that a silver coin spent by the defendants at a Mesa Grande fiesta was the very one he had given Platt two days before the murder.[46] On May 10, 1896, the case against the three men went to the white jury. Initial reports were that the jury was locked in disagreement. While ten voted to free Rodriguez and Trujillo, nine reportedly favored convicting Guavish. [47]

In the end, it may have been Molido's changing confession or Peck's attack on Molido as weak-minded and easily influenced that held sway, since only Molido, the man who turned state's evidence, was found guilty of the murder of Platt and sentenced to life in prison.[48] Judge Noyes said that only his confession saved him from the hangman's noose. The other defendants were released. Later, however, Guavish, was convicted of robbery. He spent twenty years in jail and lived out his life in Northern California, where he died in 1944.[49] Census records show Ventura Molido at San Quentin prison in 1900.

Who murdered Mary J. Platt, and why, cannot be easily determined. It may, indeed, have been a combination of many factors. Platt was at the Pechanga for several years and seemed to have an amiable relationship with tribal leadership such as Mateo Pa. The accusations of possible abuse at the Perris Indian School and Platt's unwillingness to assist frantic parents came from a "Supervisor Stewart"[50] just after the murder. Harwood Hall's 1897 report that the health of the Indian students at Perris was "deplorable" when he took over as superintendent, strongly supports the statements of Stewart and initial allegations of Guavish concerning neglect of the Indian children.

Other inconsistencies point to a motive other than just robbery or rape. It appears from Molido's testimony that Platt's alleged refusal of Guavish's demand for money occurred earlier on the same day of her murder. However, in initial reports of the crime in 1894, Indian Agent Francisco Estudillo said that he had received a letter from Platt warning of "impending trouble"[51] early on the day of her murder, obviously suggesting she anticipated a problem more sinister than just refusing to give Guavish money. It is interesting to note that Luiseño oral tradition credits the murder to Platt's violation of a tribal taboo by cutting the hair of the children at her day school. This insult, it is said, resulted in her murder and caused the murderers to cut off her hands before torching her body and the schoolhouse.[52]

The preponderance of evidence points to some infraction by Platt herself that resulted in the fatal justice meted out by members of the Pechanga tribe. This may have been the thinking of most of the two juries that could not, in the end, believe the prosecution's case against either Mateo Pa or Guavish, Rodriguez and Trujillo. Parents, when faced with a threat to their children, react instinctively. Indian parents under the pressure of being forced to surrender their children to a world beyond their control would have felt even more anxious. Violations of tribal cultural or religious beliefs such as cutting the hair of the children could only have intensified the anger of Pechanga tribal members. The people of Pechanga turned to the only option left them—violent resistance. Despite the beliefs of government officials or Christian reformers that Indian people were child-like dependents, the Luiseño parents at Pechanga knew better than most the dangers that existed in their world. They reacted as any concerned parents would react, white or Indian, when confronted with fear for their children and lack of respect for their way of life.

The violence that took the life of Mary Platt was created by a system meant to extinguish the Indian by severing their ties with those they most loved and trusted. That system did not end with the closing of the Perris Indian School. It was transferred along with the students to the new school in Riverside—now called Sherman Indian Institute. As with Perris, dissolving the ties of family and culture was often a brutal experience at the new Riverside school as well.

Little Joe Brittain of Pala was only six years old when compelled to leave his home and attend Sherman. His nephew remembered Joe speaking of the beatings he received at Sherman when caught speaking the Indian language. "After that," Willie Pink of Pala Reservation said, "my grandparents refused to teach any of the other kids the language." Pink remembered the stories of kids stealing food because they were so hungry, regardless of the punishment. They would break into the kitchen, Pink said, to get "enough food so that they could go back home—get home, then they'd be sent right back to school again."[53]

It was an arrogant system as defined by activist Charles Lummis: "The core of the 'system' …is to take the Indian from home as young as possible, 'educate' him, and turn him loose in the population—as many thousand miles from home as possible, and never let him go home again. The confessed theory is that he has no right to have a father and mother, and they no right to him; that their affection is not worth as much to him as the chance to be a servant to some Pennsylvania farmer or blacksmith, and generally at half wages."[54]

The murder of Mary Platt was certainly extreme resistance to an uncaring system. For most Indian students, escape remained the viable and practical method of resisting the forced practice of isolating Indians in boarding schools where physical want and cultural hostility was prevalent. This was the case twenty years after the founding of Sherman. Indian activists with the Mission Indian Federation spotlighted stories of heroic children who escaped Sherman to promote these acts of resistance. The Federation's publication, *The Indian*, reported in 1922 on one such incident as you would a prison break: "Albert Linton and Augustine Bersford of Santa Ysabel ran away from Sherman school. They traveled three days and three nights. At Pala both got work, and a month after both were taken back to school. The same night the latter ran away again and is now home with his folks."[55]

To the Mission Indian Federation, the government policy was a senseless abuse of the Indian family. Southern California Indians wanted educational facilities for their children but in their own communities as provided for every other American. The Federation's white Counselor, Jonathan Tibbet, wrote in 1922 that the policy "deprives the Indian parents of the companionship of their children in their younger years, and in fact for all times as the children are kept in government schools until their entire education is completed. These parents want their children with them in their younger years and are asking that schools for the teaching of the lower school grades be maintained on all reservations."[56]

"Now only a professional fool—or an Indian educator—is unaware that even an Indian child has a home," Lummis wrote, "that God was able to invent mother-love without waiting for any help from the present United States Indian Commission, and did it, hasty as His action may seem; that all humanity rests on the family and that nothing can compensate for the wreck of it."[57]

Yet, these islands of isolation imposed on Indian children were accomplishing a task that was both unwanted and unexpected by the builders of these institutions. These schools brought Indians together from all parts of America; Indians who would otherwise never have met. They shared experiences and came to understand the commonality of their desires as Indian people just as they were being educated in and about the Anglo world. "Southern tribes would have known nothing about Northern California tribes if it hadn't been for the schools," Pink said. Many of these students married, continuing the Indian blood line, Pink added, which probably would not have happened if they had stayed on the reservations.[58]

In fact, many of the men who came together in the early twentieth century to form the pan-tribal Mission Indian Federation were educated at Indian boarding schools. They included Nicholas Pena and John Ortega from Pala (Carlisle) and Samuel Rice of Santa Rosa (Hampton Normal School). Or perhaps personal experiences closer to home spurred their later activism; Joe Brittain's father, James Brittain, became a Federation judge on the Pala Reservation in the early 1920s.

Native Americans came to know the outside world through the boarding schools. Many of these educated Indians became leaders of their respective native communities. However, the understanding of white society obtained through the boarding schools created different perspectives within the various Indian communities. Some promoted citizenship, dissolution of the reservations and total assimilation into white society as the only solution to the physical misery and spiritual despair that haunted reservation life. Many of these Indians did not return to the reservations but remained in large urban settings where opportunities offered the hope of a better life. Others, however, did return to their families on the reservations where their new abilities gained under the tutelage of dogmatic white instructors, armed them with different weapons in their fight for justice for Native Americans. They organized and published their views and demands and disseminated those views to white and Indian populations. They learned of past leaders such as Olegario Calac and Will Pablo and drew strength from their struggles and those like them. Calac and Pablo had reached out past their tribal borders and created a regional network. The new leaders of resistance in Southern California would find a larger national stage on which to voice their demands for just treatment of America's first peoples.

For the Month of April, 1922   Twenty-five Cents the Copy

THE INDIAN

Published at Riverside, California

A Runner From Tribe to Tribe

OUR SLOGAN:
LOYALTY AND CO-OPERATION WITH OUR GOVERNMENT

The Magazine of the Mission Indian Federation

Front cover of *The Indian* publication, April 1922. Courtesy of A.K. Smiley Library, Redlands, CA

NOTES:

[1] Richard Pratt as quoted by Hazel W. Hertzberg, *The Search for an American Indian Identity: Modern Pan-Indian Movements* (Syracuse: Syracuse University Press, 1971), 16. Hertzberg wrote that the "melting pot" desired by reformers of American Indian government policy did not include an "Indian cultural contribution," nor was any expected. "The Indian alone was to be melted and was to come out white, in culture if not in color." Hertzberg said the name reformers gave to this process was "significant." They called it the "vanishing policy." See Hertzberg, 22.

[2] Redlands *Citrograph* newspaper, June 28, 1902, p. 10.

[3] Hertzberg, *The Search for an American Indian Identity*, 16-17.

[4] Richard Pratt as quoted by Prucha, *American Indian Policy in Crisis*, 274.

[5] Ibid., 276.

[6] Prucha, *American Indian Policy in Crisis*, 281.

[7] Horatio Rust, "Report of Mission Agency," *Sixtieth Annual Report of the Commissioner of Indian Affairs to the Secretary of the Interior, 1891* (Washington: Government Printing Office, 1891), 224.

[8] Thomas J. Morgan as quoted by Prucha in *American Indian Policy in Crisis*, 315-316.

[9] Horatio Rust, "Report of Mission Agency," 1891, 225.

[10] Jean Keller, "Stature Analysis of Perris Indian School Students, 1894-99," *Canadian Bulletin of Medical History (Bulletin canadien d'histoire de la médecine)*,(2001), 111. Water for the Perris school was always a concern but Rust's 1891 report was quite optimistic. "The outlook is fine," he said. "The Bear Valley water is piped to the land. Vineyards and orchards will surround it on all sides and my ambition is to teach the Indians to cultivate these broad acres and become good citizens. Their labor is needed here and is appreciated." The school officially was open to all Indian students within the Mission–Tule River Agency but in reality the greater majority of the students who attended resided on reservations in San Bernardino, Riverside and San Diego Counties. Access to sufficient supplies of water, however, was always a concern for administrators.

[11] Apostol, "Horatio Nelson Rust," 309.

[12] Redlands *Citrograph*, February 2, 1895, p. 8.

[13] Milner and O'Neil, *Churchmen and the Western Indians*, 155.

[14] *Banning Herald*, April 6, 1889. The Smiley Commission members were Smiley, Judge Joseph B. Moore and Charles C. Painter. Based upon their recommendations President Benjamin Harrison signed the order in December 1891, approving the creation of several small reservations in Southern California including the Morongo (village of Potrero) near Banning, California. They are credited with unraveling the complicated issues of land and water rights involving several parties, which created numerous problems for the members of the Potrero (later Morongo) Reservation. See Valerie Sherer Mathes, "The California Mission Indian Commission of 1891: The Legacy of Helen Hunt Jackson," *California History* (Winter 1993/94), 341-353.

[15] Bill Hulstrom, "Perris Indian School, circa 1893 –1902," electronic article by the Perris Valley Historical & Museum Association, http://perrismuseum/IndianSchool.htm.

[16] Apostol, "Horatio Nelson Rust," 310.

[17] Letter Harwood Hall to William A. Jones, June 2, 1897, Letterpress Book: 1 May 1897—31 August 1898, Sherman Indian High School Museum as quoted by Jean Keller, "Stature Analysis of Perris Indian School Students, 1894-99," fn 7, p.137.

[18] Apostol, "Horatio Nelson Rust," 310.

[19] Shipek, *Pushed Into The Rocks*, 48.

[20] *Riverside Daily Enterprise* newspaper, September 28, 1894, p. 2.

[21] Horatio Rust, "Report of Mission Agency," 1891, 224.

[22] Rust, "Report of Mission Agency," 224.

[23] *Riverside Daily Enterprise* newspaper, September 25, 1894, p. 1.

[24] *Riverside Daily Enterprise* newspaper, September 25, 1894, p. 1. The Redlands *Citrograph* reported that "several fathers" concerned over their children sought permits from Mrs. Platt, which were refused. See Redlands, *Citrograph* newspaper September 29, 1894.

[25] *Riverside Daily Enterprise* newspaper, January 15, 1896, p. 1.

[26] Ibid.

[27] *Riverside Daily Enterprise* newspaper, September 25, 1894, p. 1.

[28] *Riverside Daily Enterprise* newspaper, September 28, 1894, p. 2.

[29] *Riverside Daily Enterprise* newspaper, January 15, 1896, p. 1.

[30] Ibid.

[31] *Riverside Daily Enterprise* newspaper, February 15, 1896, p. 1.

[32] Ibid.

[33] Ibid.

[34] *Riverside Daily Enterprise* newspaper, February 16, 1896, p. 3.

[35] Ibid.

[36] Ibid.

[37] *Riverside Daily Enterprise* newspaper, February 16, 1896, p. 3; May 1, 1896, p. 1.

[38] *Riverside Daily Enterprise* newspaper, February 16, 1896, p. 3.

[39] *Riverside Daily Enterprise* newspaper, September 25, 1894, p. 2; May 1, 1896, p. 1.

[40] *Riverside Daily Enterprise* newspaper, February 27, 1896, p. 3.

[41] *Riverside Daily Enterprise* newspaper, March 25, 1896, p. 1.

[42] *Riverside Daily Enterprise* newspaper, March 26, 1896, p. 3; May 1, 1896, p. 1.

[43] Riverside *Daily Enterprise* newspaper, May 2, p.1.

[44] Riverside *Daily Enterprise* newspaper, May 5, 1896, p.1; May 8, 1896, p. 1.

[45] Riverside *Daily Enterprise* newspaper, May 8, 1896, p. 1.

[46] Tom Hudson, *A Thousand Years in Temecula Valley*, (Temecula, CA: Temecula Valley Chamber of Commerce, 1981), 159-161.

[47] Trial transcript, People vs. Francisco Guavish, Francisco Rodriguez & Antonio Trujillo, April 1896 in the collection of the Riverside Municipal Museum. Platt's murder was not the only unsolved case in this area. In 1906, twelve years after the murder of Platt, the body of Philip Steadman Sparkman was discovered near his Rincon store. Through personal observation and study, Sparkman compiled a dictionary and grammar of the Luiseño language published as *The Culture of the Luiseno Indians*. Francisco Calac was later arrested and accused of planning and carrying out the murder of Sparkman. Calac is listed as an inmate in Patton State Hospital in 1910 and died in 1944. In a 1978 interview Luiseño James Martinez said that "the Indians blame it [the murder] on a Mexican, but there weren't any Mexicans here. And I was told he [Sparkman] wouldn't give an Indian credit because he already had too much to pay. The Indian got drunk and killed him. That's what happened." See *They Passed This Way*, 40-41 and Robin Paige Talley, *The Life History of a Luiseño Indian: James (Jim) Martinez*, (Unpublished Masters Thesis in Anthropology: San Diego State University, 1982), 66.

[48] Riverside *Daily Enterprise* newspaper, May 8, 1896, p. 1; Hudson, *A Thousand Years in Temecula Valley*, 161.

[49] Hudson, *A Thousand Years in Temecula Valley*, 161.

[50] *Riverside Daily Enterprise* newspaper, September 25, 1894, p. 2

[51] *Riverside Daily Enterprise* newspaper, September 28, 1894, p. 2.

[52] *Riverside Daily Enterprise* newspaper, September 25, 28, 1894, pp. 1, 2; Interview with William Pink of Pala Band of Mission Indians, January 12, 2006, Murrieta, California.

[53] Interview with William Pink.

[54] Charles Lummis, "My Brother's Keeper," *Land of Sunshine*, vol. 11, No. 3 (August 1899), 142.

[55] *The Indian*, The Magazine of the Mission Indian Federation (February 1922), 6.

[56] Jonathan Tibbet in *The Indian*, (May 1922), 11.

[57] Lummis, "My Brother's Keeper," 143.

[58] Interview with William Pink.

7 "Human Rights and Home Rule"

The more one knows of the Indian as he really is, not as he appears to the tourist, the teacher, or the preacher the more one wonders.[1] —Clara True, 1909

Clara True, ca. 1909. Courtesy of Ronnie Peacock

The following article appeared in the *Redlands Review* on April 10, 1909:

CALL OF THE WILD—IT WAS TOO STRONG

Indian Girl Left Her Home at Long Beach and is Supposed to Have Gone to the Reservation Near Highland

It is surmised that a supposedly 'civilized' Indian girl, who recently left her home at Long Beach, is in hiding near Redlands. The story is told in a dispatch from Long Beach, as follows:

Because she fears that her adopted daughter, Agnawa Sandiego, a Mission Indian girl, 22 years of age, has obeyed the call of the forests and forsaken civilization, Mrs. A.B. Knowles, 1732 East Seventh street, is heart broken and has asked Chief of Police Williams to locate the girl and persuade her if possible to return to her former home.

Six years ago, Mrs. Knowles adopted Agnawa, which is 'Wild Flower of the Desert,' in the Indian interpretation of the name. The girl was left an orphan by the death of her father, himself a brave of magnificent stature, and Mrs. Knowles invited her to come and live with her. The invitation was eagerly accepted and the girl, as a rule, seemed perfectly satisfied with her home. However, Mrs. Knowles noticed that nature's moods were Agnawa's moods. When the wind blew and moaned the girl became melancholy often restless, and her eyes was a far-off look that perhaps beckoned discontent.

Only with the greatest of difficulty was Mrs. Knowles able to dispel these moods, and for house afterward, the girl would be morose and sullen. Last Friday night Mrs. Knowles noticed that the girl appeared in one of her spells— as if listening to the call of the woods. All during the evening, Agnawa hardly spoke. Mrs. Knowles thought nothing of it, however, until Saturday morning when she went into the yard to bring in some wood. She hurriedly finished her task and made her way into he house. Agnawa was not there, and upon investigation Mrs. Knowles found the girl's trunk and jewelry missing. After waiting two or three days for the girl to return, Mrs. Knowles notified Chief Williams. Mrs. Knowles is of the opinion that the girl has gone to the Indian reservation near Redlands.[2]

It takes very little effort to read this article and come to an alternative conclusion than the one proffered by Mrs. Knowles. Far from the whimsical evaluation that Agnawa was lured by some primordial instinct, it appears likely that 22-year-old Agnawa's sullen moods were indicative of a girl kept far from her home against her will and who took advantage of an opportunity to rebel against her captivity and flee to a life of her choosing as an inmate might escape her prison.

Flight remained a common act of resistance for Indians in Southern California. However, for Will Pablo resistance required political cunning and organization. He found a willing ally in his fight for leadership on the Potrero (now called Morongo) in Clara True. Commissioner of Indian Affairs Francis Leupp appointed True, former teacher of Indian children in New Mexico, as Superintendent for the Morongo Agency in 1907. True is best known as a spokesperson during the manhunt for Willie Boy in 1909. The Chemehuevi Willie Boy was accused of kidnapping and killing his 14-year-old female cousin. Anglo accounts say Willie Boy committed suicide at Ruby Mountain but Indian oral tradition commonly asserts that he escaped to Nevada.[3] Pablo's alliance with True paralleled those created with other white supporters such as John Brown Jr. and reporter John Hamilton Gilmour. The most noticeable difference was that True, who replaced Rust, was an Indian agent employed by the government.

While True had many traits similar to those of her predecessors, she was, in many ways, a unique individual and agent. The simple fact of a woman tackling the challenges of an Indian agent in an area such Banning, California, where lawless elements still roamed freely, held out special challenges. She was certainly not a typical agent or a woman for that time and place. The basis for the Pablo-True friendship (and it appears that is what it was) cannot be fully known but for Pablo this was an advantageous step in his efforts to exercise control over the affairs of the Morongo Indians and advance the rights of all affiliated Indians of the region. Pablo's tenacious resistance to the policies of Lawson and Rust forced their removal from the area. With True, Pablo's network reached inside the Office of Indian Affairs.

True's written sentiments betray a zealous belief that Indians must be protected, educated, and assimilated into American society but she clearly was less dogmatic in her approach to the Indians she encountered. While she worked tirelessly with an evangelical dedication to stop the liquor trade on the reservation, she worked just as hard to develop a rapport with strong personalities within the Indian community. "I took the strong Indians in hand," she wrote, "and had them work with me. I knew very well that if I did not, they would work against me. I am an advocate of as much individual liberty as possible rather than a great amount of centralized control."[4]

In the beginning that was not so easy. Leupp reported that one of True's duties was to attend a meeting on the reservation at which Indians, speaking in their own language, decided "whether or not they should drive her out of the agency."[5] The Cahuilla, in particular, are a patrilineal society so the idea of a female in a leadership position was initially difficult to accept. True, Leupp said, calmly wrapped herself in a blanket during the debate and "took a sound nap in the midst of the hubbub! It was a bold thing to do, and it carried the vote in her favor."[6]

That boldness was a vital attribute in an area where life could be forfeited over a disputed whiskey bottle. "Once, at a fiesta held near her school, she passed the middle of the night standing guard at a gate, six-shooter in hand, holding back a mob of half-drunken ruffians," Leupp said. True's less-than-womanly demeanor was unsettling to area whites. Leupp added that the "judges in the neighborhood were always astounded at the first appearance before them with a gang of handcuffed prisoners, as they assumed that this particularly zealous and successful fighter must be a big strapping man instead of a dainty, very feminine woman."[7]

Will Pablo was reportedly "devoted" to True.[8] A newspaper account reported that Pablo guarded True constantly and is credited with uncovering an attempt on her life. The attempt on True's life reportedly occurred at San Manuel Reservation during one of her visits. It was allegedly planned by "those who would profit by selling liquor to the Indians."[9] Pablo warned True that she "must not sleep in her cottage a certain night," a warning that she heeded. "The next morning a bullet was discovered in the wall above the pillow where she was accustomed to sleep."[10] Pablo not only showed his loyalty to True, but by uncovering the plot, proved how invaluable he was to the operation of Morongo Reservation and to True personally.

If True received loyalty where Lawson and Rust did not, it was won by her mutual respect of the people she vowed to help. In May 1909 an area newspaper reported that True, perhaps, overstepped her bounds when she approved the arrest of two white men who "destroyed a section of the [irrigation] ditch and turned the water onto the desert."[11] The *Redlands Daily Facts* reported that "Secunda, an Indian policeman…attacked the white men, and began shooting at them" when they quickly surrendered.[12] Residents telegraphed Washington, "reminding authorities of "deeds, grants, patents, and contracts which proved the white men's right to the water."[13] True received a telegram ordering the release of the man and his son. The paper said people believed True was "over-zealous" and "indiscreet" in her advice to the Indians. Concerning her choice of police she remarked that "Secunda is a bad Indian. He is not afraid to shoot and when he begins shooting he will keep on shooting. That is the reason why I have appointed him as a policeman."[14]

"Water is life here in the desert," True said. "*We* [italics added for emphasis] have the right to shoot in defense of our lives.…If they attempt to take the water you have a right to shoot."[15] Where before local newspapers had been generally supportive of agents, newspaper coverage of True's actions was not quite so warm. "She has assumed that the whites are antagonistic to the Indians," the *Redlands Daily Facts* reported, "and has counciled [sic] aggressive measures."[16] The fact that True used the pronoun "we" when referencing the right to stop theft of the water, showed the depth of commitment between True and the Indians in her jurisdiction. It is a testament to Pablo's savvy leadership that he forged such a partnership with True and certainly was beneficial for the welfare of the Cahuilla and Serrano who followed Pablo.

This alliance between True and Pablo was also positive for Pablo, personally. In 1908 True introduced Will Pablo to a remarkable gathering of scholars, activists and native leaders who met at Riverside's Glenwood Mission Inn for three days in April. John Morongo had died in 1898.[17] True's action gave political credibility to Pablo not only with the luminaries who gathered in Riverside to discuss the plight of Southern California Indians, but undoubtedly with Pablo's own people. It almost certainly elevated or solidified his status with other local Indian leaders who attended the conference. Starting with the actions of Olegario and continuing with Pablo, resistance to government policies for the Indians of Southern California required more and more the skills of an able and shrewd politician. Pablo proved worthy of the job.

This conference dubbed the "Western Mohonk"[18] sanctioned the beginning of a new epoch in humanitarian interest for Native Americans and included among its 205 participants notables such as David Starr Jordan, Charles Lummis, Alfred Kroeber, Frederick Putnam, Pliny Earle Goddard, Frank Miller, Cornelius Rumsey, Cordelia Sterling, and Albert Smiley.[19] Indian leaders included Pablo, Manuel Santos (also known as Santos Manuel) of San Manuel, Juan Lugo, Lupe Lugo, Ignacio Costo, Jim Pine, and Juan de la Cruz Norte along with leaders of Indian nations from Central and Northern California.[20] Agents and teachers from the nearby reservations also attended; besides True, they included William Stanley from Soboba and the Rev. William Weinland from Banning.[21] True's introduction to the audience received an ovation and she was "heartily cheered" by the attendees.[22] Said to be the best-known worker in California, she was dubbed "the best man among all the superintendents."[23]

The conference was an outgrowth of increased activism in California, spurred, in part, by the forced removal of the Cupeño in San Diego County from Warner's Ranch (Agua Caliente) to Pala in 1903. Debate and interest in that removal prompted Lummis to form the Sequoya League in November 1901.[24] Two years after the Cupeño removal, clerks working in the archives of the United States Senate found the "lost" eighteen California treaties. On January 18, 1905, the Senate lifted the injunction of secrecy and permitted their release to the public. This produced an escalation of sympathy for the plight of California Indians from philanthropists and the public alike.[25]

Local Riverside newspapers provided extensive coverage of the conference, in part, due to the number of prominent figures attending from the fields of academia, journalism, and business. Appeals by the various captains during the conference were delivered with "stirring eloquence," reported a local newspaper.[26] The Indian leaders spoke of the need for "more land to cultivate,"[27] more water for those lands, and schools to teach their children.

Captain Lupe Lugo of the Cahuilla Reservation, himself a graduate of Sherman Indian Institute, said that the "Indian race…can learn just as well as any other" and wanted education.[28]

Anglo speakers condemned the neglect, abuse of Native Americans, and the injustice of past government policy. It was an acknowledgement by former enemies. General S.B.M. Young recalled that 40 years earlier he led federal soldiers against "the troublesome Indians"[29]— Mohaves led by Captain Jack Jones, who now sat in the front row of the conference listening to his former adversary. Young expressed his complete sympathy with the "present movement" and added that "there are two blots on the beautiful pages of our history….One is the war we had with Mexico….The other is our treatment of the Indians which has been cruel, unwise, unmoral and a curse upon us."[30]

Frank Miller was lauded as the host and organizer of the event and presented with gifts by Ignacio Costo and others in appreciation.[31] Lummis later wrote about the conference that "it was a pleasure to watch the perhaps natural surprise of most of these delegates at the demeanor of the Indian contingent."[32] He stressed the humanity of the American Indian

Attendees to the 1908 "Mohonk West" conference at Riverside's Mission Inn.
Inn owner Frank Miller is in front, second from left. Will Pablo is third from the right.
Courtesy of Archives, Riverside Metropolitan Museum, Riverside, California.

and a hopeful awakening of a new era in the relationship between white society and the people of native America. "The Indian is no longer a freak nor a toy for philanthropy; he is a human, with some of the limitations of minority, but all the rights of humanity."[33]

The good will expressed at the conference, notwithstanding, the realities of life for California Indians was still one of desperate efforts to protect their meager resources and secure the promises made to them by the treaties of 1851-52. Their everyday life revolved around survival in a harsh land surrounded by adversaries. The greater goal was respect for tribal sovereignty and for Indian people who had been so casually discarded despite the promises of government emissaries. Resistance to repeated injustices of government policy never ceased for Southern California Indians despite the warm feelings and genuine sympathy of white benefactors such as those at the 1908 conference. Clara True was a believer in the justice deserved by the Indian people of Southern California, but her time in Southern California was brief.

True's tenure with the Morongo Agency ended in February 1910 when she announced her resignation from the Indian Service. The reason is unknown. It certainly was not because she tired of speaking out for the Indian cause. She vocally supported an uprising by Indians of Taos, New Mexico, in May 1910.[34] The Pueblo Indians "took matters into their own hands and drove the [white] squatters" off Indian lands," she said. True told the paper that the Indians were right in protecting their own lands.[35] The day after this newspaper article, True received a pen at a farewell ceremony where Pablo and others praised her accomplishments.[36]

True's core of "bad Indian" police had included Segundo Chino, Will Pablo, and Manuel Machado.[37] Machado was a "free Gabrieleño" who had found work and a home among the Desert Cahuilla.[38] After True's departure from Morongo Reservation, these men became a no-nonsense force of deputies under Special Agent Benjamin DeCreveceour, whose superior was Special Agent William "Pussyfoot" Johnson. Chino and Machado played significant roles in the Mission Indian Federation.

True's departure again changed the political dynamic of Southern California Indian reservations. Although events such as the 1908 conference heightened awareness of the problems facing area Indians, solutions proved elusive. Cahuilla on Torres Reservation in the Coachella Valley resisted efforts to force them off their land. A San Diego newspaper ran the story of the Cahuillas' refusal to obey the order of Agent Lucius Wright, ordering them to abandon five of their villages so that "land-jumpers" with the assistance of Wright, could occupy the "rich farming country" they occupied. Trouble was predicted if attempts were made to forcibly eject the Indians.[39]

The trouble reportedly arose after money was obtained, through the intervention of an attorney, to develop artesian wells in and around the village sites, creating a steady supply of agricultural water and attracting the "covetous eyes" of local Anglo farmers.[40]

Attendees to the 1908 "Mohonk West" conference at Riverside's Mission Inn.
Front row: Albert Smiley is third from the right, Charles Lummis is fourth from the right, and David Starr Jordan is fifth from the right.
Courtesy of Archives, Riverside Metropolitan Museum, Riverside, California.

Pablo continued in his role as spokesman, medicine man and political leader for the Cahuilla. Pablo's regional influence, however, kept him in a position as a vitally important leader in Southern California Indian resistance. At the same time True was announcing her resignation in 1910, Pablo was meeting with his attorney, John Brown Jr., about the rejection of a Mohave captain by the federal superintendent.[41] Pablo said that the choice of the Mohave people, Jack Harrison, came from a "long line of ancestors who ranked as chief, while the superintendent has chosen an inferior Indian for the position."[42] Past history with agents such as Lawson and Rust made Pablo keenly sensitive to attempted government manipulation of tribal leadership. As a traditional chief, Pablo fought to maintain long-standing tribal political systems.

Cahuilla captain and shaman Fernando Lugo, ca. 1890. Courtesy of
Gerald Smith Collection, Archives, A.K. Smiley Public Library, Redlands, CA

The fight continued closer to home, as well. In November 1911, a Redlands newspaper headline read, "INDIANS SEEK TO CLOSE HIGHWAY."[43] It was an act of resistance that had all the markings of one Pablo had planned. The paper reported that the "Morongo Indians at Banning are making a concentrated effort to close to public traffic the old trail over their reservation." County supervisors felt that the road could not legally be closed but were still considering building a new road farther south, off the reservation.[44]

Scholar Tanis Thorne said, "The struggle over political authority reflected broad-based disillusionment and frustration, and the desire to be free of Indian Agency interference."[45] Clashes between Indian Agency superintendents and reservation leaders or captains, she continued, occurred on reservations throughout Riverside and San Diego counties in the decade before World War I.[46] In actuality, these clashes extended back much further, dating to the unratified treaties of the early 1850s. The deceit inherent in these unfulfilled promises forced native leaders into a series of conflicts, both great and small, as they fought pernicious attacks by the Anglo majority upon their culture and land. Stanford President David Starr Jordan opined, "it was not until 1890 that the Indians knew that these treaties were not in force and that they had no rightful claim in the eyes of the law on the land which they had been occupying."[47]

Mounting tensions over control of reservation leadership, religious practices and tribal sovereignty erupted in deadly violence on May 2, 1912, on Cahuilla Reservation in Riverside County. Here, as on the Morongo Reservation and the lands of the Luiseño in San Diego County, dynamic leadership, unbowed and unrepentant, aggressively struck at their antagonist, Indian Agent William Stanley.

Stanley began his career in Southern California as a day-school teacher on Soboba Reservation under Superintendent Lucius A. Wright in 1907. Wright's home and office were at Soboba. By all accounts, Wright was indifferent to the needs of the Indian people in his charge.[48] Both Wright and Stanley viewed native celebrations of fiestas as a serious threat to their attempt to control and maintain order on the reservations. Dancing, gambling and especially use of alcohol were common at fiestas and the drinking, in particular, was viewed with serious alarm. Stanley, acting with zealous commitment, took dangerous chances to eliminate the use of liquor.[49] He and supporting officers were beaten by tribal members on Soboba, and even jailed in 1907 for interfering with fiestas.[50] It was not so much the alcohol that drove the actions of Soboba Indians but the contest over authority. They did not recognize the government's presence as binding on them or their reservation. "The matter of self-government among these Indians is an important one," Supervisor Charles L. Davis wrote in a 1908 investigative report.[51]

A reorganization of the district in 1908 placed Wright's Superintendency over the Soboba, Cahuilla, Santa Rosa, Ramona, and Santa Ynez reservations.[52] The unrest at Soboba was mirrored on other reservations, in particular Cahuilla, after Francis Swayne was made superintendent in 1909. Swayne immediately encountered problems with the traditional system and well-supported leadership of the reservation.[53] Emerging as a force on the reservation was Leonicio Lugo, son of the hereditary ceremonial leader (net) Fernando Lugo.[54] Fernando Lugo, called the last of the "old time" captains, (1820-1905)[55] succeeded Manuel Largo, lieutenant of Juan Antonio and the staunch ally of Olegario Calac in the fight to protect Indian lands in the 1860s and 1870s. Largo stepped down as chief in 1877. In reporting his retirement, the *San Diego Union* abandoned its antagonism of a few years earlier when Largo led a fight to secure a land base for his people. "He is an excellent

Leonicio Lugo ca. 1890. Courtesy of Gerald Smith Collection, Archives, A.K. Smiley Public Library, Redlands, California

old man and is deservedly respected," the paper wrote. "His authority over his tribe was absolute, and it was ably and justly used."[56]

The rise of Leonicio Lugo followed long-established lines of leadership among the Cahuilla and came at a time when government agents were attempting to politically reform the traditional system and control tribal leadership. Lugo received his education at the first reservation school at Cahuilla. He was a prize student of teacher Mary Ticknor and as a young man was dubbed a "progressive"[57] by agents such as Horatio Rust, who made Lugo his interpreter, a police officer and supported his elevation to captain after the death of Pablo Cassaro in 1890.[58] Lugo supported his wife, two children, and other family members. In 1887 he farmed five acres along with twenty-two head of cattle. Lugo was literate, capable of speaking both Spanish and English, but also relied upon the advice of his nephew Lupe Lugo, who was educated at Sherman Indian Institute.[59] As captain of the Cahuilla, Lupe Lugo was a major figure at the 1908 conference in Riverside.

Thorne noted that after 1906, pressure mounted for agents to exercise greater power, including the right to depose those Indian leaders deemed "troublemakers" or obstructionist to Agency goals.[60] However, Anthropologist Lowell Bean believes that such pressure occurred very quickly after the 1891 Act for the Relief of the Mission Indians and the Smiley Commission Report of the same year.[61]

By 1907 the population at Cahuilla had dropped markedly to roughly 150 people.[62] Despite the depleted condition of the reservation, the Cahuilla there united in an effort to stop government-mandated allotment of their land and disregard of boundaries. "The boundary issue was a very serious concern," for the Cahuilla, Thorne wrote.[63] Monetary fines were levied against Anglo trespassers who sometimes found themselves confined to a new reservation jail. "There were repeated requests from the Cahuilla Reservation for fences, boundary markers, and a new survey. It was reported in 1909 that the Cahuilla Reservation people were 'much exercised' over the ill-defined boundary.[64] When the new survey was made at last, its results were unsatisfactory to the Cahuillas," Thorne wrote, and reportedly Will Stanley "favored the white ranchers' interpretation of where the boundary lay." As tensions heightened, threats of violence against the continued trespassers were made.[65] The arrest and punishment of white trespassers paralleled the action taken on Morongo Reservation by Will Pablo and Agent Clara True. Unfortunately, Swayne and Leonicio Lugo lacked a relationship like that of Pablo and True.

Friction between Swayne and Lugo developed over Lugo's collection of small financial tributes from tribal members and the extent of Swayne's authority. The problem escalated in the fall of 1910 when Swayne deposed Lugo as captain despite issuing him a commission the previous July.[66] Swayne moved to make an "example" of Cahuilla leadership as personified by Lugo and harassed Lugo by prosecuting him for minor offenses.[67] This action was indicative of a larger purpose by Swayne and by extension the Indian Bureau, which was the destruction of Indian culture and dissemination of their land holdings. The short-term goals of this were expressed at a conference of Mission Indian superintendents in Temecula in June 1910 where Swayne gave a paper that called for the abolishment of "enemy songs and immoral and degrading chants."[68] The use of fiestas to organize political resistance to government authority was an even greater worry to Mission Indian Agency officials. Government investigator Frank Thackery later reported that Leonicio Lugo had "been shrewd enough to grasp the opportunity, and has made it a point to visit these fiestas or other gatherings of the Indians for the purpose of uniting the malcontent element as his followers."[69] Indian activists with the Mission Indian Federation would emulate this use of fiestas as a venue to organize resistance a few years later.

With the departure of Swayne in 1911, the oversight of Cahuilla Reservation near Anza fell to Stanley. A variety of opinions about how to solve the problems which existed on the reservation only led to government vacillation. "The Cahuillas remained cordially uncooperative to Stanley," Thorne wrote.[70] Stanley was not known to have an "authoritarian personality"[71] and one historian wrote of his successes on behalf of Native Americans, including the development of more water for irrigation, better water for domestic use and water for pumping plants.[72] However on the issue of reservation authority, Stanley, like those before him, was adamant that the government through the agent controlled tribal government, land and water usage and property rights, negating any respect for tribal sovereignty. The accumulative effect of the long-simmering dispute between the Cahuillas and the agent came to a head in May 1912.[73]

Reports indicate that Stanley was invited to an annual fiesta celebrating the Cahuillas' patron saint.[74] He arrived the evening of May 1 along with agency farmer Henry Pedersen, Indian policemen Celso Serrano, and John Largo. They met with day-school teacher Carl Stevens.[75] Stanley had sent word that he wished to speak to Cornelio Lubo and Adolph Lugo about a property dispute. Lubo had "changed a public road which had been worked and used by the public for many years...in defiance of the authority of Supt. Stanley," according to government investigator Thackery.[76] Reportedly Stanley also planned to deal with the issue of branding bulls for the government that the Indians felt belonged to them.[77]

That evening, tribal members gathered at the home of Juan Acosta for the annual celebration and feast. There was singing and dancing and a mass conducted by Leonicio Lugo after decoration of the graves in the reservation cemetery.[78] Stanley did not attend but sent policeman Largo to tell Lubo to report to the schoolhouse the next morning. Largo later testified that it was at the fiesta that "rebellion against the rule of Stanley was hatched" and arrangements made for an attack the next day.[79] Largo named "medicine man" Juanita Casero as inciting those present. According to Largo, Stanley prohibited Casero from practicing his traditional medicine.[80] Stanley's wife corroborated Largo's statement. May Stanley later testified that she remembered a quarrel between her husband and Cahuilla tribesmen when Stanley prohibited treatment of Juan Tortes by Casero.[81] The *Redlands Daily Facts* reported that "the Indian doctor wanted to employ incantations and weird ceremonials for the use of the sick man and Stanley took no stock in that school of medicine."[82] Largo also insisted that the men at the fiesta performed "an old fashioned war dance" and were still dancing when he left at midnight. This allegation was also contained in the government's brief accompanying the appeal of the defendants filed with the United States Supreme Court in October 1913.[83]

The morning of May 2, about twenty-five Cahuilla men led by Leonicio Lugo arrived at the schoolhouse and teacher Steven's home, where Stanley had spent the night.[84] Stanley

Clara True with Segundo Chino (far left) and Ben DeCreveceour (far right), ca. 1909.
Courtesy of Ronnie Peacock.

greeted them and suggested that everyone meet in the schoolhouse. He was joined there by Serrano, Pedersen, and Stevens. Largo and Adolph Lugo came a little later. Ignacio Costo, "a regular interpreter for the malcontent element," acted as interpreter for the Indians, according to investigator Thackery. Lugo immediately challenged Stanley for summoning Cornelio Lubo, saying that he, Lugo, had full authority and that if he wished to discuss Lubo's actions, "it must be done only through him [Lugo]." Lugo also disputed Stanley's right to brand the bulls then residing on the reservation.[85]

The government statement of the incident reported that one Cahuilla in attendance, Pio Lubo, was heard by Largo, Serrano and Adolph Lugo saying in Cahuilla, "if you fellows are afraid of Mr. Stanley, I will drive him out by his hair," or that "you must do what you said this morning. Let us drag him out by the hair." These statements were not translated to the non-Indians present.[86] Receiving no satisfaction from Stanley, Leonicio Lugo abruptly ended the meeting and told everyone to leave. Stanley sent officer Largo to bring Cornelio Lubo back inside the schoolhouse after Lubo ignored the superintendent's verbal orders to stay.[87] Finding Lubo outside, Largo grabbed him by the shoulder, prompting a scuffle as Lubo physically resisted. Several other Cahuilla came to Lubo's aid. Pio Lubo, Pablino Lubo, and Francisco Lubo began severely beating Largo, and wrestled his revolver from him. Serrano, the other policeman, ran to assist Largo but reached the door to find the barrel of Ambrosio Apapas' gun aimed at him. Serrano pulled his own weapon and the two exchanged shots, with Francisco Lubo receiving a minor wound to the knee from Serrano's weapon.[88] Apapas emptied his own gun at Serrano, and, receiving Largo's pistol, continued to fire, striking Serrano below the heart.[89]

By this time Stanley and Stevens had reached the little porch of the school, where Investigator Thackery wrote that Stanley yelled for his men not to shoot.[90] According to Thorne and Cahuilla oral history, Stanley shouted, "shoot that goddamn Indian," referring to Apapas.[91] Apapas allegedly advanced on the white men and opened fire as they retreated into the school, striking Stanley in the back.[92] The shot reportedly passed through Stanley, hitting his heart.[93] Apapas pursued them into the school where he continued to fire at Pedersen and Stevens who, unhurt, escaped through the rear of the building.[94] Outside, a badly beaten Largo was saved from a worse fate by the intervention of Charlie Arenas. Investigator Thackery wrote that Apapas exited the schoolhouse, approached Largo, leveled his pistol and began pulling the trigger on the empty revolver. Realizing his gun was empty, Apapas asked the crowd for more cartridges to finish the job. At that point, Thackery said, Arenas intercepted Apapas and stopped the attack on Largo. According to Thackery, Arenas was "closely associated with the malcontents" but also related to Largo.[95]

The parties separated and went to their homes. Those involved in the attack met with Captain Lugo and it was decided to leave that evening for Riverside in order to consult their attorney, Miguel Estudillo.[96] The men, including Apapas, Francisco Lubo, and Leonicio Lugo, Juan Costa and Felix Tortes, were stopped at Perris by Riverside County Sheriff Frank Wilson, who took Apapas and Francisco Lubo into custody. The others continued to Riverside, where they talked with their attorney and Lugo obtained warrants for the arrest of Largo and Serrano for assault with a dangerous weapon.[97]

Francisco Lubo and Apapas were initially charged with Stanley's murder but two months later a federal grand jury indicted eight more Cahuilla as co-conspirators: Leonicio Lugo, Pio Lubo, Pablino Lubo, Cornelio Lubo, Charlie Arenas, Patrick Casero, Agapito Lubo and Cervantes (Santos) Lubo. The trial began in Los Angeles in early March 1913. The federal courtroom and courthouse hallways were packed with a large crowd, who attended either in support of the Cahuilla or were there as witnesses.[98] Many of the spectators were tribal members who were forced to sell off most of their possessions to pay the expense of traveling to and from the trial.[99] Condina Hopkins acted as an interpreter for the government with Will Pablo as "special judge" to check the accuracy of Hopkins' translations. Gabe Acosta was brought in by the defense to verify the work of both Hopkins and Pablo.[100] A Redlands newspaper reported that a number of jurymen openly said they would not take an Indian's word over that of a white man.[101]

Newspapers reported that the accused showed no emotion during the trial but sat "like stones."[102] The government's case, as argued by United States Attorney Dudley W. Robinson, was that the accused conspired to assassinate Stanley, something all the defendants consistently denied. The defendants and attorney Estudillo countered that a stray bullet from the gun of Celso Serrano killed Stanley during the confrontation outside

Indian agent William Stanley at Soboba Reservation.
Schoolteacher Mary Sheriff Fowler is front row center. Undated.
Courtesy of Charlene Ryan, Soboba Band of Luiseño Indians.

the schoolhouse.[103] Reservation schoolteacher Ada Light swore that she heard Francisco Lubo threaten to kill Stanley after the agent had Lubo jailed in 1907 and finally banished him from Soboba after a second offense in 1908.[104] Stanley's 13-year-son, said to have an expertise in Spanish, corroborated Light's story, stating that he was present when Lubo came to the Stanley house and made the threat.[105] Leonicio Lugo and Cornelio Lubo testified they considered themselves friends of Stanley and on the best of terms with him.[106] An attempt by Apapas to claim diminished capacity or insanity due to a medical condition (goiter) was rejected by the court.[107]

After several hours of deliberation, the jury, not surprisingly, found for the government with six of the ten defendants receiving a sentence of ten years in prison for second-degree murder. Charlie Arenas, Patrick Casero, Agapito Lubo, and Cervantes Lubo were acquitted.[108] The jury accepted the government's argument that a conspiracy existed. Oral history of the

Cahuilla discounts any conspiracy and believes the accused were "railroaded."[109] An appeal to the United States Supreme Court in October 1913 for a new trial was denied.

Those convicted were sent to the federal penitentiary at McNeils Island, Washington. Pio Lubo died there a year later. Pablino Lubo, Francisco Lubo, and Ambrosio Apapas were released for good behavior after six years. Cornelio Lubo moved to Syracuse, New York. Leonicio Lugo, the alleged head of the conspiracy and tribal captain, apparently returned to the tribe, where in 1924 he was elected a judge of the Mission Indian Federation.[110]

Stanley was buried at San Jacinto on May 7, 1912. Newspaper accounts said that the funeral was "attended by hundreds of people from all over the country, many going from Riverside. The cortege to the cemetery was fully a mile long. Many Indians attended the services, for the officer was much esteemed by the Sobobans."[111] Soboban Charlene Ryan said that on the first-year anniversary of Stanley's death, 60 people from the reservation went to the burial site; "the grave was covered in flowers because the people loved him so much." His fight to get a hospital for the Soboba reservation and develop water sources and irrigation won him many native friends. Many testified on behalf of the prosecution at the trial.[112]

The Bureau of Indian Affairs retaliated against Cahuilla Reservation for its association with the ring of "insurgents,"[113] as Celso Serrano called them. After Stanley's death, the agency buildings and the school were abandoned and fell into disrepair. Other tribes "didn't want to be associated with us," Cahuilla tribal member JoMay Modesto said, "and the BIA cut us off…Cahuilla were shunned. We lost Bureau services." Modesto added that they did not receive any benefits from federal-revenue sharing until the 1960s, when BIA involvement began again.[114] This did not dampen efforts to maintain and organized resistance to government policy or to reach allies on other reservations. Lupe Lugo was one of those who began circulating petitions on different reservations, detailing ongoing injustices against Southern California Indians, demanding citizenship as a way "to free themselves from the yoke of the Indian Agency."[115] Similar calls for unity would be heard over the next few years, giving rise to organizations such as the Mission Indian Federation.

The repercussions from Stanley's death were not over, however. The Cahuilla would exact revenge on John Largo, who was a chief witness against Stanley murder defendants. On March 22, 1921, Largo, now Chief of Police on Cahuilla, and Dr. Eugene W. Hawkins, Indian Service physician for the Cahuilla, went to the home of Francisco (Chico) Lugo. They were there reportedly to verify additional money Lugo owed the government for the purchase of stock.[116] During the buggy ride, Largo made mention that Felix Tortes was riding horseback from Chico's home to that of Adoph Lugo, "who was known to be a captain of the Tibbet forces."[117] As they approached, Largo noted that Tortes was returning to Chico Lugo's home. As they reached the home, Tortes entered Lugo's house while Lugo met the two men at the front gate. Tempers flared over the exchange of paperwork at which time Lugo began shouting in the Indian language, prompting a nervous Largo to begin unbuttoning his coat.[118] Hawkins said he then became aware that Felix Tortes was standing just inside the gate at a distance of roughly fifteen feet with a rifle leveled at both him and Largo. Hawkins said as he ducked down, Tortes opened fire. As Hawkins ran for the cover of a nearby adobe structure, he saw Tortes shooting and advancing upon Largo, as the officer, revolver drawn, ran backward. Hawkins then continued his rapid exit from the area and later testified that a couple of bullets had uncomfortably whistled past him.[119]

Hawkins could get no help from other Cahuilla but returned later with Anglo authorities to find Largo's body. Hawkins reported that Largo was shot through the thigh and just above the pelvis.[120] Tortes and Lugo went straight away to the Soboba home of Adam Castillo, who, at that time, was Grand President of the Mission Indian Federation. Castillo notified the authorities and arranged for the immediate surrender of the two men.[121] Largo's pistol and cartridge belt were later provided by Chico Lugo from their hiding place.[122]

Witnesses, including Lugo's wife, testified that Largo pulled his pistol and only then did Tortes fire at the men. Newspaper stories immediately linked the killing of Largo to the feud stemming from the Stanley affair on Cahuilla Reservation. Largo was described as close to the government and as one who had antagonized the tribe by his opposition against the tribe's rebellious spirit.[123] Since witnesses swore that Tortes reacted in self-defense, both Tortes and Lugo were exonerated of any guilt in November 1921.[124] This is probably the same Tortes who rode with Leonicio Lugo and the others when stopped by Riverside County sheriff's officers shortly after Stanley's murder.[125]

The government prosecuted ten Cahuilla Indians for conspiracy to kill William Stanley but it wasn't the killers of an agent that truly worried the Indian Bureau. The true conspiracy on Cahuilla Reservation was the same conspiracy hatched on Portero Reservation and before that in the Luiseño villages of San Diego County or the Cupeño village of Agua Caliente—a conspiracy by Native Americans to hold onto their own lives, protect their property from outside thieves, secure their precious resources of water and arable land, teach their traditions in their own way, and remove the yoke of an oppressive bureaucratic boot from the necks of the Indian people of Southern California. It was a fight for sovereignty.

This does not mean that all native peoples spoke with one voice. The factions within the Indian community were as varied as human nature itself, and as contentious. But, when leaders with daring and spiritual strength spoke out, they found many who responded. Most were heirs of a long tradition of leadership, passed on as a precious responsibility from one generation to the next. They were not always guiltless in their efforts but they believed in themselves, their culture, and the Indian people.

Antonio Garra, Juan Antonio, Olegario Calac, Manuel Largo, Will Pablo, [126] and Leonicio Lugo—all laid the foundation for the next wave of resistance in the twentieth century with the formation of new Pan-Indian movements. New leaders emerged from the ranks of the so-called Mission Indians with links to the leadership clans of the past and a new willingness to continue the fight.

NOTES:

[1] Clara True, "The Experiences of a Woman Indian Agent," *The Outlook Magazine* (May- August, 1909), 336.

[2] *Redlands Review* newspaper, April 10, 1909, p. 4.

[3] True oversaw the Morongo, Palm Springs (Agua Caliente), Twenty-Nine Palms, San Manuel and Mission Creek Reservations. See the *Riverside Enterprise*, April 29, 1908, p. 2

[4] Clara True, "Experiences of a Woman Indian Agent," The Outlook," 335. Clara Davis True was born in New Columbus, Owen County, Kentucky in August 1868. Her father, George, was a clerk and salesman for a novelty vendor. She had two sisters, Elizabeth and Joan. In 1887 she graduated from the Synodical College of Fulton, Missouri with a Mistress of Arts degree. She lived in and around the Springfield, Missouri, area where her family had moved. She worked as a teacher for several years. In 1893, True joined the Indian Service and was assigned to teach at the Pine Ridge Agency in South Dakota. This was three years after the massacre of Big Foot's people at Wounded Knee and the same year as the Columbian Exposition in Chicago where a young professor named Frederick Jackson Turner declared that the American frontier was closed. From 1893 through most of 1907 True ran day schools or boarding schools at a number of Indian agencies across the West, including the Sac and Fox in Missouri, Pueblo schools in New Mexico, and the Colville Agency in Washington. While teaching in New Mexico, she was seen by Commissioner of Indian Affairs, Francis Leupp, who later wrote of the encounter. True "weighed one hundred and five pounds when I chanced upon her for the first time in a low mud schoolhouse," Leupp wrote. "What stuck me at once in Miss True's school was the well-groomed look of the children: the hair of the girls was brushed to such a gloss that you could almost see your face in it; the boys, though naturally more rough-and-ready in appearance, were marvels of general cleanness and the clothing of all the children was neatly patched.…When I went away, the governor of the village, an aged Indian, collected some of his chief councilors and trailed me several miles, till he found a place where our conversation could not be overheard, and there confided to me that his heart was heavy with feat lest I might be going to take Miss True away." Leupp added that he studied the traits of this diminutive woman. Word came to him of her "prowess in riding and shooting." The Potrero [also called Morongo] Agency in Southern California, having become disagreeably notorious for its record of Indian and Mexican outlawry, I concluded that a man of about Miss True's build was needed to manage it." Some of this information came from e-mail correspondence with Ronnie Peacock, a scholar at the University of Northern Colorado who was completing a dissertation on the life of Clara True, June – August 2001.

[5] Francis Leupp, in the *Redlands Daily Facts* newspaper, May 13, 1910.

[6] Ibid.

[7] Ibid.

[8] *Redlands Daily Facts* newspaper, March 4, 1910.

[9] Ibid.

[10] Ibid.

[11] *Redlands Daily Fact*, newspaper, May 22, 1909, p. 3.

[12] Ibid. The "Secunda" mentioned here is undoubtedly Segundo Chino.

[13] Ibid.

[14] Ibid.

[15] Ibid.

[16] Ibid.

[17] *Riverside Daily Enterprise* newspaper, April 29, 1908, p. 2. True also introduced Jim Pine, Juan Lugo, Manuel Santo and Juan de la Cruz Norte. John Morongo had died in 1898. Hanks interview with Ernest Siva, February 20, 2008.

[18] Charles Lummis, "Getting Together," *Out West* magazine (June 1908), 505.

[19] Ibid., 507.

[20] *Riverside Daily Press* newspaper, April 28, 1908, p. 4.

[21] Ibid.

[22] *Riverside Daily Enterprise* newspaper, April 29, 1908, p. 2.

[23] *Riverside Daily Press* newspaper, April 28, 1908, p. 4.

[24] Edwin R. Bingham, *Charles F. Lummis, Editor of the Southwest* (San Marino, California: The Huntington Library, 1955), 113-115.

[25] Robert W. Kenny, Attorney General of California, *History and Proposed Settlement Claims of California Indians* (Sacramento: California State Printing Office, 1944), 24-26.

[26] *Riverside Daily Press* newspaper, April 28, 1908, p. 4.

[27] Ibid.

[28] Ibid.

[29] *Riverside Daily Enterprise* newspaper, April 30, 1908, p. 1.

[30] Ibid.

[31] Ibid.

[32] Lummis, "Getting Together," 505.

[33] Ibid.

[34] *Redlands Daily Facts* newspaper, May 16, 1910, p. 1. According to the newspaper, "the trouble was caused by the encroachment of white settlers upon lands of the Indians. The Indians, after warning the settlers, finally took matters into their own hands and drove the squatters off the lands, and it was this action which caused the sensational articles to be sent abroad. According to Miss True the Indians were in the right and their action will be upheld by the authorities in Washington should there be further complications." Attempts to usurp Pueblo Indian lands in New Mexico, however, continued, leading to another outbreak of violence and intimidation in 1922. Secretary of the Interior Albert Fall supported the Bursum Bill that proposed to surrender large sections of Indian lands to non-Indian squatters. The controversy gave rise to the American Indian Defense Association and brought John Collier to national attention. See Chapter 9 of this work.

[35] Ibid.

[36] *Redlands Daily Facts* newspaper, May 17, 1910, p. 5. True and life companion Mary Bryan moved to New Mexico where True continued to work for an end to the alcohol trade on the reservations. Despite her continual fight to protect Indian land at California's Morongo Reservation, a True biographer says her motivations changed by the 1920s. Margaret Jacobs wrote that True supported the Bursum Bill, perhaps for personal reasons since True's New Mexico ranch was on land belonging to the Santa Clara Pueblo. The True described by Jacobs has a disdain for traditional native life and custom, considering Indians backwards and ofen treating them as mere children. See, Margaret Jacobs, "Clara True and Female Moral Authority," an essay in *The Human Tradition in the American West*, no. 10, Benson Tong and Regan A. Lutz (eds.) (Wilmington, Delaware: Scholarly Resources Inc., 2002), 99-115.

[37] Oral tradition of the Gabrieleño family of Machado. Interview with Dorothy Machado Mathews, council member of the Gabrieleño Band of Mission Indians, September 19, 2004, Banning, California.

[38] Ibid.

[39] "Torros Indians Aroused Over Agent's Order," unidentified newspaper article in Constance Goddard DuBois Papers, Miscellaneous Clippings, Microfilm Reel 3. The approximate date for this news article was determined from the reference by its author that "all the Mission Indians of California have become fearful lest the inroads of the white settlers should oust them from their reservations. This order coming as it does so soon after the unfortunate removal of the Warner's Ranch tribes, is well calculated to arouse suspicion." The Cupeño at Warner's were removed to Pala in 1903.

[40] Ibid.

[41] *Redlands Daily Facts* newspaper, February 11, 1910.

[42] Ibid.

[43] *Redlands Daily Facts* newspaper, November 27, 1911, p. 1.

[44] Ibid.

[45] Tanis Thorne, "The Death of Superintendent Stanley and the Cahuilla Uprising of 1907-1912," *Journal of California and Great Basin Anthropology* (2004), 233.

[46] Ibid.

[47] David Starr Jordan, "Helping the Indians: What the Riverside Indian Conference Accomplished—Demand for Homes, Physicians, Educators and Protection," *Sunset, Magazine of the Pacific* (January, 1909), 59. This is likely an overstatement on the part of Jordan. Scholar Richard Carrico wrote that Luiseno leader Olegario Calac was "aware of the government's rejection of the 1852 treaties and…harsh dealings with the northern California Modocs" in 1870. See Carrico, "The Struggle for Native American Self-Determination," 204.

[48] Thorne, "The Death of Superintendent Stanley," 240-241.

[49] Ibid., 240.

[50] Ibid.

[51] Charles L. Davis, "1908 Report on Soboba and its superintendent Will Stanley, 1 July," copy in the The Rupert and Jeannette Costo Archive of the American Indian, Box 93, University of California, Riverside Special Collections.

[52] Thorne, "The Death of Superintendent Stanley," 240.

[53] Ibid., 241.

[54] Ibid., 236.

[55] Ibid.

[56] Robinson and Risher, *The San Jacintos*, 106.

[57] Thorne, "The Death of Superintendent Stanley," 237.

[58] Ibid.

[59] Thorne, "The Death of Superintendent Stanley," 237, 239; Frank A. Thackery, "Report of 21 June to Commissioner of Indian Affairs," copy in Rupert and Jeannette Costo Collection, Box 109, University of California, Riverside Special Collections, 2. Thackery reported that the Cahuilla were "stubborn, independent and self-confident people."

[60] Ibid., 235.

[61] Bean, "Morongo Indian Reservation: A Century of Adaptive Strategies," 170.

[62] Thorne, "The Death of Superintendent Stanley," 237.

[63] Ibid., 239.

[64] Ibid.

[65] Ibid.

[66] Ibid., 241-242.

[67] Ibid., 242.

[68] Robinson and Risher, *The San Jacintos*, 116.

[69] Thackery, "Report of 21 June to Commissioner of Indian Affairs," 3. All agreed that the government ban on alcohol use by Indians must be strictly enforced.

[70] Thorne, "The Death of Superintendent Stanley," 243-244.

[71] Ibid.

[72] Elmer Holmes as quoted in Robinson and Risher, *The San Jacintos*, 117.

[73] Thorne, "The Death of Superintendent Stanley," 244-245.

[74] Ibid., 245.

[75] Robinson and Risher, *The San Jacintos*, 117.

[76] Thackery, "Report of 21 June to Commissioner of Indian Affairs," 9. Lubo's act emulated a similar action on the Potrero Reservation a few years earlier (see page 9 of this chapter) as local Indians blocked long-used roadways across their land to emphasize their right of sovereignty and control of their own land.

[77] Thorne, "The Death of Superintendent Stanley," 245; *Ambrosio Apapas, et al., v. The United States, In the Supreme Court of the United States, October Term, 1913, In Error to the District Court of the United States for the Southern District of California*, copy in Rupert and Jeannette Costo Collection, Box 109, 6.

[78] Thorne, Thorne, "The Death of Superintendent Stanley," 245; Testimony of Leonicio Lugo as reported in the *Redlands Daily Facts*, newspaper March 12, 1913, p. 3.

[79] Testimony of John Largo as reported by the *Redlands Daily Facts* newspaper, March 8, 1913, p. 1.

[80] Ibid.

[81] Testimony of May Bessie Stanley as reported by the *Redlands Daily Facts* newspaper, March 7, 1913, p. 3.

[82] Ibid.

[83] Largo in the *Redlands Daily Facts* newspaper, March 8, 1913, p. 1; *Ambrosio Apapas, et. al., v. The United States, In the Supreme Court of the United States, October Term, 1913*, 6.

[84] Thackery, "Report of 21 June to Commissioner of Indian Affairs," 8.

[85] Ibid., 9. Ignacio Costo, the interpreter for the "malcontents" was the same praised at the 1908 conference in Riverside and who presented gifts to Frank Miller.

[86] *Ambrosio Apapas, et. al., v. The United States, In the Supreme Court of the United States, October Term, 1913*, 9-10.

[87] *Ambrosio Apapas, et. al., v. The United States, In the Supreme Court of the United States, October Term, 1913*, 10-11; Thackery, "Report of 21 June to Commissioner of Indian Affairs," 10-11.

[88] Ibid.

[89] Ibid., *Ambrosio Apapas, et. al., v. The United States, In the Supreme Court of the United States, October Term, 1913*, 11.

[90] Thackery, "Report of 21 June to Commissioner of Indian Affairs," 11.

[91] Thorne, "The Death of Superintendent Stanley," 246. Thorne received her information from Cahuilla tribal member JoMay Modesto during an interview in 2004. Modesto related the incident as told her by her father who was a young boy at the time of Stanley's killing. Modesto told Thorne that according to her father Stanley was killed in the agency house where teacher Stevens lived and not in the schoolhouse as indicated in the official reports. It should be noted that Modesto's father and another boy, Sylvester Costo, were only "six or seven" years of age and were playing some yards away when the fight broke out. They "did not get too close because they knew there was trouble," Modesto said, but hid nearby amid rocks. Hanks interview with JoMay Modesto (Cahuilla), Celeste Hughes and Charlene Ryan (Luiseño), May 23, 2005, Soboba Reservation.

[92] Thorne, "The Death of Superintendent Stanley," 246; Thackery, "Report of 21 June to Commissioner of Indian Affairs," 11.

[93] *Redlands Daily Facts* newspaper, May 2, 1912, p. 1.

[94] Thackery, "Report of 21 June to Commissioner of Indian Affairs," 11.

[95] Ibid., 12.

[96] Ibid.

[97] Thackery, "Report of 21 June to Commissioner of Indian Affairs," 12; *Ambrosio Apapas, et. al., v. The United States, In the Supreme Court of the United States, October Term, 1913*, 12.

[98] *Redlands Daily Facts* newspaper, March 5, 1913, p. 5.

[99] Hanks interview with JoMay Modesto, Celeste Hughes and Charlene Ryan, May 23, 2005, Soboba Indian Reservation. According to Modesto this financial burden precipitated the leasing of Cahuilla land to local ranchers without BIA approval, an action continued to this day on the Cahuilla Reservation.

[100] *Redlands Daily Facts,* newspaper, March 8, 1913, p. 1.

[101] *Redlands Daily Facts*, newspaper, March 5, 1913, p. 5.

[102] Ibid.

[103] *Redlands Daily Facts*, newspaper, March 20, 1913, p. 1; Thorne, "The Death of Superintendent Stanley," 247.

[104] Ada Light testimony as reported by the *Redlands Daily Facts,* newspaper, March 7, 1913, p. 3.

[105] Ibid.

[106] *Redlands Daily Facts,* newspaper, March 8, 1913, p. 1; *Redlands Daily Facts,* newspaper, March 12, 1913, p. 3.

[107] *Redlands Daily Facts* newspaper, March 18, 1913, p. 2.

[108] *Riverside Daily Press* newspaper, March 28, 1913, p. 1; Thorne, "The Death of Superintendent Stanley," 247.

[109] Hanks interview with JoMay Modesto, Celeste Hughes and Charlene Ryan, May 23, 2005, Soboba Indian Reservation.

[110] Thorne, "The Death of Superintendent Stanley," 247; It should be noted that Robinson's account in *The San Jacintos* , 118, states that it was Francisco and not Pio Lubo who died in prison and that the last to be paroled was Apapas in 1919. The men were eligible for parole after serving one-third of the ten-year sentence. It was reported that Prosecutor Robinson was inclined to grant an early release to Cornelio, Pio, Pablino and Francisco Lubo since they were considered "least culpable of the entire sextette." "Upon Leonicio Lugo's shoulders was placed the blame for the killing of Stanley...He is referred to as the leader of the conspiracy, and the man who, above all others, should be held responsible for what happened that fateful morning." See *The San Jacinto Register* newspaper, May 8, 1913. Cornelio Lubo's move to Syracuse, New York (Thorne, 247) was likely a desire to be near Antonio Lubo who is listed as living there in the 1910 federal census. In 1900 Antonio Lubo was a Mission Indian attending Carlisle Indian School in Pennsylvania. Francisco Lubo died on Cahuilla July 5, 1925. Ambrosio Apapas died July 2, 1924.

[111] *Redlands Daily Facts* newspaper, May 7, 1912, p. 1.

[112] Hanks interview with JoMay Modesto, Celeste Hughes and Charlene Ryan, May 23, 2005, Soboba Indian Reservation. See also, The *San Jacinto Register* newspaper, May 8, 1913.

[113] *Redlands Daily Facts* newspaper, March 8, 1913, p. 1.

[114] Hanks interview with JoMay Modesto, Celeste Hughes and Charlene Ryan, May 23, 2005, Soboba Indian Reservation.

[115] Thorne, "The Death of Superintendent Stanley," 247.

[116] Deposition of Eugene W. Hawkins, July 15, 1921, in Rupert and Jeannette Costo Collection, Box 109, University of California, Riverside, Special Collections; *Redlands Daily Facts* newspaper, November 2, 1921, p. 6

[117] Deposition of Eugene W. Hawkins, July 15, 1921. Jonathan Tibbet at this time was the white counselor

for the Mission Indian Federation, which formed in the fall of 1919 during meetings with Southern California Indian captains at this Riverside home.

[118] Ibid.

[119] Ibid.

[120] Ibid.

[121] *The Indian*, Magazine of the Mission Indian Federation (April, 1921), 9.

[122] Deposition of Eugene W. Hawkins, July 15, 1921.

[123] *Redlands Daily Facts* newspaper, November 9, 1921, p. 4.

[124] *Hemet News* newspaper, November 11, 1921 as quoted by Robinson and Risher, *The San Jacintos*, 118.

[125] *Redlands Daily Facts* newspaper, November 2, 1921, p. 6; November 9, 1921, p. 4; Robinson, *The San Jacintos*, 118

[126] Will Pablo was clearly a man of cunning and charisma along with certain manipulative qualities. He also changed and adapted his positions over time. His work with True and later as a special federal officer with Ben De Crevecoeur may have also instilled some pragmatism. By the time his children were born in the early 20th century Pablo had decided that they should not learn their native Cahuilla language. One can only surmise that Pablo recognized the changes around him and wanted his children to learn English to assist in their survival and progress in the larger world. As he aged, however, his defiant character emerged again. Cahuilla oral traditions speak of Pablo violating a taboo by taking tribal artifacts including sacred objects and displaying them at local fairs. "He invited non-Indians to come to the reservation to see [and] to learn about Indians," Morongo elder Ernest Siva said. From this start, his daughter Jane Pablo later started collecting items in her house which became the Malki Museum on Morongo Reservation. According to Siva, Pablo became ill because of his actions—an illness no American doctors could cure. He was dying. Cahuilla shaman Pedro Chino agreed to heal Pablo if he promised never to repeat his actions of displaying sacred objects. Siva said that Pablo later ignored Chino's admonition and was again struck ill. This time Chino refused to treat him and Pablo died. According to available records Pablo died some time around 1936. Hanks interview with Ernest Siva, February 20, 2008.

8 They Called Him "Buffalo Heart": The Birth of the Mission Indian Federation

And dark days shall come to the Indian. Dark days when the light of the future shall shine no more to the people, and the road ahead [will] be lost in the gloom of the shadows. They shall seek a white leader; when such days are here, a white leader to find the trail for the people. —Indian Legend[1]

Federation Crier calling Federation members to a meeting.
Courtesy of the Machado Family Archives.

The following article ran in the *Redlands Daily Facts* on February 14, 1914:

The unmistakable evidences of the white man's civilization have appeared at the Soboba Indian reservation near San Jacinto. The International Order of Wont Works has nothing whatever on the women and girls at this reservation who have recently taken up the occupation of lace making, for the latter have been on a real strike. It is written in the past tense advisedly for the strike, modeled after the white man's as it was, genuine and real in purpose and action, came to a speedy end, through careful and expert handling.

Mrs. E. C. Sterling of the city was appraised of the fact the other day that those engaged in the lace making had refused to work longer for the rates paid and had 'struck.' Mrs. Sterling went at once to the reservation, took hold of the situation with a firm grasp, and the women and girls are back at their useful occupation again, happy and contented.

With the Pala lace making well under way with the women happy and satisfied, and with the arrangements which the promoters had made for the payment of the women for their product and the subsequent disposal of it by themselves, working smoothly, there seemed to be an opportunity for the further branching out along these lines, and it was decided to begin operations at Soboba. Plans were made and less than three months ago, Miss Lawrence was established at Soboba to teach the women to make lace with a view of earning some money on their own. There was a very clear working plan outlined at the beginning of the lessons. The ladies of the lace making committee were to provide looms, needles, bobbins, thread and patterns for the pupils. The finished lace was to be paid for at prices agreed upon in advance, and the women were to be paid at once without waiting for the sale of the lace.

The teacher began her work, and the Soboba women and children took so readily to the art, that by the time they had worked little over a month they were turning out saleable lace. As fast as it was turned out it was taken by the committee and the women were paid for it. They seemed to be more than satisfied, and the committee was encouraged in the belief that the work was going to fill a long felt want.

Teacher Mary Fowler, Cordelia Sterling and native lace makers on Soboba Reservation, ca. 1914
Courtesy of Gerald Smith Collection, Archives, A.K. Smiley Public Library, Redlands, California

Like a thunderbolt out of a clear sky came word from the lace teacher at the reservation recently, to the effect that Mrs. Sterling's presence was urgently needed. Without a thought of trouble Mrs. Sterling obeyed the summons. She went to the Soboba the early part of the week and suddenly found herself with a strike on her hands.

It is by no means an easy matter to agree with men who believe they have a grievance. One would hardly look, however, for keen logical argument on the part of Indian women, and the magnitude of the task spread our before her did not dawn on Mrs. Sterling until the arguments were well underway. One woman had undertaken to be spokeswoman for the whole class all excepting three of whom had evidently been talked into the belief that they were downtrodden and oppressed, and that they must at once make a stand for their rights. The spokeswoman was backed by another who, while she had little to say, had formed some radical opinions which were really more disconcerting than the voluable speech of the ring leader.

Dramatically and with no regard for the fact that the ladies had assumed a great deal of trouble and expense in order to help them to help themselves, the women expressed themselves as having decided not to work any longer unless their pay should be increased. Mrs. Sterling pointed out that they were reaping all the benefits which were accruing from the work, and the promoters had no interest beyond helping them.

The incident is a striking one (no pun intended) as it is probably the first time on record that the Indian man or woman has shown that this race was drawing abreast of the times in matters of this nature. The women had evidently made some study of what other people do in circumstances which they may regard as similar, but which are in reality widely different.

It needed a firm hand and an expert one—one thouroughly familiar with the Indian nature and a personality endeared to the Indian by long years of beneficial association, to solve the problem. Fortunately, these requirements were available, and in the great confidence felt in Mrs. Sterling because of her good works for them extending over many years, the women accepted her statements and returned to work. The strike was over.[2]

The February 1914 strike by the women lace-makers of Soboba is indicative of the continuing tension that existed on the reservations of Southern California one year after the imprisonment of the Cahuilla rebels for killing William Stanley. Although short-lived, it was just one more act of defiance—resistance—against what these women believed were exploitative practices. All the more telling is that this act challenged so-called "friends" of the Indians—the philanthropic white women of the Redlands Indian Association.

Carlotta Lubo of the Soboba Band of Luiseño Indians and unidentified girl, ca. 1914. Courtesy of Gerald Smith Collection, Archives, A.K. Smiley Public Library, Redlands, CA.

One of the key members of the Redlands Indian Association was Mrs. Cordelia Sterling. Although a report said that Mrs. Sterling was able to "market their product to much advantage" the *San Jacinto Register* reported that the women struck because "the price paid for their lace products was less than that originally fixed." The price was set artificially high to encourage the women, according to the newspaper.[3]

In 1910, news stories began touting the efforts of Sterling to introduce the teaching of lace making to Indian women in Southern California. Connection was made with the Indian Mission and Lace Association in New York, which had been teaching the art to eastern Native American women for 25 years.[4] Pala Reservation was chosen to be the central point for the area's spread of this craft. Teachers also were sent to Soboba, Mesa Grande and La Jolla in San Diego County.[5]

The *Redlands Review* newspaper of October 25, 1910, reported: "sales of Indian laces at a single afternoon tea in New York sometimes amount to more than $5,000." By that time, the reports continued, "the work of the Indians [had] been awarded gold medals" at three previous World Fairs and were "equal to the best importations."[6] Although well meaning, descriptions of the ability of the Indian women were patronizing at best, and demeaning at worst. Sterling claimed that lace-making "fit the aboriginal mind and natural adeptness of the hand better than anything else."[7] The "snow-white condition" of the lace made by the Indian women was reported with astonishment, since those who knew "the lives of the aborigines under usual condition…[knew that] dirt and disorder form an integral part thereof."[8]

By early 1914, locally made Indian lace was being exhibited at the Mission Inn in Riverside, Hotel Del Coronado in San Diego, and at the National Orange Show in San Bernardino. Postcards of the women making lace, with Sterling observing, were made to sell at the Orange Show in 1914, and were produced at around the same time the strike occurred on Soboba reservation.[9]

The Indian women obviously felt they were not adequately compensated for their lacework but another possible source of tension and ill-feeling may be due to the generous publicity and credit given Sterling and the Anglo lace instructors. Ironically, although Sterling and others took credit for introducing lace-making to Southern California Indian women,[10] there is evidence that these women already knew the skill and were producing startling examples of fine lace well before Redlands was even a city. At the March 1913 trial of the six Cahuilla charged with killing Superintendent William Stanley, rancher Charles Thomas said that he first knew the Cahuilla in 1861. "They made coarse blankets. The women used to make this drawn-work. When I went there the first time I stopped at the place of old Victoriano [Soboba]. He was of the old captains, and the bed that I slept on had lacework, that wide (indicating) on the pillow cases and sheets. His granddaughter made it and her name was Rosaria."[11] From her travels through Southern California in 1883, Helen Hunt Jackson produced the book *Glimpses of California and the Missions*. Throughout the book, Jackson makes note of the "hand-wrought lace, made by the Indians themselves. This is one of their arts which date back to the Mission days. Some of the lace is beautiful and fine, and of patterns like the old church laces."[12] Jackson makes note of the lace and its creators at reservations in Temecula, Cahuilla, San Juan Capistrano, Pala, Carmel, and Soboba.[13]

News accounts of the strike, unfortunately, do not identify any of the Indian women who struck for better wages. Exactly how the controversy was resolved, likewise, is not known. However, it may be more than just coincidence that ten months after the Soboba women struck for better wages, the Redlands Indian Association declared victory in its efforts to assist local Native Americans and virtually disbanded. The consensus of opinion was "that the need for the work done by the Indian association has largely gone by." With most Indians on allotments, association members felt Indians had sufficient land and water and for those "not fortunately situated" they were able to earn wages by working for people.[14]

There is very little chance that the Indians of Southern California would have agreed with the assessment of the Redlands Indian Association. Government agents still asserted control over tribal politics and the social and religious day-to-day activity of native California people. Tribal leaders still complained of the lack of "sufficient land and water" despite the assurances of the Redlands organization. The strike by Indian women in February 1914 was centered on the Soboba Reservation, but underscored an anger that was prevalent throughout the reservations of Southern California.

The vital need for water, in particular, was a never-ending struggle along with demands for control of a well-defined land base. Seeking relief or at least support from the agents proved futile and relations with government representatives was just as acrimonious as when Agent Stanley was killed. The old men of the tribes, following the prophecy of the legend, told at the beginning of this chapter, sought a white man who would speak for them. Their choice was a 63-year-old product of the American West named Jonathan Franklin Tibbet. On an October day in 1919, Tibbet was approached amid the bustle and sounds of the Riverside County Fair.[15] A conversation was conducted in English and in the ancient tongues of Alta California. The dialogue ended as abruptly as it started. A few days later more than a dozen of the captains of the "Mission people"[16] led by Chief Joe Pete of the Cahuilla and Serrano people journeyed to Tibbet's Riverside home. More talks ensued. This led to the first large-scale gathering of what would become the Mission Indian Federation when more than two hundred Southern California Indians met in November 1919 at Tibbet's home.[17]

It is likely that those captains who approached Tibbet and now asked him "to assume the duties of counsillor" [sic][18] saw him as a bridge between their two worlds with experience in both. Tibbet's character was forged on the raw frontier of the nineteenth century. The man the Indians would name "Buffalo Heart,"[19] was born near the old San Gabriel Mission on January 4, 1856. His father, by the same name, had first seen the San Bernardino and San Gabriel valleys in 1848 before moving on to the northern gold fields, where he found profits in selling supplies to adventuresome wealth seekers.[20] After a short return to the Midwest the family returned and settled in Southern California. There were seven Indian villages on the Tibbet ranch, and Indians were always in and around the household as servants and laborers but also friends.[21] Jonathan Tibbet the younger grew up in this atmosphere learning eleven different Indian dialects along with Spanish. As a boy he began collecting what was to become an extensive array of Western Americana.[22]

Like others who later championed Indian rights, Tibbet was on the other side of the conflict as a young man. During a time in Arizona, he was a civilian Indian scout for the army, later Chief of Scouts, a deputy United States marshal, as well as chief of vigilantes. He assisted, according to one writer, in "carrying on wars with the Indians of Southern California, Arizona and New Mexico, especially the Apache Indians."[23] The same writer described Tibbet as "a large man, weighing perhaps over two hundred pounds, erect and of commanding presence and poise. He was an expert with fire arms, and could shoot a pistol equally well with either hand. As was said, he was 'quick on the trigger.' "[24] However, it was also said that Tibbet was responsible for saving many Indian lives during this time due to his sympathy for them nurtured from his youth.[25]

He returned to Riverside in 1891 where he became a broker of farms, homes and mines. One author wrote that Tibbet seemed "to have had a knack of accumulating property and money."[26] He closed his office in 1912 at the urging of his wife Emma but continued to list himself a money lender and operated out of his home on Prospect Avenue. He remained an active member of the San Bernardino, Riverside and Los Angeles Pioneer societies. [27] Members of the local Pioneer Society gathered in the large yard behind the Tibbet home under a canopy of eucalyptus trees. This area beginning in 1919 provided shelter for an encampment of Native Americans. A ramada was built under the trees and there was a council room for business meetings. A fire pit dominated the center of the property where the people gathered at night for dances and ceremonial activities.[28] Julio Norte "of the Morongos" was elected grand president of the group on the second day.[29]

It is not surprising that this first gathering was prompted by mainly Desert and Pass Indians since they were very vocal in opposing government allotment plans. In particular Coachella Valley ranchers were sinking wells that sapped the more shallow government wells dug for the Indians, resulting in declining productivity of their fields.[30]

In March 1918, Chief Pete and his people appealed for assistance to President Woodrow Wilson "with scores of petitions." Pete accused the Indian Service of trying to reduce the size of allotments from 160 acres to just five acres, which Pete said was absurd in an arid country. Cahuilla water rights were constantly being challenged, Pete told government inspectors, and Anglo farmers were given preference in leasing tribal farm land.[31]

Communal resources were vital for the success of the Agua Caliente Indians. "Our land is desert," one leader said, "and there is not enough good farming land for everyone. If the land is allotted, then there is no grazing land left and we could not keep cattle."[32] The lack of arable land would later result in additional problems with those white farmers who received cheap leases of Indian land from the government.[33] Securing and protecting precious water rights remained a dominant theme of this first gathering by leaders throughout Southern California.

Even as Southern California Indians were struggling to obtain basic property rights, their young men were being asked to fight and die for America in the ongoing world conflict. Chief Joe Pete struck at this hypocrisy by counseling young Cahuilla men to ignore government questionnaires which registered them for conscription into the United States Army. A year before Pete approached Tibbet, government prosecutors arrested him on a charge of "obstructing the draft law." Indian Agent J. E. Jenkins called Pete a "mischief maker" among the Indians with a personal grudge against the agent.

During a hearing in Los Angeles, a newspaper reported that Pete "sat at his ease, his gleaming eyes missing nothing that occurred, and a Mona Lisa sort of smile playing over his dusky features." Chief Pete was armed. It was reported that Pete produced numerous documents and letters along with "data regarding the case and the status of the reservation Indians under the draft laws." These included letters from officials in the Department of the Interior and a member of the Bureau of Indian Commissioners, Isidore Dockweiler. Dockweiler was also a prominent attorney and well-connected Democrat politician. Dockweiler advised Pete that his people were exempt from the draft and that the young men should not "put hands on papers" which registered them. All charges against Pete were dropped. [34]

A year after this victory, Pete was still seeking justice for the Indian farmers of Coachella Valley through an alliance with Jonathan Tibbet. Even before the first large gathering in Riverside in late November 1919, Tibbet joined with the Serrano and Cahuilla of the low desert to reclaim the land dispersed by the agents to local white farmers. In Thermal, California farmer J. Robertson swore that Tibbet and Joe Pete confronted him on November 17, 1919, telling him he must consult with Pete on "all matters relating to the Indian in the vicinity"[35] and that government agents should not interfere. In December 1919, farmer Philip Shelton stated that Tibbet and Pete were among a group of Indians who chased his workers from the fields he had leased, removed his equipment, and posted signs warning that trespassers faced being arrested.[36] He also asserted that he was told to vacate the property unless he paid a fee to Tibbet's association, which had as much authority in Washington as did government officials.[37] This was just the first of such confrontations that would occur over the next year as members of the Mission Indian Federation began asserting an alternative authority over native lands and resources in direct defiance to the government and Indian Bureau police.

While unity of purpose was certainly a driving force behind the gathering in Riverside, total unity proved elusive. A group of "younger" Indians led by Ignacio Costa (or Costo) and Lupe Lugo of Cahuilla, who were central figures at "Mohonk West" in 1908, argued for a different priority—citizenship for all Native Americans.[38] This splinter group appears to have been following the lead of the Society of American Indians and leaders such as Dr. Carlos Montezuma and Charles Eastman, who were preaching abolishment of the Bureau of Indian Affairs, citizenship for all Indians, an end to reservations, and complete assimilation of the Native American.[39] This tension between the so-called "progressives,"[40] as they were quickly hailed, and older traditionalists among the tribes would redefine the goals of the initial organization.

The old men of the tribes sought to honor the sacrifices of their fathers who signed the California treaties and the culture they wished to preserve. "They are dying fast, those old chiefs, old captains and the things of their life as they lived it," a federation publication stated.[41] "To the customs and language of their people. Still living in days that have passed from reality to the pages of history. They will never change, those old Indians, heedless to the stream of the times that flows at their feet."[42] Figures such as Figtree John (Juan Razon) were symbolic of California's Indian past. "They speak in the words of their people and live in the past," the magazine continued.[43] "They have seen much in the rising suns over the length of a century. Beyond them, the young Indian keeps step with modern life."[44]

Jonathan Tibbet, ca. 1920.
Photo courtesy of Archives, Riverside Metropolitan Museum, Riverside, California.

These elders opposed the change in their status as wards of the nation, a newspaper reported. "What they desire is protection in the rights they claim and the privilege of living on their own land in their own way; they are against any change what would tend toward concentration."[45] The fear of government spies or dissenting voices immediately created concern with Federation leadership. Tibbet lobbied for a Credentials Committee to insure that only friends and supporters be allowed into meetings.[46] Defining those supporters would prove difficult and controversial.

Thirty-five-year-old Joseph DePorte attended the next conference in January and February 1920 at the Tibbet home. DePorte and his wife Rilla were Indians from Oklahoma and in 1920 DePorte was employed by Sherman Institute as a "disciplinarian."[47] He came at the invitation of Tibbet but soon found himself at odds with his host and critical of Tibbet's manipulation of the meeting. At a small organizational meeting on January 26, 1920, Tibbet reportedly pushed for the Indians to mount a dramatization called, "Soul of Rafael" after being approached by a promoter of the play. This proposition was dismissed by President Norte, who moved on to other business. To DePorte, Tibbet seemed "the usual run of Indian exploiter."[48] In his report filed with the government, DePorte stated that from then on he did his best to "discredit"[49] Tibbet with other participants. He believed that Tibbet wished to use local Indians to commercially support his own aims, particularly a museum. Along this line, Tibbet allegedly sounded out local Indians about creating a village where they could live as they did before the white man came.[50] DePorte saw that, along with several references to Tibbet's extensive curio collection, as a means of promoting a Tibbet museum. He also accused Tibbet of "mummery" by appealing to the "superstitious nature of the old people," through his encouragement of dancing, ritual, and ceremony.[51]

DePorte cited news reports of the conference that were anything but flattering. The *Los Angeles Examiner* published a story mocking the ceremonial aspects of the gathering, stating that dancers "began a jazz shimmy…a weird thing, a series of grunts, leaps, steps back and forth…a veritable graveyard of grunts. It was the original fox trot to the tune of 'The Vamp.'" It continued that the dancers had for headdresses "a few cabbage-like growths."[52] Certainly within this atmosphere the progressives felt emboldened in their desired path for the new organization. While not counted among the young progressives, Tibbet came to see DePorte as a threat.[53]

Tensions mounted when the *Riverside Daily Press* published an editorial condemning discussion at the convention about eliminating the Department of Indian Affairs, labeling such talk as "bunk.…In general there seems to be a disposition on the part of certain agitators to 'bust things wide open' without offering any constructive program," the paper continued.[54] DePorte, of course, endorsed the editorial. Perhaps to defuse the situation, members of the progressive wing delivered a resolution to the newspaper endorsing the paper's editorial and denying that they "advocated or are advocating the abolition of the Indian bureau."[55] DePorte's notes indicate that the young men argued all night with the elders convincing them of the need for the resolution.[56]

Much of the controversy developed following after speeches made by invited celebrities, such as Osage representatives from Oklahoma led by Charles Trumbly, Sioux actor Luther Standing Bear, Comes With the Dawn (Ono Anpo Hinapa), and particularly Red Fox

James, a northern Blackfoot lecturer.[57] James was a member of the Society of American Indians and the addresses of these participants reflected directly the feelings and policies of the radical wing of the Society of American Indians as represented by Montezuma. The dissension this created among Mission Indians was identical to that which marked the debate within the Society of American Indians over the ways, means, and timing of securing equal rights for Native Americans.[58] This debate ultimately led to the dissolution of the Society of American Indians and would be the basis of continuing dissent within the Mission Indian Federation.

Above all else, the guest speakers argued that the Bureau of Indian Affairs was the root of problems facing American Indians. Red Fox James also made an appeal for the younger progressives in the conference. "I want to see the young folks in with you," he said. "Let them have a voice. Do not keep them out."[59] Ono Anpo Hinapa condemned exploiting Indians for commercial purposes "through museums, tribal dances and other exhibitions" that perpetuate "aboriginal conditions." Allot Indian lands, give them full citizenship, and abolish the Indian Bureau, he added.[60] Their arguments were countered by an Inspector Sweet, who was in Riverside reporting on Sherman Institute. Sweet stated that the work of the Indian Bureau was unfinished. "This Indian question has a great many misunderstandings…differences of purpose…You Indians have referred in this convention to some resolutions you want to pass, some things you want the government to do for you. Some of these things are right and proper, but if the Indian Bureau were abolished, there would be nobody to bring about the good things you want done."[61] During the debate, which at times became heated, Tibbet voiced what many of the older men were thinking. "It is not a question in my mind whether or not it is advisable to abolish the Indian Bureau but it is this agent system that we all know works to the disadvantage of the Indians on the reservations and elsewhere….The agent comes on your reservation and surrounds himself by three or four policemen and he then rides up to your house and says, 'Here, I want your little boy or your little girl.' He never consults the parents whether or not he should tear that child from the house….That system, friends we propose to abolish first. Do away with your abolishment until you get results direct at home. That's my advice."[62]

Scholar Hazel Hertzberg, in speaking of the middle-class Indians who were members of the Society of American Indians, wrote that, "much as they resented the Bureau, [they] could not reconcile themselves to a policy which they feared would deliver older Indians in the hands of rapacious enemies and destroy forever the possibility of protecting the Indian land base." Immediate abolition of the Indian Bureau fell to "a small band of true believers."[63] For Southern California Indians, the financial thread was much thinner and the repercussions much more severe.

Consensus was not to be had at this conference. Debate at the 1920 conference mirrored the factionalism within the Federation's ranks, with government supporters such as DePorte vying for leverage against invited, and homegrown radicals such as Lupe Lugo, Alex Tortes, and Ignacio Costo of the Cahuilla. When the young men attempted to insert language into

Sketch from "Proceedings of the Second Annual Conference of the Society of American Indians, held at Ohio State University, Columbus, Ohio, October 2-7, 1912," in the Quarterly Journal of the Society of American Indians, vol. 1, no. 1, 1913.

a federation constitution, a final argument between DePorte and Tibbet occurred. DePorte is not specific, but from earlier remarks, the young progressives, inspired by rhetoric from speakers such as Red Fox St. James, sought organizational language that more closely mirrored the tenets of the Society of American Indians. According to DePorte, Tibbet complained that "an organization already existed and that this [proposed] constitution took its very heart out."[64] Tibbet also objected to opening active membership in the federation to any Indian who could pay the minimal membership dues and permitting, both Indian and white, to become non-voting associates (again modeled after Society of American Indians' guidelines).[65] DePorte was then ordered to leave the conference by a tearful elder who pleaded for cooperation with Tibbet. DePorte rejected this. Two elected officers of the conference, Cahuillas Lupe Lugo and Ignacio Costo, also left along with all the younger contingent and some elders. Arrangements were made for these members to "properly organize under their own selected leadership."[66] At the conference's conclusion, many provisions sought by the young "progressives" were incorporated into the federation constitution, including active (voting) and associate (non-voting) membership. Only Native Americans could be active members.[67]

Carlos Montezuma and members of the Society of American Indians, from
"Proceedings of the Second Annual Conference of the Society of American Indians,
held at Ohio State University, Columbus,Ohio, October 2-7, 1912," printed in
Quarterly Journal of the Society of American Indians, vol. 1, no. 1, 1913.

Tibbet's motivations do beg scrutiny. His avowed interest was to assist Southern California
Indians in achieving the justice promised them under the treaties of 1851-1852, including
secure and protected boundaries, water rights and control over their own affairs on the
reservations. Why then invite outside speakers whose message was the radical dismantling
of the entire reservation system, and the complete assimilation of native peoples into the
American society? If he was playing off the celebrity of these well-known lecturers to
validate and energize the conference he got a result he didn't plan on—the energizing of a
factional offshoot of boarding school-educated young men who rallied to the words of Red
Fox James and others. DePorte's more cynical analysis, that Tibbet was merely a huckster
looking to commercially exploit Indians for profit, seems unlikely, since Tibbet and Joe Pete
continued to escalate their war of resistance through repeated clashes with authorities.

In late February, Agency Superintendent Robert Burris fired off telegrams to the Indian
Office in Washington that Pete and twenty followers "overpowered" an Indian Bureau
policeman and removed a prisoner from the Indian court on Martinez Reservation.[68]
Pete was later arrested at Torres Reservation "after strenuous resistance" and sentenced to
forty days of labor at the Malki jail.[69] As Pete's attorney filed writs for his release, Tibbet,
according to Burris, consulted with Mission Indians, including Julio Norte, and planned to

"liberate" Pete.[70] Burris then requested permission to remove Tibbet from the reservation and authority to hire additional Indian guards.[71]

The debate over direction of the new pan-tribal movement would again take center stage in the fall of 1920. In September, Tibbet wrote Montezuma directly, telling him of the conference and complained that "agents have started a regular campaign of throwing Indians into the dirty filthy vermin infested jails on the reservation. They do this too without any warrant – trial or law." This new battleground may be just where Montezuma believed his presence could have an effect. The local newspapers heralded his attendance at the 1920 conference. Divisions within the Society of American Indians, however, were beginning to unravel the organization. Varying attitudes toward the Indian Bureau, growth of the peyote religion, and tribal factionalism were taking their toll. Montezuma had envisioned the fight to abolish the Indian Bureau as a source of "Indian common ground," Hertzberg wrote, but it failed to provide the desired inspiration for a unified front among Native Americans.[72] The new battleground for this question shifted to Southern California in the fall of 1920 with the next conference of the Mission Indian Federation.[73] Divisions among Southern California Indians persisted with two conventions being held that fall.[74]

Progressives headed by Cahuilla Ignacio Costo met in early October at the First Congregational Church in Riverside. The organization, now dubbed the "Progressive League of Mission Indians," discussed a resolution calling for the government to give Southern California Indians title to their reservation lands, as now constituted, along with full citizenship.[75] Members also voiced support for the Raker Bill, providing for a Court of Indian Claims in California.[76] Costo wrote Commissioner of Indian Affairs Cato Sells, soliciting support for his organization.[77] A letter from the Indian Bureau was read to the gathering, supporting the Progressive League and warning of the "selfish gain" inherent in the Tibbet movement.[78] William Pablo, "the prominent member of the Morongo Reservation," is mentioned as cautioning against any hasty action and [suggested they] forego a vote "until the League's membership had reached a number that would have some influence."[79]   Others in attendance who offered encouragement were the Rev. William Weinland and attorney and State Senator Miguel Estudillo, defender of the Cahuilla convicted of killing Agent Stanley in 1912.[80]

The gathering later that month at the Tibbet home was again a mixture of fiesta (referred to as Pow Wow by the local press) and political organization. As with earlier conferences, Tibbet opened the proceedings to interested whites, who were instructed and entertained by traditional dances and ceremony. "Indian tepees, costumes and a 'campfire' lent realistic touches to last night's gathering," reported the *Riverside Daily Press* on October 29, 1920.[81] This practice of using the long tradition of Indian fiestas as a staging area for fundraising and political rally would be a federation characteristic for many years.

Building good will with the public at large became an important part of the conference. In part, this may have been due to rumors that circulated accusing the Indians of organizing

In first of two parts, Mission Indian Federation's first convention at Jonathan Tibbet's Riverside home, January 1920. Courtesy of Archives, Riverside Metropolitan Museum, Riverside, CA.

"against the white people." These charges were said to be "the work of agitators," which was a clear reference to the Progressive League.[82] For his part, Montezuma interjected a theme of patriotism into the meetings. He advised those gathered to promote their loyalty to the United States government as a way to ennoble and aid their cause.[83]

Tibbet returned the favor granted him by Montezuma by attending the ninth annual conference of the Society of American Indians in St. Louis, Missouri, in mid-November 1920. Tibbet presented an address called "Human Rights and Home Rule," which became the motto for the Mission Indian Federation.[84] The St. Louis conference very likely completed Tibbet's conversion to the policies of Montezuma. According to Tibbet, the "sentiment at the conference indicates the early elimination of the present Indian agency system and the substitution of some sort of home rule."[85] Unfortunately, the Society of American Indians could not determine what that "substitution" was to be. The Mission Indian Federation would have the same problem over its lifetime.

The St. Louis conference of the Society of American Indians was characterized as "a sad affair" and "disappointing;" most criticism focused on wrangling between its officers and Montezuma.[86] In the meantime Montezuma's hope for "Indian common ground" found possibility in the Federation. Montezuma later wrote to Richard Pratt: "I went up to Riverside and spoke briefly at the meeting of the Mission Indian Association…They were generally a fine looking lot of men. They passed strong resolutions to go to the President, the Department, and to Congress, and also provided that Tibbet should go to Washington to present their resolutions and to their claims. That they have not realized their own difficulties and the true way out is very plain to me. I did the best I could to put them on the right track."[87]

Second photo half, Mission Indian Federation's first convention at Jonathan Tibbet's Riverside home, January 1920. Courtesy of Archives, Riverside Metropolitan Museum, Riverside, CA.

As the Riverside conference was ending, government Indian Agency Superintendent Paul Hoffman was publicly talking about seeking complaints against "certain Indians on a charge of conspiring to incite insubordination." [88] Hoffman may have found the culminating incident needed to secure indictments with the murder of federal Indian policeman John Largo on March 22, 1921. It appears that Tibbet also took time from his journey to St. Louis to recruit for the Federation. Hoffman discovered that Tibbet had visited other Indian agencies in Arizona, New Mexico, and along the Colorado River "for the purpose of inducing the Indians to join his organization."[89] Eleven days after the killing of Largo, a federal Grand Jury charged Tibbet and B. H. Jones of "having alienated the confidence of the Mission Indians of California in the Federal Government."[90] A newspaper account in the *New York Times* continued that "the organization (Mission Indian Federation) was said to have been responsible for insubordination among the Indians and the instigation by them of a 'strike' for government entirely free from the United States."[91] In another report, Hoffman accused the Federation of organizing a power paramount to that of a government on the reservations.[92]

Newspapers clearly connected the indictments with the killing of Largo. The *Los Angeles Times* noted that it was the first time in years that federal officials were compelled to quell disturbances and added that "the bitterness among the mission Indians broke out...when John Largo, a reservation policeman was killed."[93] Tibbet visited the Cahuilla Reservation shortly after his indictment was announced.[94] He may have consulted with Adolpho Lugo, neighbor of the accused and a strong Federation supporter. Government officials through the media accused Tibbet of preaching "Bolshevistic" doctrines and encouraging the Indians to rebel with "many of the older Red Men...on the point of insurrection."[95]

News of the indictments spread quickly throughout Southwest reservations in particular, drawing Native Americans to what was expected to be the largest conference to date in April 1921. Besides local Southern California tribes, Yuma, Supai, Walapai and Mohave made up some of the estimated 1,500 Indians in attendance.[96] Carlisle Indian School founder Richard Pratt, who was personally invited by Tibbet, was in attendance from his home in La Jolla, California.[97]

The government unwittingly gave the Federation a rallying point; a blatant example of the diminished status Indians held in this country. If the Federation had fumbled in its first attempts to define itself, the arrest of Tibbet and an estimated 56 others, was a galvanizing incident. During the conference in late April 1921 the government announced additional indictments that included Grand Chief Joe Pete, Buell H. Jones and F. U. S. Hughes.[98] Much of the conference was the same as it had been with open sessions for visiting whites to experience native dancing and ceremonials including a deer dance and fire eating. However, government attacks brought change. New Federation police patrolled the grounds guarding access during business sessions.[99]

A leadership change had transpired as well. By April 1921, Adam Castillo from the Soboba Reservation became Grand President of the Federation. Exactly when Castillo replaced Julio Norte is not known but it is likely that it happened shortly after the January/February 1920 conference. Joseph DePorte made note at that time that Norte was beginning to doubt Tibbet and his leadership.[100] From existing evidence, Castillo came from a leadership clan of the Soboba, being the great-grandson of the well-respected Soboba Chief Victoriano, one of the signers of the 1852 treaty.[101]

The Federation coordinated its spring conference to coincide with hearings held by the Congressional Committee on Indian Affairs at the Mission Inn where Federation members offered testimony.[102] They sent a petition representing thousands of Indians in the Southwest to President Harding asking for patents for each tribe for their reservation land in lieu of allotment. They again sought "home rule" and respect for their elected captains and reservation schools to educate Indian children.[103]

Federation publications continued to make the case that Native Americans were the most loyal Americans and had answered the call of its government, most recently in the Great War. One resolution stated, "the sincerity of this love for our country was proven on the battle fields of France and Germany by the valor of thousands of our boys in khaki, who sacrificed their health and lives in responding to the President's Call, seventy-five of whom were furnished by the Sherman institute near our council grounds."[104] It offered patriotic poetry and stories of heroism such as Joseph Oklahombi, a Choctaw Indian who captured 171 German prisoners single handedly and was decorated by French Marshal Petain to become the second greatest American hero of World War I after Sergeant Alvin York.[105] The Federation began its conferences with a ceremonial raising of the American Flag. Leaders incorporated the flag and symbols such as the Bald Eagle and American presidents such as Lincoln into their literature—symbols that embodied Americanism, regardless of ethnicity, as a means of soliciting support from mainstream white Americans.[106]

Not everyone responded well to this, especially among the Cahuilla. "It wasn't as traditional as they wanted," JoMay Modesto, a Cahuilla, said. "The Cahuilla didn't like the harshness of the regimen…And they didn't like it because they marched in with the flag."[107]

The Cahuilla "wanted to live the way they wanted to live and didn't want anyone telling them what to do," Annie Hamilton of the Ramona Band of Cahuilla said.[108] As a girl she visited with friends at La Jolla Reservation and remembered hundreds gathering for a Federation meeting and fiesta. Hamilton said her mother didn't believe in the Federation. The Cahuilla "had their own traditions and culture that they followed."[109] They wanted to be left alone, by the Federation and the Bureau of Indian Affairs. Cahuilla oral tradition even referred to killing priests, Hamilton said. "Years ago," she said, "when they came walking up, the Indians would kill them because they didn't want them there."[110]

Raising money for Federation activities also became a source of friction among Federationists and those opposed to the Federation. In the beginning the people sacrificed in order to contribute to the Federation. They would pass the hat, Hamilton said, and the "old Indians would put all their money in there. They didn't have no money afterwards. It was hard."[111] Modesto said that when she was growing up, "they were always passing the hat."[112]

Pauline Murillo of the San Manuel Serrano remembered the well-dressed man in the brown suit with the little brown derby and the gold chain who visited their home when she was a child.[113] "Every week…the old people, grandmothers and everything, they would put money up here, in this jug or a jar on top, and they'd always say, 'that's for Adam Castillo'… Lots of times we didn't have enough to get meats or bread or something, because we had to save the money for him. And when he'd come, why, they'd get it down and pour it all out, and he'd get it and put it in his pocket and go away."[114]

Neither Hamilton nor Murillo understood what was going on at that time. Later Murillo said she came to understand that the money was to support Castillo's work for the Indian people, including trips to Washington.[115] For the Cahuilla, Annie's son, Manuel Hamilton, said, "lots of promises, but through time it ended with the same outcome as before."[116]

The Federation still ran up against other organizations, many of them created by well-to-do Anglos who were suspicious and competed with the Federation for attention and resources. Carlos Montezuma wrote to Richard Pratt that the Mission Indian Federation and the Indian Fellowship League of Los Angeles, comprised of prominent citizens, "are tangled up against each other. The Mission Federation thinks the organizations at Los Angeles are using the Indians and the Indian Bureau, double crossing and not really working in the best interest of the Indians. So far as I can arrive at the Los Angeles League thinks that Mr. Tibbet is no good."[117]

Charles Ellis took over as Superintendent of the Mission Indian Agency in 1922 and became the next in line to wage war against the culture of Southern California Indians. Ellis attacked Indian dancing, as it has been over the years, along with traditions such as "give aways"[118] and other ceremonies. Ellis' public statements read like an aged father scolding children at a junior high dance. "Dancing, as done in the ballroom or even in the open air, under favorable conditions is all O.K. But when the light fantastic is tripped to the rhythm of a rattlesnake orchestra and when bodily injury is the result of such dances, the office of Indian Affairs at Washington draws [the] line."[119] If Indian religion was looked upon as the acting out by mischievous children, getting the government to recognize the sovereignty of reservations and tribal self-determination must have seemed a distant possibility.

Tibbet wrote Ellis reporting of complaints from the Campo Reservation of Kumayaay in San Diego County that white men were encroaching on their lands and that government officials were unlawfully entering houses and forcibly searching personal effects.[120] Montezuma's cries that reservations were prisons was certainly validated by such actions. The *Riverside Enterprise* reported in the spring of 1924 that "thousands of Mission Indians …chafing under what they regard as unfair treatment by Washington bureaucracy, have been reported to be planning an uprising to protest against an order barring their ancient tribal religious rites."[121] Supervisor Ellis, of course, denied the reports were true.[122]

The greatest point in of Jonathan Tibbet's life, however, surely came on May 2, 1923, the opening day of the annual conference of the Mission Indian Federation in Riverside. The day before, the government announced the "complete acquittal of Tibbet and the score or so of Indians indicted" the year before "on charges of conspiring against the government…. The officials have practically admitted the Red Men were guiltless."[123]

A reporter for the *Riverside Enterprise* (whose byline was Mister X) recorded the reaction to the news of those at the conference. His description was not just reporting, but provided an eloquent interpretation to what must have been a pinnacle of elation, if only momentary, for all who had fought and suffered to secure Native American rights. The news report deserves to be fully presented:

> That night "gathered around the fireplace, circled with its tall eucalyptus trees, were throngs of Indians with here and there their white friends. At a wooden table, painted red, directly in front of the fireplace sat the chieftains, grave men …whose long, straight black hair was unacquainted with the barber's shears. At the end of the table sat Jonathan Tibbet….It was a proud day for Tibbet and his pride was reflected in his beaming countenance. Everywhere there were flags—the Stars and Stripes, for in spite of the efforts of certain Indian officials to prove the Red Men seditionists that is the only banner they ever have known and a spirit of intense loyalty was marked.

> "Tibbet, the beloved white counsellor [sic] rose to this feet, almost with the deliberations of the chiefs at his side, there was not a sound to be heard, save

the rustle of the wind through the tall eucalyptus trees. Then came the shrill whoop of an Indian—and another and another. The grove was full of them. It might have been a century ago, when the fathers of these same Indians were the rulers of all this Southern land. But it was only a good-natured tribute to the white man who for years has devoted his time to the cause of his red cousins.

"Tibbet, his head bare, his face slightly flushed, and his eyes flashing, said it was a great day, a day of triumph. The indictments brought by the authorities were dismissed, the Indians were vindicated….Then he asked all who had been indicted to raise their hands. Instantaneously, the air was filled with hands. It looked as though nearly every Indian present had been called into court. Dramatic and strikingly effective was the close of Tibbet's address. Calling to his side a feeble old Indian said to be 128 years old, he presented him as having been dragged from his home by Indian agents, but now happily vindicated and at peace with all the world. You could have heard the cheering for many blocks."[124]

The government, however, did not need sedition charges to succeed. They could just simply allot reservations out of existence. While some activists favored dismembering the reservations, the methods and favoritism revealed the practice as further punishment of Native Americans, particularly in Southern California. Two pieces of government legislation, the latest in March 1917, refueled governmental zeal to force allotment of lands in severalty.[125] Historian Van H. Garner wrote that the president was responding specifically to the "needs of developers in Palm Springs" by signing the 1917 law authorizing "even commanding" allotment.[126] Indians such as the Agua Caliente of Coachella Valley renewed their protest against allotment while the potential unjust distribution of land enraged all Southern California Indians.[127]

As usual, stories of threats and physical abuse by government agents made their way to the media. The aged Yuma chief George White, wearing a faded blue army coat complete with brass buttons and numerous medals, told the Federation faithful numbering near 700 of being "handcuffed…seized and taken to the Los Angeles jail with nine others protesting against the division of our tribal lands."[128] The feeble elder, his voice shaking with emotion, said the protest failed. "We were forced to make our thumb marks or put our signatures on the allotment papers."[129]

Petitions and letters were sent to Secretary of the Interior Hubert Work and white supporters such as Congressman Phil Swing and Mrs. Stella Atwood, California chairwoman of the Indian Welfare Committee of the General Federation of Women's Clubs.[130] In the October 1923 convention, Mission Indian Federation resolutions were passed that once again pointed with pride to the number of Indian boys who recently defended the nation and confirmed the loyalty of Southern California Indians to "our country and to its flag and to the constitution of the United States,"[131] while condemning the actions taken by that country's government against these loyal first Americans. They recounted a sad history of abuse at the hands of the white race of which allotment was the just the latest threat. "We have never secured any land or lands under any allotment plan nor do we want any," read a resolution.[132] "We are unalterably opposed to allotment of our reservations as being against our future interest."[133] Agents who "were cold, dominating and brutal," and who treated them inhumanely, reward few Indians who cooperated. "Now the favorites and sycophants on each reservation are permitted to select their allotments [and] in many instances they are given the old home of another. What do our white friends think of this injustice?"[134] Lines were being delineated on the reservations that would lead to even more violent confrontations.

Legislation in the year 1924 changed the political dynamic on the reservations. In June 1924, the Congress passed the Indian Citizenship Act. Ironically this date, marking a goal so long sought by the Society of American Indians, was symbolically seen as the point where it ended as an organization. The bill reportedly granted citizenship to native-born Indians without effecting native property rights or tribal status.[135]

Many saw this law as a natural progression toward assimilating Native Americans into mainstream society and a concluding element to the Dawes Act of 1887 that initiated allotment of native lands. For others it was also a reward for the continual sacrifice of America's first people, who bled and died for this country, most recently in the Great War in Europe. Dr. Joseph K. Dixon, a former minister and advocate of Indian assimilation, wrote that "the Indian, though a man without a country, the Indian who has suffered a thousand wrongs…threw himself into the struggle to help throttle the unthinkable tyranny of the Hun. The Indian helped to free Belgium, helped to free all the small nations, helped to give victory to the Stars and Stripes. The Indian went to France to help avenge the ravages of autocracy. Now, shall we not redeem ourselves by redeeming all the tribes?"[136] The *New York Times* cynically reported that "not even the new legal status afford them (Indians) practical protection from the jealousy and ignorance of white men determined to 'civilize' them by gradual elimination."[137]

Citizenship was just what many within and outside the Mission Indian Federation were seeking. With equal protection of the law, Native Americans surely believed that they could now control their own property and lives free from government interference. However, citizenship did not bring control of the demanded land patents for the tribes of Southern California. While the jurisdiction of the agents was muddied by this new status, agents still argued that they had the final say over reservation life and activities.[138]

The Federation moved forward to make itself the primary authority on reservations in Southern California. By the mid-1920s the area's 30 reservations all contained Federation elected captains, judges and police officers. The officers, while not armed, carried clubs if necessary and sported six-pointed stars stamped with "Mission Indian Federation."[139]

Mission Indian Federation convention at Jonathan Tibbet's Riverside home, October 1920.
Carlos Montezuma is seated to the right of Tibbet.
Courtesy Archives, Riverside Metropolitan Museum, Riverside, California.

The Mission Indian Federation police continued to exercise their authority. In September 1924 Escondido City Marshal F. M. Hewson wrote to California's Attorney General and Charles Burke, Commissioner of Indian Affairs, seeking legal clarification after accepting prisoners from Mission Indian Police. The "drunks" were arrested by the Mission Indian Federation at a Rincon Reservation fiesta. "I would appreciate knowing...just what their authority is and where did they originate."[140]

Commissioner Burke informed Hewson that the Federation had "no authority under federal law to make arrests, try cases or commit to jail...or act as officers on the Indian reservations."[141] Burke again exposed the continual bias that Indians could not think for themselves. The organization, he wrote is "largely controlled by certain parties, some of whom are of white blood, who influence the Indians to oppose or resist the regular constituted authorities."[142]

At approximately the same time, Federation police confronted federal Prohibition Officer Charles Cass on the Soboba Reservation, "the headquarters of the Federation."[143] Cass had

Believed to be a picture of Mission Indian Federation police, with Adam Castillo seated in the front row, third from right.
Courtesy of Bud Mathewson Collection, Banning Public Library District, Banning, California.

received word of "liquor violations" and subsequent trouble at a Soboba fiesta. Federal police attempted to search a car and the home of Bernardo Resvoloso, the Federation captain, upon the suggestion of Superintendent Ellis.[144] Cass and three officers were surrounded by "at least forty-five" Federation police, all wearing stars. Informed they could not search without Resvoloso's permission, Cass skirted serious trouble by agreeing to the close scrutiny of the Federation officers as he looked around.[145] Finding nothing incriminating, he scolded Federation policemen for interfering with federal officers and warned of future consequences. Cass was clearly told that all arrested on the reservation would be tried by Indian judges and no arrests or searches could be conducted without Federation consent. Cass' job, he was told, was to assist them in suppression of alcohol violations as stated in Cass' commission as a special officer.[146]

The Indian courts were again active settling disputes during the spring 1925 conference in Riverside. The Reverend Joseph E. Fisher was honored by the attendees as being only the second white man, after Tibbet, to be adopted by each of the fifty-seven tribes of the association. This was done in appreciation of his assistance during "recent Federal indictments."[147]

These relationships represented the present status of the Federation but connection was made as well to the struggles of past resistance leaders who fought to preserve the lands that the Federation now protected. *Los Angeles Times* convention coverage featured pictures of many current Federation officers and captains. Federation members named Segundo Chino, the ally of Clara True, as "head of the Indian police department."[148] One picture stands out, however. Proudly held in full display was "the first [American] flag given to the Indians by the government."[149] It was the flag given to Olegario Calac, "the first Indian general…who received the flag when he and a delegation of Mission Indians were guests of the government in Washington, D.C. more than fifty years ago."[150]

The Federation held up that flag as a mantle of the continuing fight, which now confronted them on the reservations. Arrests by Mission Indian Federation police were sometimes met with counter complaints; Kumeyaay Marcelino Staggs, for example, won a $60 judgement against Federation police after his arrest for adultery imposed by a Mission Agency judge.[151] In contrast to common stories about the immorality of Indians, the Federation imposed and enforced a strict moral code of behavior. Joe Guachino, a Diegueño (Kumeyaay) born on Santa Ysabel, remembered that if you "got together" with a girl from another reservation and the captain found out, you were forced to get married.[152]

Reservation fiestas continued to be a cross-roads of interaction and potential violence between Federation and federal Indian police. At issue, as always, was the use of alcohol which officials zealously enforced under the new ban of national prohibition. Mission Agency farmer George Robertson along with federal Indian police officers Mariano Blacktooth and Jim Banegas (Venegas) set up a "sting" at Pala in June where several Indian people were arrested for possession of alcohol.[153] Indian people complained of the often brutal tactics used by federal Indian police. Banegas was said to be unfit for his job.[154] Another officer, Juan Leo, had a reputation for being "extremely brutal."[155] "People did not have much respect for him because he would tie people up and beat them," said Luiseño Willie Pink who often heard stories told about Leo from his family.[156] Contempt of Banegas and Blacktooth reportedly led to them being assaulted at a Santa Ysabel fiesta.[157]

Paul Cuero, tribal chairman of the Campo Band of Kumeyaay Mission Indians in 2004, said his people remember how the federal Indian police actually ran the illicit liquor trade on the reservations.[158] "You had police selling it [liquor]," Cuero said. "They were in control of it. They'd allow some bootleggers who [were] paying them off."[159]

These allegations had been made before. In 1911 William "Pussyfoot" Johnson, the chief special officer of the Indian Service in charge of suppressing the liquor trade, resigned his commission, citing a "cabal"[160] within the Interior Department that blocked his efforts to stop the illegal sale of alcohol by Indian officials to the Pueblo Indians of New Mexico. Johnson specifically named Indian Superintendent C. J. Crandall as running the operation and encouraging attacks upon Johnson and his police officers.[161]

As with the killing of William Stanley, a pressure point fed by anger and frustration was building with only the right spark to create an explosion. That spark came on July 16, 1927, at a fiesta at Campo Reservation in San Diego County. Robertson suspected alcohol use at the fiesta. Accompanied by three San Diego County deputy sheriffs and three Indian officers, Banegas, Blacktooth and Leo, they arrived at Campo late that evening.[162] Deputies King Powell and Murray stayed with Leo at the entrance to the reservation from the county road in order to check cars for contraband. The other went to an identified hut, where they spied Tom Hilmiup (pronounced Hesh-me-up) and a man named Lucas making "canned heat."[163] Hilmiup was the younger brother of Campo's Captain Marcus Hilmiup. The two men were arrested; the noise attracting the attention of fiesta goers. As Robertson, Deputy Ralph Kennedy, Blacktooth and Banegas moved to their cars, four Federation officers carrying clubs, and led by Santiago (Jim) Mesa, challenged the authority of the federal officers.[164] Things immediately escalated when Tom Hilmiup attempted to escape and was clubbed to the ground by Robertson and Kennedy. Clubs and fists soon filled the air as Mission Indian Federation officers tackled Blacktooth and took his pistol. Banegas fired off a couple of warning shots before being overwhelmed and taken into Federation custody and dragged away inside the fiesta ramada, where he was to face Captain Hilmiup and where some remember him being tied to a pole.[165]

Outnumbered, Robertson and Kennedy awaited the arrival of Powell, Murray and Leo before attempting Banegas's rescue.[166] According to government reports the Indians began chanting in Kumeyaay and opened as a fan to the federal officers who entered the "darkened ramada."[167] Juan Leo later said Hilmiup was ordering his men "to finish it."[168] Deputies Kennedy and Powell made a move to release Banegas but Captain Hilmiup ordered Kennedy to be restrained. Powell reacted at once by shooting and wounding one or two Federation policemen, forcing Kennedy's release.[169] Campo Indian Frank Cuero then rushed at Powell "like a mad bull"[170] according to reports and was shot dead by the deputy. Captain Hilmiup, who may have been given Blacktooth's confiscated weapon, exchanged shots with Robertson and Leo, striking each three or four times before receiving a fatal wound to the neck.[171] At least five other Campo Indians were injured in the melee. Santiago Banegas was hospitalized and later died from his wounds, according to a government report.[172]

Despite the accounts of the San Diego sheriffs who accused Mission Indian Federation police of being the aggressors, a San Diego County coroner's inquest found that "Robertson, Kennedy and Powell acted with 'homicidal intent' in the deaths of both Cuero and Hilmiup."[173] Witnesses such as Mrs. P.M. Moore stated that while attending the fiesta, "she saw not a single drunken person and no evidence that any of the Indians had any liquor or were armed."[174]

Members of the Mission Indian Federation meet under the trees and an array of flags
at the Riverside home of Jonathan Tibbet.
Courtesy Archives, Riverside Metropolitan Museum, Riverside, California.

The important question of jurisdiction, however, remained unresolved. Federal agent C. B. Winstead was assigned to question witnesses and collect further evidence. The government again singled out Tibbet as an instigator of the conflict and sought another indictment against the Grand Counselor.[175] Government efforts to connect Tibbet to the shootout failed but on October 5, 1927 ten Indians, mostly Mission Indian Federation police officers, including Jim Mesa, were indicted for conspiracy to commit an offense using dangerous weapons.[176] The federal prosecutor Thomas Sloan was clearly disappointed by Tibbet's absence from the indictment. "It will be a shame to prosecute the Indians without the man who advised them what to do in the way of organizing a local government on the reservation and taking over the government from both the state and federal governments."[177]

In a bizarre twist, this Sloan, in all likelihood, is Thomas L. Sloan, a past president of the Society of American Indians and an Omaha Indian.[178] Census records show Sloan practicing law in Southern California in 1930. In another irony, Sloan at that time was living in El Cajon, California, the same town as Purl Willis who later will replace Tibbet as Grand Counselor of the Mission Indian Federation.[179]

Realizing the difficulty of proving a conspiracy, United States Attorney Emmett Daugherty secured additional indictments of assault with dangerous weapons against the accused a month later.[180] Shortly afterward most of the defendants were released on their own recognizance, with Tibbet paying a reduced bail for three of the men.[181] As they did with the 1921 indictments, government officials let the threat of a court trial linger for the purpose of intimidating activists among Southern California Indians. Daugherty finally recommended dismissal of the charges in 1936, explaining that the case had remained open because of the "moral effect upon the Indians."[182] "A situation…serious but disgraceful," is how former agent James Jenkins saw the tragic affair. In a letter to John Collier, then executive director of the American Indian Defense Association, Jenkins said that Robertson "saw, or thought he saw, an opportunity to do something heroic, so he swooped down upon the camp,"[183]

In the aftermath of the bloodshed at Campo, Federation leadership was challenged. Less than a month after Campo, Federation President Adam Castillo was defied in a meeting at Soboba Reservation. Juan Elenterio accused Castillo of giving only a "fragmentary" report relative to the finances collected from the people.[184] Elenterio said later that Castillo was "reticent and evasive…and when members of the tribe insisted on hearing a full report from the collections, Castillo became angry and threatened to invoke his power to make arrests."[185] When Elenterio argued with Castillo the Federation president and a Soboba judge had the man arrested and jailed in the Hemet city jail.[186]

Castillo later filed a complaint with Agent Ellis, charging that seven days before the incident, Elenterio and Steve Arenas made an unprovoked attack upon Gervasio Romero.[187] According to Castillo he served a warrant for both men at that time and had them jailed in Hemet. Their attorney, Mr. Sloan, arranged for their release.[188] Elenterio later sued Castillo for false imprisonment in Riverside Superior Court, naming Tibbet and two Mission Indian Federation policemen in the suit.[189] Edward Davis wrote Superintendent Ellis about the inciden, predicting "this will probably be a battle to a finish, with the dissolution of the Federation, if successful, as the result."[190] Davis, like many others, underestimated the strength and resolve of a people long oppressed.

The Federation continued to spread its control over reservation life and affairs through elected tribal leaders, supporting, but not directing, the respective captains and judges. "The Captains are elected by the people and they work for, and with their people, Castillo wrote to Ellis. He appealed to Ellis "to recognize the rights of the old Indians. Because they are wiser; the younger people may be smarter, but they are often misled and so easily influenced and often make mistakes."[191]

There were defections, however, among the older leaders. Shortly after the Riverside conference in November 1925, the Cahuilla of the Torres Reservation, including their Chief Joe Pete who had first contacted Tibbet, left the Federation. They appealed to John Collier, seeking support for the immediate needs of the low desert Indians.[192] Pressure from developers was mounting on the Indians of Coachella Valley. "What we want is more water on Indian lands and better living," Captain King George wrote.[193] George and Pete complained of Tibbet's dominance of the Federation and Pete was frustrated over the use of money collected from poor Indians.[194]

Money was to take on added importance after the passage of the California Indians' Jurisdictional Act of 1928 (Lea Act). This established a Court of Claims to consider a suit for reparations to California Indians for lands lost through the eighteen unratified treaties.[195] Several provisions, however, guaranteed that any award for Native Americans would be artificially low. This was essentially acknowledged by a Department of Interior report ,which said that "the bill is designed to afford only a modest amount of relief as will take care of their most essential needs....So we have in effect arbitrarily reduced the claim in behalf of the Indians."[196] It also prevented Indians from hiring their own attorneys,

Ruins of the jailhouse on Campo Reservation in San Diego County.
Courtesy of the author.

requiring the California attorney general, mistrusted by most Indians, to argue the case on behalf of the state's native population.[197] This action reduced a settlement worth billions of dollars to one that would eventually amount to little more than five-million dollars for acreage comprising most of California.[198] An intense legal battle to force the government to provide fair compensation, through subsequent legislation, marked the next decades. At issue was fair and true compensation for the loss of most of Southern California. The Mission Indian Federation would play a central role in this struggle.

Those battles would be waged without Jonathan Tibbet, christened "Buffalo Heart," by the Federation.[199] As Federation members gathered for the spring 1930 convention in Riverside, Tibbet became ill and died on April 22, 1930, at the age of 74.[200] Four days later Tibbet's casket was borne by eight Indian captains to his grave in Riverside's Evergreen Cemetery.[201]

Jonathan Tibbet had provided just what was asked of him by those first Indian captains who came to his home in the fall of 1919—a link to the Anglo world that surrounded them. His motivations may have shifted along the way, as did the motivations of many who joined the Federation, but his intentions were always a better life for the Indian people he knew in his youth and respected as an adult. His death marked another shift in leadership for the Federation and more controversy over purpose and practice waited in the wings. But, the Mission Indian Federation was now an organization of some standing. Its impact throughout Southern California was already felt and its presence on the national stage of pan-Indian activism was just beginning.

Tibbet's wife Emma continued to offer their Prospect Avenue home for Federation meetings, but attendance began to slowly diminish over the next few years. Some writers point to the harsh conditions for local Indians brought on by the Depression as the cause. Emma Tibbet died in early January 1947 and was buried alongside her husband.[202]

In February 1932, Adam Castillo addressed a fact-finding committee investigating the condition of San Diego County Indians.[203] He told them of the creation of the Federation. "We could not speak effectively as Indians and had to get a white man who was friendly to us to do some of the talking. Our old people found a white man living in Riverside who was willing to take up our cause. His name was Mr. Tibbet. We now know that we have heard a lot of bad reports about him from the white people. But perhaps when his story is all known there will be a lot of good that can be said about him too. He is dead now. He was our friend." [204]

NOTES:

1 *The Indian,* Magazine of the Mission Indian Federation, v. 1, no. 1 (April 1921), 1.

2 *Redlands Daily Facts* newspaper, February 14, 1914, p. 1.

3 *San Jacinto Register* newspaper, February 19, 1914, p. 1. Two months after the strike, Sterling again displayed "four squares of beautiful filet of lace work" at the Redlands Chamber of Commerce produced by children from Soboba. However, the children involved, it was pointed out, were part of a family which had not struck for higher wages—one of two Soboba women who did not go on strike. Clearly the exhibit was a reward for the family. See *Redlands Review* newspaper, May 13, 1914, p. 3.

4 *Redlands Daily Facts* newspaper, October 25, 1910, p. 3; *Redlands Review,* newspaper, October 25, 26, 1910, p. 3

5 *Redlands Review,* newspaper, October 25, 1910, p. 3.

6 Ibid.

7 *Redlands Daily Facts,* newspaper, April 15, 1916, p. 5.

8 *Redlands Review,* newspaper, October 26, 1910, p. 3.

9 *Redlands Daily Facts,* newspaper, February 18, 1914, p. 6. If one studies the images, there is a distinctly different feeling between the two groups with an inherent anger shown among many of the Soboba women. It is also interesting to note that no Soboba women are recorded to have attended the exhibit at the Orange Show four days after the report of the strike. A teacher from Soboba was present along with two Indian lace makers from Pala. See also, *Redlands Daily Facts* newspaper, March 7, 1914, p. 6.

10 *Redlands Review* newspaper, January 11, 1914, p. 3; April 15, 1916, p. 3.

11 Trial transcript, *U.S. v. Ambrosia Apapas et al., In the District Court of the United States, Southern District of California, Southern Division,* 174, copy in the Rupert and Jeanette Costo Collection, Box 109, University of California, Riverside, Special Collections.

12 Helen Hunt Jackson, Glimpses of California and the Missions (Boston: Little, Brown & Company, 1923), 121.

13 Ibid., 121, 139, 142, 145, 151, 157. The woman Jackson described as the lace maker at Soboba was the daughter of Chief Victoriano. Rosaria, described by Charles Thomas was Victoriano's granddaughter and sister to Victoriano's grandson, José Jesus Castillo. It is the writer's belief that José Castillo was the father of Adam Castillo who, in 1920, became President of the Indian activist organization, Mission Indian Federation. See footnote 99, this chapter.

14 *Redlands Daily Facts,* December 8, 1914, p. 1.

15 *The Indian,* Magazine of the Indian Federation, v. 1, no. 1 (April 1921), 1. In this edition, Joe Pete, Chief of several clans in the Coachella Valley, recounted the story of an Indian council at Mathews Grove in San Bernardino in July 1883 where Marcus Morongo "known among the whites as General," was elected chief. Pete was made "inspector for the tribes in this country." Upon his death, Pete became chief of over 3,000 desert and valley Indians covering the reservations of "Torres, Alimo, Martinez, La Mesa, Augustine, Cabezon, Palm Springs, Malki and Santa Manuel." This again shows a political networking of, in this case, primarily Cahuilla and Serrano peoples. Scholar Anna Rose Monguia wrote that Tibbet contacted Julio Norte of the Morongo Reservation in April 1918 and suggested the creation of a "'Southern California Pioneer Association' with a membership of Indians, pioneers and native sons of California." See Anna Rose Monguia, *The Mission Indian Federation: A Study in Indian Political Resistance,* Master's Thesis, University of California, Riverside, 1975. Tibbet's desire may have been to incorporate the Native American element into the existing Pioneer Association. This may have precipitated the encounter as described in the *The Indian.*

[16] Ibid.

[17] Ibid.

[18] Ibid.

[19] *Riverside Enterprise* newspaper, April 18, 1921, p. 1; April 23, 1930; *History of San Bernardino and Riverside Counties*, Brown and Boyd, eds., 881.

[20] *History of San Bernardino and Riverside Counties*, Brown and Boyd, eds., 880; Tom Patterson, "The Tibbet House hosted colorful gatherings of Southwest Indians," *Riverside Press-Enterprise*, September 28, 1980, B-2.

[21] *History of San Bernardino and Riverside Counties*, Brown and Boyd, eds., 881.

[22] Ibid. Tibbet's retirement was said to allow him to concentrate more time on Indian affairs. Tibbet hoped to create his own museum featuring his incredible collection of over 5,000 objects and artifacts relating to Native American and early Western American history. Its value in 1929 was placed at $250,000. In 1927, President James A. Blaisdell of the Claremont Colleges formally solicited the Tibbet collection. Blaisdell wrote of the advantages of having an educational institution administer the collection where "the care of specialists and students would always be available." Tibbet agreed and following some legal clarifications, the Tibbet collection was unveiled to the public on October 29, 1929 in the Claremont Colleges Museum—the seminal collection of the museum. The collection was utilized for many years as a teaching tool to students and was "well publicized in the surrounding communities." In 1987 or 1988, Claremont Vice President Eleanor Montague arranged for the collection's "permanent loan" to Riverside County. To this date, inquiries as to the whereabouts and status of the Tibbet Collection to Riverside County officials, including the Riverside Metropolitan Museum, have proven futile. Some artifacts in this extraordinary collection included weapons once owned by Jesse James, Wild Bill Hickok, Bill Cody and George Custer, a jacket worn by Sitting Bull and an extensive basket collection. Information obtained from *A History of the Claremont Colleges Museum, 1929-1976*, excerpt provided the writer in 2000 by Nancy Kohl, a Tibbet family descendant in personal communication with the writer.

[23] Jonathan Tibbet as Told to Frank D. Thomson, "California Reminiscences of Jonathan Tibbet, Jr.," *The Quarterly, Historical Society of Southern California*, (March 1945), 81.

[24] Ibid.

[25] *History of San Bernardino and Riverside Counties*, Brown and Boyd, eds., 882.

[26] Tom Patterson, "The Tibbet House hosted colorful gatherings of Southwest Indians," *Riverside Press-Enterprise* newspaper, September 28, 1980, B-2.

[27] Ibid.

[28] Joan Hall, "The Prospect Avenue Pow-Wows," *Riverside Press-Enterprise*, n.d., from the collection of the Riverside Metropolitan Museum.

[29] *Riverside Enterprise* newspaper, December 1, 1919, p. 1.

[30] *Riverside Enterprise* newspaper, December 2, 1919, p. 5.

[31] *Redlands Daily Facts* newspaper, March 26, 1919, p. 2.

[32] Joan Hall, "The Prospect Avenue Pow-Wows."

[33] *Riverside Enterprise*, November 30, 1919, p. 1.

[34] *Redlands Daily Facts* newspapers, April 13, 1918, p. 2. Isidore Dockweiler was appointed by President Woodrow Wilson to the Board of Indian Commissioners. He was a politically well connected, having been the candidate in 1902 for Lieutenant Governor of California.

[35] Memorandum, excerpts of affidavits, compiler unknown, Rupert and Jeanette Costo Collection, Box 109.

[36] Ibid.

[37] Ibid.

[38] *Riverside Enterprise*, December 2, 1919, p. 5; *Los Angeles Times*, February 3, 1920, p. II 6; News article, n.d., (approximately February 6, 1920) in Joseph DePorte, *To the Hon. Commissioner of Indian Affairs Through Superintendent F. M. Conser, A Report in Three Parts on a Gathering of Over Two Hundred Mission Indians of Southern California from Twenty-Six Different Reservations, at the Home of one, Jonathan Tibbet, a Resident of Riverside, California, upon his Personal Solicitation & Invitation*, February, 1920 in National Archives, Washington, D.C. Office of Indian Affairs Received, copy provided the writer from the archives of Dr. Lowell Bean, Palm Springs, Califor17a.

[39] Armand S. La Potin, *Native American Voluntary Associations* (New York, Westport, Connecticut: Greenwood Press, 1987), 147-148. Dr. Carlos Montezuma was a Yavapai Apache raised and educated in Chicago by Carlos Gentile and after his death as a protégé of the Chicago Press Club. At the age of four, Montezuma was captured by the Pima Indians and sold to Gentile for $50. Following his medical training he entered the Indian Service as a physician working on various reservations before accepting an invitation to work at Carlisle Indian School headed by Richard Pratt. Montezuma became a devotee of Pratt adopting the philosophy of public education and assimilation for the Native American. He, like Pratt, despised the reservation system which he saw as an Indian prison and fought to dismantle the Bureau of Indian Affairs. He was "by temperament and conviction a factionalist," according to one writer. After helping to form the Society of American Indians in 1911 he became one of its severest critics in succeeding years. His influence would have a direct impact on the Mission Indian Federation. He attended at Tibbet's request, the Federation conference in Riverside in October of 1920. His newsletter entitled Wassaja was published from April 1916 to November 1922 and was an important clearing house for information effecting the lives of Native Americans. Montezuma died January 31, 1923. He is buried on the Fort McDowell Reservation in Arizona. See Hertzberg, *Search for an American Indian Identity*, 43-44.

[40] *Riverside Daily Press*, October 2, 1920, p. 3.

[41] *The Indian*, Magazine of the Mission Indian Federation, v. 1, no. 1 (April 1921), 1.

[42] Ibid.

[43] Ibid.

[44] Ibid.

[45] *Riverside Enterprise*, December 2, 1919, p. 5.

[46] Deborah Dozier, "Tales of Hoffman or how I learned to stop worrying and love the Mission Indian Federation," Paper presented at the 12th Annual California Indian Conference, Berkeley, California, 1993, copy given to the writer by the author.

[47] 1920 federal census for Riverside, California.

[48] DePorte, *To the Hon. Commissioner of Indian Affairs*, 1. The DePorte document is a hodge-podge of opening narrative, clippings, narrative and miscellaneous documents referring to the January-February 1920 conference of the Mission Indian Federation. Numbering of the individual pages is inconsistent at best. References to the DePorte report, therefore, indicate material within the generic body of the document. Any page number designation for a specific citation is general in nature and given for approximate reference. The dramatization referred to as, "Soul of Rafael," was actually an adaptation of a 1906 book by Marah Ellis Ryan called *For the Soul of Rafael*. The story is set in old California during the time of the missions. A young aristocratic Spanish woman name Marta Estavan leaves the convent and falls in love with a young American after he is saved from attacking Indians. After all their trials of life, love and conscience, the two finally marry. The movie based on the book was made in 1920 and starred Clara Kimball Young.

[49] Ibid., 3.

[50] Ibid., 4.

[51] Ibid., 16.

[52] *Los Angeles Examiner* newspaper, January 29, 1920 in DePorte, *To the Hon. Commissioner of Indian Affairs,* Exhibit W.

[53] DePorte, *To the Hon. Commissioner of Indian Affairs,* 11.

[54] *Riverside Daily Press* newspaper, n.d. in DePorte, *To the Hon. Commissioner of Indian Affairs,*7.

[55] Ibid., Exhibit G, 8.

[56] Ibid.

[57] Ibid., 21. Francis Red Fox St. James was a rancher from Montana whose Indian blood was often questioned by critics. He made a living from his lectures and running camps. St. James was anti-immigrant and anti-Negro wrote Hazel Hertzberg. After the demise of the Society of American Indians, St. James continued with his own "brand of fraternal Pan-Indianism" in the form of the Tepee Order and the American Indian Association which faded from existence by the end of the 1920s. See Hertzberg, *Search for an American Indian Identity,*128-129, 170, 184, 228-231. Luther Standing Bear is purported to be the brother of Henry Standing Bear, the Ponca Sioux who in 1879 led a small group of followers from Indian Territory to traditional lands in Nebraska to bury a young son who had died. Arrested by the army, whites rallied to Standing Bear and the courts (Standing Bear v. Crook) ruled that Standing Bear was a person "within the meaning of the laws of the United States" and had the right to personal freedom. His people were able to stay in Nebraska and Standing Bear became a celebrity, traveling the country speaking out about the injustice of the reservation system. His talk was seen by Helen Hunt Jackson which inspired her to write her groundbreaking work, *Century of Dishonor.* See Trafzer, *As Long as the Grass Shall Grow,* 317.

[58] Hertzberg, *Search for an American Indian Identity,* 43-45.

[59] Red Fox St. James in DePorte, *To the Hon. Commissioner of Indian Affairs,* 22.

[60] *Riverside Daily Press* newspaper, February 2, 1920 in DePorte, *To the Hon. Commissioner of Indian Affairs,* exhibit J, 30.

[61] Inspector Sweet in DePorte, *To the Hon. Commissioner of Indian Affairs,* 26-27. The first name of Inspector Sweet could not be identified.

[62] Jonathan Tibbet in DePorte, *To the Hon. Commissioner of Indian Affairs,* 35.

[63] Hertzberg, *Search for an American Indian Identity,*177.

[64] Tibbet in DePorte, *To the Hon. Commissioner of Indian Affairs,* 11. According to Deporte, the "elders" actually decided on January 31, 1920 to "turn the work of the constitution over to the younger element." (DePorte, 9).

[65] Ibid., *Riverside Daily Press* newspaper, February 2, 1920 in DePorte, *To the Hon. Commissioner of Indian Affairs,* exhibit J, 30.

[66] *Riverside Daily Press* newspaper, February 2, 1920 in DePorte, *To the Hon. Commissioner of Indian Affairs,* exhibit J, 30.

[67] Ibid.

[68] Telegram, Indian Agency Superintendent Robert Burris to Indian Office, February 26, 1920 in DePorte, *To the Hon. Commissioner of Indian Affairs,* miscellaneous documents, 70.

[69] Ibid.

[70] Telegram, Indian Agency Superintendent Robert Burris to Indian Office, February 27, 1920, March 4, 1920 in DePorte *To the Hon. Commissioner of Indian Affairs,* miscellaneous documents, 70.

[71] Ibid., Joe Pete and his wife appealed in March 1920 for help from attorney Isadore Dockweiler, member

of a local Indian Commission. They complained they were threatened by Burris who accompanied by heavily armed police burst into their homes. Rose Pete wrote that she and her aged mother were manhandled and thrown into the yard by William Pablo. See Letter, Joe and Rose Pete to Dockweiler, March 2, 1920, Carlos Montezuma Papers, University of California, Riverside microfilm, Reel 8.

[72] Hertzberg, *Search for an American Indian Identity*, 183.

[73] Letter, Jonathan Tibbet to Carlos Montezuma, September 8, 1920, Montezuma Papers, microfilm, Reel 5.

[74] *Riverside Daily Press* newspaper, September 29, 1920, p. 2; October 26, 1920, p. 4.

[75] *Riverside Daily Press* newspaper, October 2, 1920, p. 3.

[76] *Riverside Daily Press* newspaper, September 29, 1920, p. 2

[77] Letter, Ignacio Costo to Cato Sells, February 4, 1920 in DePorte *To the Hon. Commissioner of Indian Affairs*, miscellaneous documents, 68.

[78] *Riverside Daily Press* newspaper, October 2, 1920, p. 3

[79] Ibid.

[80] Ibid.

[81] *Riverside Enterprise* newspaper, October 29, 1920, p. 5. A key speaker at the Mission Indian Federation conference was Frederick G. Collett, founder and representative of the Indian Board of Cooperation in San Francisco. He also stressed the work done with California Congressman John Raker to secure legislation for a Claims Commission to hear complaints and make reparations to California Indians. Collett spoke of the millions of dollars involved for the 75,000,000 acres of land promised protection by the eighteen unratified treaties. See *Riverside Daily Press*, October 28, 1920, p. 6.

[82] *Riverside Enterprise* newspaper, October 26, 1920, p. 5

[83] *Riverside Daily Press* newspaper, October 26, 1920, p. 5.

[84] *Riverside Enterprise* newspaper, December 5, 1920, p. 8.

[85] Ibid.

[86] Hertzberg, *Search for an American Indian Identity*, 193.

[87] Letter, Carlos Montezuma to Richard Pratt, April 29, 1921, Carlos Montezuma Papers, University of California, Riverside, microfilm, Reel 5. Although Montezuma wrote this letter just after the annual spring conference in 1921, there is no evidence that he attended that specific conference and was still referring to his visit in the fall of 1920.

[88] *Riverside Enterprise* newspaper, November 9, 1920, p. 6.

[89] Dozier, "Tales of Hoffman."

[90] *Riverside Enterprise* newspaper, April 3, 1921, p. 1. B.H. Jones was Buell H. Jones, called "Arrowhead" by the Federation, a mulatto teacher in Los Angeles. His father was a black railroad porter. His mother was a full-blood California Indian, possibly low desert Cahuilla from the Indio area although she is identified as Serrano in the notes of anthropologist John P. Harrington. See also, *The Indian*, Magazine of the Mission Indian Federation (April 1921), 4. According to Lario Ramon, Jones spoke to the people on the Martinez Reservation against allotments and the denial of liberty to Indian people. Ramon also complained of arbitrary arrests on the reservation by federal police including a captain who prevented one such arrest only to be jailed himself for 30 days. See letter, Lario Ramon to Carlos Montezuma, April 12, 1921, Montezuma Papers, microfilm Reel 5.

[91] *New York Times* newspaper, April 3, 1921, p. 25.

[92] Dozier, "Tales of Hoffman."

[93] *Los Angeles Times* newspaper, April 3, 1921, p. IV 13.

[94] *Redlands Daily Facts* newspaper, April 5, 1921, p. 8.

[95] *Riverside Enterprise* newspaper, April 3, 1921, p. 1. *The Indian* magazine, April 1921, 2.

[96] *Riverside Enterprise* newspaper, April 15, 1921, p. 10; April 18, 1921, p. 1. At this time newspaper accounts estimated the membership of the Mission Indian Federation at between 5,000 and 20,000 Indians at this time. See *Riverside Enterprise* newspaper, April 10, 1921, p. 3; *Los Angeles Times* newspaper, April 3, 1921, p. 25.

[97] *Riverside Enterprise* newspaper, April 21, 1921, p. 1; Letters, Jonathan Tibbet to Richard Pratt, March 21, 1921, April 13, 1921, Richard Henry Pratt Papers, Yale Collection of Western Americana, Beinecke Rare Book and Manuscript Library.

[98] *Riverside Enterprise* newspaper, April 23, 1921, p. 1. Charges against the men included conspiring to organize the American Service Club League and Indian Betterment Association (a Los Angeles based group), created to destroy the good will of the Indians. A third charge was levied at Jones for conspiring to destroy the good will of the Indians at Torres and Martinez Reservations. See Dozier, "Tales of Hoffman."

[99] Ibid.

[100] DePorte, *To the Hon. Commissioner of Indian Affairs*, exhibit F, 75.

[101] Castillo was born on December 28, 1885 on the Soboba Reservation near San Jacinto, California. His mother, Doloros "Sayish" Resvoloso, died in 1890 and Castillo was raised by his maternal grandmother Polonia (or Paulina) Lubo. On his 1929 enrollment forms (for the 1928 Indian Jurisdictional Act) he lists his father as Jesus (Joseph) Castillo and his grandmother as Villiano Castillo Morales. In her dealings with the family of Victoriano in 1883, Helen Hunt Jackson referred to his grandson as Jesus Castillo. However, in a letter to Secretary of the Interior Henry Teller Castillo signs his name José Jesus Castillo. See Helen Hunt Jackson, *Glimpses of California and the Missions*, 141-142. Adam Castillo was an important informant for anthropologist J.P. Harrington. Castillo could speak Luiseño and Cahuilla and could understand Gabrieleño which was spoken by his grandmother. It is believed that the Resvolosos (Castillo's maternal grandfather) were Gabrieleño. See J.P. Harrington notes, vol. 3, Reel 107. See also Richard Hanks, "Sketch of Adam Castillo," *Standing Firm, The Mission Indian Federation fight for basic human rights* (Banning, California: Ushkana Press, 2005), 27. Ushkana is the publishing arm of the Dorothy Ramon Learning Center of Banning, California, a native run non-profit organization dedicated to the promotion and preservation of local native culture.

[102] Dozier, "Tales of Hoffman;"*The Indian*, Magazine of the Mission Indian Federation (November 1921), 3.

[103] *Riverside Enterprise* newspaper, June 4, 1921.

[104] *The Indian*, Magazine of the Mission Indian Federation, v. 1, no. 3 (April 1921), 3

[105] *The Indian*, Magazine of the Mission Indian Federation, v. 1, no. 4 (November 1921), 6.

[106] *The Indian*, Magazine of the Mission Indian Federation, v. 1, no. 4 (November 1921); (April 1922) among others.

[107] Hanks interview with JoMay Modesto, May 23, 2005.

[108] Hanks interview with Annie Hamilton, Ramona Band of Cahuilla Indians, July 30, 2004, Redlands, California.

[109] Ibid.

[110] Ibid.

[111] Ibid. Annie Hamilton only remembered Frank Lubo being a member of the Federation. Obviously, there were other members of the Mountain Cahuilla who joined including Adolpho Lugo. Leonicio Lugo returned to the Cahuilla Reservation after his release from prison and was a made a Federation judge in 1924.

[112] Hanks interview with JoMay Modesto, May 23, 2005.

[113] Hanks interview with Serrano elder Pauline Murillo, December 3, 2000, Morongo Indian Reservation. See also Pauline Murillo, "Man With The Brown Derby," in *Standing Firm*, 26.

[114] Ibid.

[115] Ibid.

[116] Hanks interview with Manuel Hamilton, at that time Tribal Chairman of the Ramona Band of Cahuilla Indians, July 30, 2004, Redlands, California.

[117] Letter, Carlos Montezuma to Richard Pratt, June 13, 1922, Montezuma Papers, Reel 5.

[118] *Riverside Enterprise* newspaper, March 23, 1923, copy in Tribal Archives of the Soboba Band of Luiseño Mission Indians.

[119] Ibid.

[120] Letter, Tibbet to Charles Ellis, March 26, 1923, National Archives, Pacific Region (Laguna Niguel), RG 75, Mission Indian Agency, Central Classified Files, 1920-1953, Box 16.

[121] *Riverside Enterprise* newspaper, May 7, 1924, copy in Tribal Archives of the Soboba Band of Luiseño Mission Indians.

[122] Ibid.

[123] *Riverside Enterprise* newspaper, May 5, 1923, section two, p. 1.

[124] Ibid. The reporter's mistaken spelling of Tibbet's name as "Tibbetts" has been corrected in the quote for clarity.

[125] Shipek, *Pushed Into the Rocks*, 50. According to Shipek, "after 1917 the Indian Bureau reactivated the allotment program for Southern California based on two acts of Congress: Section 17 of the act of June 25, 1910, 36 Stat. L., 859 and the act of March 2, 1917, 39 Stat. L,. 969-76 which authorized "the allotment of irrigable lands to Mission Indians of California in such acres *as may be in their best interest.*" (Emphasis added by the writer).

[126] Garner, *The Broken Ring*, 124.

[127] *Riverside Enterprise* newspaper, May 4, 1923, p. 7; Garner, *The Broken Ring*, 124-125.

[128] *Riverside Enterprise* newspaper, May 5, 1923, clipping in files of National Archives (Laguna Niguel), RG 75, Mission Indian Agency Central Classified Files, 1920-1953, Box 24.

[129] Ibid.

[130] *Riverside Enterprise* newspaper, May 4, 1923, p. 7.

[131] *Riverside Enterprise* newspaper, October 28, 1923, clipping in files of National Archives (Laguna Niguel), RG 75, Mission Indian Agency Central Classified Files, 1920-1953, Box 24.

[132] Ibid.

[133] Ibid.

[134] Ibid.

[135] Hertzberg, *Search for an American Indian Identity*, 205.

[136] Joseph K. Dixon quote from website http://www.historicaldocuments.com/IndianCitizenshipAct1924.htm.

[137] *New York Times*, newspaper as quoted by Hertzberg, *Search for an American Indian Identity*, 206-207.

[138] Thorne, "On the Fault Line: Political Violence at Campo Fiesta and National Reform in Indian Policy," *Journal of California and Great Basin Anthropology,* (1999), 195-196.

[139] Ibid. 193, 195.

[140] Letter, F.M. Hewson to California Attorney-General, September 3, 1924, National Archives (Laguna Niguel), RG 75, Mission Indian Agency, Central Classified Files, 1920-1953, Box 16.

[141] Letter, Charles Burke to F.M. Hewson, September 1924, National Archives (Laguna Niguel), RG 75, Mission Indian Agency Central Classified Files, 1920-1953, Box 16. It is interesting to note that in both the letter from Hewson to the California Attorney General and Burke's response, they refer to the outlaw group as the "American Indian Federation" not the Mission Indian Federation. A national Pan-Indian reform movement under the name of American Indian Federation would not appear officially for another ten years. The Mission Indian Federation would be a key component of the American Indian Federation. Possibly just a coincidence or perhaps even as early as 1924, the seeds for this national organization was subtly making itself known through use of the name.

[142] Ibid.

[143] Letter, Charles Ellis to S. McNabb, November 14, 1927, National Archives (Laguna Niguel), RG 75, Mission Indian Agency Central Classified Files, 1920-1953, Box 16.

[144] Ibid.

[145] Ibid.

[146] Ibid.

[147] *Los Angeles Times* newspaper, April 11, 1925, p. 6.

[148] Ibid.

[149] Ibid.

[150] Ibid.

[151] Thorne, "On the Fault Line," 196-197.

[152] Hanks interview with Joe Guachino, February 18, 2001, Morongo Indian Reservation.

[153] Thorne, "On the Fault Line," 198.

[154] Ibid.

[155] Hanks interview with Willie Pink, January 12, 2006, Murrieta, California

[156] Ibid.

[157] Thorne, "On the Fault Line," 198.

[158] Hanks interview with Paul Cuero, July 12, 2004, Campo Indian Reservation.

[159] Ibid.

[160] *Redlands Daily Facts* newspaper, October 3, 1911, p. 6. One of Johnson's deputies, Juan Cruz, was tried for murder following an attack where he killed his "principal assailant Jose Garcia." Johnson vehemently criticized the Indian Service for its refusal to support Cruz. Former Morongo Indian Agent Clara True, now living in New Mexico, took up the cause of Cruz's defense, soliciting funds from friends in Redlands.

Johnson and True received assistance from W.C.T.U. attorney J. H. Crist and succeeded in winning Cruz's freedom.

[161] Ibid.

[162] Thorne, "On the Fault Line," 199.

[163] Ibid.

[164] Ibid.

[165] Ibid.

[166] Ibid., 200.

[167] Ibid.

[168] Ibid.

[169] Ibid.

[170] Ibid.

[171] Ibid.

[172] Ibid.

[173] Ibid., 201.

[174] *Los Angeles Daily Times*, July 18, 1927.

[175] Thorne, "On the Fault Line," 201.

[176] Ibid., 202.

[177] Ibid.

[178] Hertzberg, *Search for an American Indian Identity*, 46.

[179] 1930 federal census records for San Diego County.

[180] Thorne, "On the Fault Line," 202-203.

[181] Ibid.

[182] Ibid., 206.

[183] Letter, James Jenkins to John Collier, August 3, 1927, Rupert and Jeannette Costo Collection, University of California, Riverside, Special Collections, Box 6.

[184] *Redlands Daily Facts* newspaper, October 27, 1927, p. 12.

[185] Ibid.

[186] Ibid.

[187] Letter, Ellis to Dr. W. L. Chilcott, August 15, 1927, National Archives (Laguna Niguel), RG 75, Mission Indian Agency Central Classified Files, 1920-1953, Box 16.

[188] Ibid.

[189] *Los Angeles Times* newspaper, October 6, 1927, p. A 8.

[190] Letter, Edward Davis to Ellis, October 5, 1927, National Archives (Laguna Niguel), RG 75, Mission Indian Agency Central Classified Files, 1920-1953, Box 16.

[191] Letter, Adam Castillo to Charles Ellis, April 28, 1925, National Archives (Laguna Niguel), RG 75, Mission Indian Agency Central Classified Files, 1920-1953, Box 16.

[192] Letter Captain King George and Joe Pete to John Collier, November 8, 1925, Rupert and Jeannette Costo Collection, Box 6.

[193] Ibid.

[194] Letter Captain King George and Joe Pete to John Collier, November 8, 1925, Letter, Joe Pete to unknown recipient, January 17, 1926, Rupert and Jeannette Costo Collection, Box 6.

[195] Garner, *The Broken Ring*, 155-156.

[196] Ibid., 155.

[197] Ibid.

[198] Ibid., 156.

[199] *The Indian*, Magazine of the Mission Indian Federation, v. 1, no. 1 (April 1921), 5

[200] Hall, "The Prospect Avenue Pow-Wows."

[201] Hall, "The Prospect Avenue Pow-Wows."

[202] *Riverside Enterprise* newspaper, January 4, 1947.

[203] Adam Castillo in *Fact-Finding Study of Social and Economic Conditions of Indians of San Diego County California and Reports From Specialists in Allied Fields,* 1932, 54.

[204] Ibid.

For the Month of Nov. 1922   Twenty-five Cents the Copy

THE INDIAN

Published at Riverside, California

**OUR SLOGAN: LOYALTY AND COOPERA-
TION WITH OUR GOVERNMENT**

The Magazine of the Mission Indian Federation

9 THE SALESMAN FROM SAN DIEGO: PURL WILLIS AND THE TRANSFORMATION OF THE MISSION INDIAN FEDERATION

The slow vanishing of the Indian race through oppression carried into the hearts of the people the flame which had been burning in those ...who believed a conflagration was necessary to reveal to our continental congress the real death race toward which we are traveling. Our future success will depend on our ability to stand together.[1] —Mission Indian Federation, 1922

Pin of Mission Indian Federation. Courtesy of the Machado Family Archives

The 1920s were a decade of change for Native Americans in California and across the country. Government oppression through attacks on native land tenure and control of resources and attacks on religious and cultural activities such as dancing galvanized the attention of liberal white reformers. Figures emerged on the national stage who would play key roles in the lives of American Indians for years to come. Many were associated with several new Indian support organizations. These national developments had an impact on many American Indians, including those in Southern California.

John Collier created the American Indian Defense Association in 1923 specifically to contest the proposed Bursum Bill.[2] This measure, supported by Secretary of the Interior Albert B. Fall, sought to resolve the dispute over Pueblo Indian lands in New Mexico.[3] The threat of violent conflict was very real as local Indians clashed with Anglo and Hispanic squatters who, over time, had claimed sections of the Pueblo Indian lands. The intimidation and destruction of property mirrored the actions taken by the Mission Indian Federation in California to regain control of their Indian land base. The Defense Association took shape in New York City in May 1923. Its board of directors included Charles Lummis, Walter Woehlke and Stella Atwood.[4]

Much of Collier's troubled childhood was spent in the Atlanta area where he was born in 1884. As a young man he became interested in the writings of utopians and anarchists who praised the values of communal and cooperative societies. His avid interest in human relationships led him to pursue a career in social work in the New York City area.[5] Collier was attracted to a dynamic group of radical intellectuals of the city, including Max Eastman, John Reed, Isadora Duncan, and Emma Goldman. They met at the salon of the wealthy Mabel Dodge.[6]

Collier biographer Kenneth Philp wrote that Collier "worried about the impact of industrialization and urbanization on the quality of human life, believing that organic society with its sense of community was being replaced by one in which the individual found himself isolated."[7] His work in community service and adult training finally led him to California as the state's director of adult educational programs and later as a lecturer at San Francisco State College.[8] Collier was already familiar with the Pueblo people, having accepted an invitation in 1920 from Dodge to visit her at her Taos home. In the Pueblo

One of two parts, panorama: Mission Indian Federation Convention, October 9. 1924. Photo courtesy of the Machado Family Archives.

people, Collier felt he found the secrets of a democratic communal form of existence.[9] He developed a passion for culture as an answer to social cohesion over politics and became an advocate for tribal institutions and property rights.

Collier's zealotry for answers inherent in Native American culture drove him later, as Commissioner of Indian Affairs, to fight for a government policy that radically altered American Indian policy. The Indian Reorganization Act, that marked his administration, did much to preserve native culture and stop forced assimilation of native people and the destruction of their way of life. Collier embraced a romanticism about the imagined answers inherent in Native American communal society. What Collier did not anticipate was the widespread discontent or anger by many Indian people at the programs he sought to implement. Collier's efforts fell far short of the demands by such groups as The Mission Indian Federation. The clear problem to the Federation and other activist groups, was that despite improvements enacted through the Reorganization Act, Washington still governed life on American Indian reservations. The Federation did not seek more liberal federal policies; Federation leaders demanded that the mammoth bureaucratic Indian Service cease control over their lives altogether. The argument between Collier's romantic notions of native life and the harsh reality that fueled the Federation's rebellion would take center stage for much of the 1930s and 1940s. Some believe this period of activism was the pinnacle of the Federation's long battle for justice, equality, and sovereignty for American Indians and specifically for Southern California Indians.

Collier's attraction to Native American life and the fight for Native American rights led to him to solicit assistance for Indian people from the General Federation of Women's Clubs where was he introduced to Mrs. Stella Atwood of Riverside, California.[10] Mrs. Atwood formed and chaired the Federation Indian Welfare Committee. With financial backing from members, Atwood hired Collier as her field agent in their effort to defeat the Bursum Bill, which eventually led to formation of the American Indian Defense Association with

Second half, panorama: Mission Indian Federation Convention, October 9. 1924.
Photo courtesy of the Machado Family Archives.

Collier as Executive Director.[11] The American Indian Defense Association's agenda was a complete rejection of the assimilationist policies that guided nineteenth-century reformers such as Herbert Welsh and the Indian Rights Association. Collier's organization proposed Indian education which promoted group loyalties, development of native arts and crafts as well as religious and ceremonial practices. Most importantly, the American Indian Defense Association demanded an end to the allotment program begun under the Dawes Act of 1887.[12]

Opposition by Collier, the American Indian Defense Association and others proved successful in defeating the original bill. The compromise of the Pueblo Lands Act did provide some safeguards and greater oversight in deciding title of disputed Indian land. Collier saw this as "the difference between honest adjustment and mere theft."[13] The heavy-handed tactics of Secretary Fall and the administration energized the reform movement with an increased concern for the rights and welfare of America's First People.

This concern led to a government-supported investigation of the conditions on the country's Indian reservations headed by Lewis Meriam, which in 1928 produced *The Problem of Indian Administration.*[14] Some of the committee members were former members of the Society of American Indians, including Henry Roe Cloud and Fayette McKenzie.[15] The report labeled a failure the efforts to allot Indian lands and assimilate and acculturate Indian people. Health conditions of Native Americans were deplorable and the report called for immediate reforms in the area of housing, sanitation, and public health. Many people, including Collier, saw the report as the most significant indictment of the Indian Bureau since Helen Hunt Jackson's *A Century of Dishonor.*[16]

For Collier the walls that hid the dirty secret of abuse of Native Americans crumbled with Meriam. He believed the American Indian Defense Association had brought about "a provisional revolution"[17] in American Indian policy. Collier and the American Indian Defense Association put Indian policy reform on the front pages. That success led to

Collier's elevation to Commissioner of Indian Affairs on April 21, 1933 after the election of Franklin Roosevelt to U.S. president.[18]

As in the past, the voices still missing from the discussion on reform were those of Native Americans themselves. Many, including those in the Mission Indian Federation, came to believe that their desires and opinions in the planning of their own lives were still being ignored. The Claims Commission, established by the 1928 act, did not solve the problems of Southern California Indians but created new problems as debate intensified over fair compensation and justice. Collier's appointment was initially viewed by most Southern California Indians as the answer to breaking free from the oppressive hold on their lives by the Office of Indian Affairs.

Initially, the Federation's leadership put their faith in Collier to deliver the kinds of sweeping reforms they fought for, including a dismantling of the Indian Bureau. Collier's administration, while performing a critical service in preserving Native American culture, doubted the ability of Indian tribes to adequately run their own affairs without Bureau assistance. This drove a wedge between activists of the Mission Indian Federation and John Collier.

At the time of Collier's appointment, the Mission Indian Federation had proven that it was a dynamic force in the political life of Southern California Indians. The aged elders of the various tribes of the region continued to be the backbone of the organization supported by a new generation of emerging leaders such as Adam Castillo. Many who initially worked on the Mission Indian Federation executive committee and ran its day-to-day operations were educated at white-controlled boarding schools with a different understanding of twentieth-century demands on Native Americans.

Samuel Rice, Bentura Watta, Nicholas Pena, Andrew Moro, and John Ortega had all spent time in Anglo institutions that taught assimilation as the only way of survival in the white world. The problems facing Native Americans in the early twentieth century were as complicated and varied as the number of tribes in the United States. There was no monolithic thought among native peoples about the certainty of any solution. Federation members, like Native Americans across the country, developed their ideas about helping their people based on one absolute--change must happen. The Federation provided them a voice for change.

Cahuilla Samuel Rice was initially put in charge of editing the organization's publication, *The Indian*.[19] He and Watta were Sherman Institute graduates and Rice also attended the Hampton Normal School in Virginia. Pena, Moro, and Ortega were all Cupeño who attended Pratt's Carlisle Indian School in Pennsylvania.[20] Moro, early on, was the Branch President of the Federation in Los Angeles and represented the enclave of urbanized Indians struggling to make a living in industrial Anglo-dominated centers.[21] Samuel Rice's uncle Bartisol Rice was a Federation captain at Morongo Reservation where he, Segundo Chino, and Manuel Machado maintained a strong Federation presence.

Bartisol Rice and family, undated.
Courtesy of Weinland Collection, Huntington Library, Pasadena, CA

John Ortega was an early supporter. By 1922 he was listed on the Executive Committee: chairman of the constitution committee.[22] John's stepson remembered him as a decent and hard-working farmer who was greatly respected by the Pala people. Described as a "quiet" and "thoughtful" man, with an undeniably dignified bearing, Federation members voted in 1921 to choose his image "to use as the Indian cut," on the logo of the Federation. His face for many became the face of the Mission Indian Federation.[23] John's wife, Juanita Rosetti Machado Ortega, also became a force inside and outside the Federation over the next 30 years.[24]

Juanita Ortega took an active part in Federation affairs along with fellow Juaneño Marcus Forster, who in 1935 was Federation captain for the Juaneño and Secretary/Treasurer of the Federation. Both Juanita Ortega and Forster received updates from Castillo in Washington where, in 1935, he also represented a national Pan-Indian organization The American Indian Federation.[25] Juanita was listed as an American Indian Federation vice-president.[26]

John and Juanita Ortega, undated.
Photo courtesy of the Machado Family Archives

Agitation by groups such as the Mission Indian Federation helped initiate government action such as the limited 1928 Jurisdictional Act but greater challenges lay ahead, particularly after the death of Tibbet. Just days before Tibbet's death, Castillo complained to Commissioner of Indian Affairs Charles Rhoads about the belligerence of the enrolling agent Harry E. Wadsworth, particularly as it concerned the wrongful incarceration of Patricio Tortes.[27] The agent still refused to recognize the head-men of the tribes, which Castillo said "seems to be the main difficulty, between the government and the Indian."[28]

Castillo's chief complaint dealt with the poor conditions at the government-operated Indian hospital at Soboba. The hospital was opened through the lobbying efforts of former Agent William Stanley. The physician, W. L. Chilcott, and his nurse were rarely at the hospital, which resulted in the negligent deaths of patients some who, along with their families, had waited through the night for the doctor to return. Patients were forced to work to earn room and board, wrote Castillo, and were forced to leave before they were well.[29] This gross negligence on the part of government administrators was typical of the problems that drove Southern California Indians to fight for a larger voice in their own affairs. The consistent alternative, as practiced by the government was indifference, neglect and, in this case, death. Castillo again insisted that the Indians themselves must have a say in hiring a doctor and asked "if the government could only in some way co-operate with the Indian tribes."[30] Coming just two years on the heels of the Meriam Report, these complaints were particularly egregious.

Federation members again gathered at the Tibbet home in October 1930, where resolutions were yet again passed that restated Federation allegiance to this country while seeking decent reservation schools for children and the right of self-determination, including the right to elect officers.[31] Federation leadership continued to counsel against accepting allotments of reservation lands and complained that many times improved sections were being given to those who had not worked the land. In retribution for the refusal of opponents to accept allotted land, the Federation accused Agent Wadsworth and others of giving away the land "which their fathers before them had held" to Federation opponents.[32] In San Diego County, Federation members met with a special committee appointed by the Board of Supervisors to investigate conditions on San Diego County reservations. One of the three-member panel was Purl Willis, a non-Indian clerk and deputy in the county treasurer's office.[33] Willis took a personal interest in the plight of San Diego County natives and began advocating on their behalf within and outside of county government.[34]

Willis' later critics complained of his criminal background as proof that his motive in working for local Indians was self-serving. Federation opponent Tómas Arviso of the Rincon Reservation wrote that Willis spent five months at the Ohio Reformatory in Mansfield, Ohio, in 1907 after being convicted of forgery.[35] A February 1906 newspaper article in the *Washington Post* stated that Willis at the time of his indictment was a former deputy probate judge and captain of the Seventh Regiment of the Ohio National Guard. The report stated that Willis allegedly forged the name of a board member of the Memorial Hall.[36]

By May 1932, Willis appeared frequently in San Diego area newspapers, citing the shameful facts discovered during his committee's nine-month investigation and condemning the treatment of local Indians.[37] The removal of the federal agent—this time Charles Ellis— was a chief concern for the Federation and Willis. Food, housing and control of their own lives through Indian self-rule were likewise demanded.[38]

The Federation at this time claimed more than 2,500 members. Investigators found the Federation to have a strong presence on all San Diego County reservations.[39] Nearly 83 percent of the families at the La Jolla, Los Coyotes, and Santa Ysabel reservations declared themselves to be Federation members.[40] A handful of people claimed loyalty to Collett's Board of Indian Cooperation and the Mission Indian Cooperative Society.[41] This latter anti-Federation group included Indians mainly from La Jolla and Rincon and had approximately 50 members in 1932.[42] As the name entails, they supported allotment and self-improvement "through cooperation with Governmental agencies."[43] Members included Tómas Arviso, Ben Amago and Sam Calac.[44] Calac and Amago had been members of the

Mission Indian Federation and attended the 1920 conference and signed the resolution that rejected abolition of the Indian Bureau.[45]

Besides government apathy and denial, opposition took shape in San Diego newspaper editorials which alleged to speak for the "more intelligent Indians."[46] Traditional Anglo hostilities to native activism are apparent in the rhetoric. "Certainly, we have to recognize the fact that there are a number of dissatisfied Indians" Edward H. Davis wrote, "because, no matter how much is done for them they would want more, and if any other man was superintendent they would jump on him as on Mr. Ellis....A strict scrutiny of these discontented Indians no doubt would disclose the fact that they are members of the Federation, a well-organized clicque [sic] of Indians who have consistently held up to scorn and ridicule the government work among them, and the Indian officials." The paper accused the Federation of intimidation and sabotage in its efforts to maintain the organization.[47]

The election of U.S. President Franklin Roosevelt in 1932, and the anticipated changes in the Indian Service were, at first, seen with great optimism. The Federation realized an immediate success in July 1933 when Indian Agent Charles Ellis was replaced with John Dady. The Federation openly supported the bid of John Collier to become the new Commissioner of Indian Affairs.[48] Collier's appointment in April 1933 by Secretary of the Interior—and former American Indian Defense Association member—Harold Ickes[49] was viewed with great hope for an "Indian New Deal." For the Federation, this meant nothing less than a dismantling of the Office of Indian Affairs, unqualified citizenship and complete, unfettered Indian control of Indian lives and fortunes.

To his credit, Collier immediately began seeking reforms to dilute missionary influence on reservations, encourage the practice of traditional religion and culture, and abolish archaic espionage and gag rules used against Native Americans.[50] However, author Philp wrote that while Collier worked to expand his reform program, he believed that all achievements would be "temporary structures built on sand" unless he altered the Dawes Allotment act.[51]

Ironically, the allotment issue would drive a wedge between John Collier and Southern California Indians, particularly Low Desert Cahuilla. Joe Pete and other Cahuilla had turned to Collier's American Indian Defense Association in the 1920s in an effort to stop the efforts of Agent Wadsworth to force allotments. By the early 1930s many had returned to the Mission Indian Federation, including tribal leader, Marcus Pete, son of Joe Pete.[52]

Nearly half of the Agua Caliente in the Coachella Valley, considering themselves progressive, agreed to take the land in severalty. The other half, affiliated with the Federation, refused and vilified the rival Cahuilla.[53] In an action typical of government incompetence, many of the awarded tracts were withdrawn from Cahuilla ownership when they were deemed too valuable for Indians and vital to the growing resort of Palm Springs.[54] If the two factions disagreed on land ownership they came together in their mutual disgust and antagonism toward government handling of the entire mess.[55]

Federation efforts to stem a tide of forced allotments was meeting with success in San Diego County, where the people of Pala refused allotments on Federation advice.[56] Continued incidents of civil disobedience by Federation members frustrated local officials and non-Federation natives. The *San Diego Sun* reported in February 1933 that Castillo and 50 others were arrested and indicted for "interfering with the allotment plan." These cases, however, were "never pushed," according to the paper, although tribal people primarily at Rincon and La Jolla were able to get permanent restraining injunctions issued against Federation members.[57] Indian Bureau Field agent Mary McGair stated: "I am quite willing to admit that the allotment should be modified in many instances."[58] The newspaper acknowledged the efficacy of Federation strategy. "So, after all," reporter Virgil Wyatt wrote, "the federation may yet accomplish one of its chief purposes—to 'restore the lands to original owners.'"[59]

In his zeal to create a "Red Atlantis"[60] Collier forged ahead with his package of reforms labeled the Indian Reorganization Act, otherwise known as the Wheeler-Howard Act. The measure did offer limited home rule for reservations, curb the powers of bureau agents, increase aid through the states for education and social services, provide loans to encourage Indian students to seek higher education, promote native arts and crafts, and most importantly, put an end to the forced allotment program.[61] Although many of these reforms had been sought since the inception of the Federation, they stopped short of the Mission Indian Federation members' ultimate goal to rid themselves of government involvement in their lives. The bill actually created more divisiveness within the greater Indian community.[62] The Federation publication, *The Indian*, revived with Castillo as editor and Samuel Rice as associate editor, attacked Collier's plan as just another way to "further enslave our race." [63] Full citizenship was still denied Indians. Indians were to remain wards of the government under Office of Indian Affairs control with no legal standing to make their own decisions without government oversight. Other Indians believed that to accept the Indian Reorganization Act was to risk giving up lands already allotted to them.[64] Many saw Wheeler-Howard as just another bad attempt by whites to control Native Americans. To progressives, Collier's beliefs, like the legislation, were a back-to-the-blanket program conjured from his own romantic and "communistic" views of Indian life and culture.[65]

Ten national meetings or congresses were held around the country, including in Riverside and San Diego, to receive comment on the proposed measure.[66] Hostility to the bill, especially in areas such as Oklahoma, and among the Sioux and Navajo, was vocal and passionate. In Oklahoma and the Great Plains, reversing the effects of years of allotment by recreating tribal community was severely problematic.[67] Navajos bristled over a provision mandating range management through reduction of the tribe's sheep herds.[68] This overt opposition to major portions of the bill led to intense Congressional debate and subsequent changes to the legislation. A key element of the amendment stated that the measure would be inapplicable on any reservation where the majority of voters rejected it. This, of course, also excluded that reservation from economic incentives concurrent with acceptance such as access to a revolving credit fund.[69]

Collier's chief adversaries in California were the Mission Indian Federation and Frederick Collett's Indian Board of Cooperation, renamed Indians of California, Inc. Collier attacked both organizations and particularly their fund-raising techniques during a 1934 Congressional hearing.[70] Collier claimed that the two groups aligned themselves in 1933 and conducted joint solicitations from needy California Indians.[71] Between 1920 and 1922 Collett alone raised over $30,000 from poor Indians, primarily in Northern California.[72] The actual total of his collections was not publicly known, Collier said. He criticized Mission Indian Federation and Indian Board of Cooperation efforts to pass legislation which, he said, would allow "certain attorneys a claim of unpredictable amount against the forthcoming judgment" pending in the Court of Claims when the California attorney general carried the litigation free of charge.[73] Collier accused Willis and Collett of inciting a rebellion and referred to a Justice Department report that Willis' activities were an "organized racket."[74]

Rachel Barker, Executive Secretary of the American Indian Defense Association, testified that while efforts were underway to replace Agent Charles Ellis in 1931, Purl Willis and his associate, San Diego hosiery salesman and businessman H.R. Prather, made it clear that they "would not rest" until they replaced Ellis with Willis as superintendent of the Mission Agency.[75] Willis bragged that he "controlled the Indians absolutely."[76] Barker was also critical of the "notorious" Collett "for his exploitations of our California Indians."[77] Supporters of Collier included Stella Atwood and John Myers, former professional baseball player and spokesman for the Santa Rosa Band of Indians.[78] The Federation's future credibility among whites and Indians would suffer from its association with Collett.

The president signed into law the amended Wheeler-Howard Act (Indian Reorganization Act) in June 1934.[79] Scholar Lawrence Kelly, however, noted that "Congress made clear that it had little desire to encourage a revival of Indian tribal identity."[80] Collier's chief success was in stopping the forced allotment of Indian lands, but Kelly wrote that his law "sought not so much to reverse the nation's historic attitude toward the Indians as to freeze it where it was in 1934."[81] Passage of the bill was a tenuous victory from a skeptical Congress. This became quite apparent when in February 1937, the bill's author, Senator Burton K. Wheeler, reacting to continuing native opposition, proposed repealing the Indian Reorganization Act.[82] In his autobiography, Wheeler wrote that he introduced the initial Indian Reorganization Act only upon Collier's request, without even reading the measure and was "not proud" of getting it passed. Once he read the bill, Wheeler said he did not like it.[83] Collier's ideal of "Red Atlantis" prevailed as long as Franklin Roosevelt held the office of the presidency. World War II, Roosevelt's death and the advent of the Cold War brought change to the federal government and a reversal of the well-intentioned, if flawed, plans of John Collier.

Believed to be a delegation of the Mission Indian Federation, undated.
Jonathan Tibbet is in the back center (wearing hat) and John Ortega is on the far left.
Courtesy of the Machado Family Archives

Independent and diverse Native American groups from across the country openly voiced their opposition to implementation of most of the Indian Reorganization Act. Organizations such as the Indian National Confederacy of Oklahoma (Five Civilized Tribes), the Intertribal Committee for the Fundamental Advancement of the American Indian (Iroquois), the Black Hills Treaty Council (Sioux) and the Mission Indian Federation all sent representatives to Washington to lobby against Wheeler-Howard.[84] Here, amid the white marble pillars of Anglo-American control and power, these representatives sought out each other for an alliance against the perceived threats to American Indians' future.

They met "in the very shadow of the capitol," Adam Castillo wrote. He claimed to have issued the "original call …to a few Indians in various sections of the nation." [85] The result was the creation of The American Indian Federation, which historian Laurence Hauptman believed was one of the "least understood political organizations in Native American history."[86] The temporary organization founded in Washington held its first convention in Gallup, New Mexico, the following August where a preamble was drafted.[87] Castillo said that he declined becoming the American Indian Federation's first president; that title went to Joseph Bruner, a full-blooded Creek Indian and self-made businessman from Sapulpa,

Oklahoma.[88] Despite Bruner's traditionalist background and upbringing, he was an avowed assimilationist who sought complete integration into mainstream America.[89]

The American Indian Federation represented a significant step forward in Pan-Indianism and according to Hauptman, was "one of the earliest Native American militant efforts that tried to influence national policies."[90] The organization, initially, had a clear and focused agenda: the removal of John Collier as Commissioner of Indian Affairs, repeal of the Indian Reorganization Act and emancipation from the Bureau of Indian Affairs.[91] Other members of this diverse alliance included North Carolina Cherokees and particularly the Navajo, infuriated over Collier's herd reduction plan, under the leadership of missionary Jacob C. Morgan.[92]

Some of the dynamic leaderhip involved in the American Indian Federation included Castillo, Juanita Ortega, Vivian Banks and Rupert Costo from the Mission Indian Federation; Thomas Sloan and Delos K. Lone Wolf, formerly with the Society of American Indians; and Seneca, Alice Lee Jemison, the "brains" of the early organization and its most prominent lobbyist and voice in Washington during the early years.[93]

Never far away from the central philosophy of the American Indian Federation was the spirit of Carlos Montezuma, who had also greatly influenced the Mission Indian Federation. According to Hauptman, the American Indian Federation "practically deified him." His arguments against the Bureau of Indian Affairs were inculcated in American Indian Federation attacks against the same bureaucracy. Costo, Jemison and Sloan saw themselves as "disciples of Montezuma," Hauptman wrote.

Southern California Indians clearly rejected Collier's plan to reorganize the lives of Native Americans, with only the reservations of Capitan Grande and Mesa Grande accepting the program.[94] Collier's actions in the controversy surrounding allotment of Agua Caliente lands in the Coachella Valley seems a contradiction to his avowed promise to prevent such injustice. After having valuable tracts reclaimed by the government, Desert Cahuilla, with the assistance of Thomas Sloan, sued the Secretary of the Interior in 1935. According to historian Garner, Collier responded with fury. Collier's "solitary goal from 1935 on was to dissolve the entire reservation."[95]

Garner makes a case that Collier was acting in his own personal interest in his treatment of the Palm Springs Indians. As early as 1924, Collier was working with local promoters to convert Indian canyon lands into a national monument and in 1935, Garner noted, Collier was engaged in a scheme to lease large sections of Cahuilla land for development.[96] White migration to the area along with a desire to create a resort community in the desert created an elitist Anglo population which considered the poverty of local Indians a detriment to the "aesthetic standards of the community" [97] they wished to create. Indians also increased charges on the tollgates leading to the scenic canyons in line with the large profits being taken by resort owners busing tourists to the sites; the move drove the Palm Springs Chamber of Commerce "to distraction" and caused the chamber to seek remedy from the Interior Department.[98] Collier joined the chamber as an ally in efforts to curb this Indian entrepreneurial endeavor.[99] Collier's antipathy toward the desert Cahuilla increased when rival Cahuilla factions joined together in 1934 to uniformly reject Collier's Indian Reorganization Act.[100]

In retaliation, Collier refused to recognize elections on the reservation and told Agent Dady to choose someone to run the reservation in place of the native residents. [101] Dady's choice was a former Palm Springs narcotics and alcohol agent named Harold H. Quackenbush, who was paid from tribal funds without Indian permission.[102] To the Indians of the low desert, Collier's 1937 initiative to repeal the "making of allotments" to California's Mission Indian reservations was a direct attempt to legally defuse cases pending by Agua Caliente.[103] At the same time Collier introduced legislation permitting him to sell parts of Indian land that, Garner argued, was specifically aimed at seizing Indian canyons for a national monument.[104]

Quackenbush "did all he could to break the resistance of these Coahuilla [sic] Indians," Garner wrote. He took over collection of tribal fees received from tourists and seized Indian businesses, including a thriving business owned by "Marcos Pete."[105] Pete, assisted by Thomas Sloan, fought back, winning a ruling from the United States Supreme Court and a restraining order against the Department of the Interior.[106]

With backing from the Mission Indian Federation, the Agua Caliente reformed its Tribal Committee and began collecting tribal revenues in direct opposition to Quackenbush.[107] In a move reminiscent of previous years, Quackenbush ordered the arrest of Castillo, Willis, Willie Marcus, Borrisco Sol and respected Cahuilla elder Francisco Patencio.[108] The charges were conspiracy to defraud and treason. Specifically, they were accused of embezzling $11,000 in tribal funds and conspiring to overthrow constituted government authority.[109] Garner wrote that since Willis and Castillo were from outside the Palm Springs area, Quackenbush called upon various law enforcement agencies for help. However, still short of assistance, Quackenbush even deputized his wife to search the Soboba home of Castillo.[110]

Both Collier and Secretary Ickes realized the questionable nature of such arrests and began immediately to defuse the situation. Collier ordered the men released on their own recognizance and ultimately the United States Attorney did not pursue the charges, citing lack of evidence. Moreover, as Garner pointed out, the charge of treason smacked of earlier oppression and Collier knew "it could not stick."[111] Prosecution of Tibbet in 1922 made him a hero among Southern California Indians. Willis' reputation could only benefit in the same way.[112]

On January 1, 1936, Castillo, as district president of the American Indian Federation, sent a letter to followers titled "District Order No. 1."[113] He "called upon loyal members of the Mission Indian Federation to show their loyalty to our race and cause" by registering their names with the Federation. "With very few exceptions, the Mission Indians are all of one kind," he continued—"UNITED BEHIND OUR COURT OF CLAIMS BILL."[114]

One of two, panorama: Members of the Mission Indian Federation, ca. 1940s.
Courtesy of the Machado Family Archives

Castillo presented an optimistic assessment of the events of the past year: "The year 1935 has shown us that by intelligent and loyal action of a united Indian race, we can accomplish great things for our people. Never in the history of our country have such constructive progress been made as during the past year. However, our enemy is strongly entrenched in the century of bureaucratic despotism over our race and he is fighting with all the wealth and power at his command to block us from achieving our rights under law—the freedom of full CITIZENSHIP."[115]

Unity was a grave concern for Castillo and the Federation as 1936 dawned. The previous year saw some defections from the Mission Indian Federation that had to give him worry. Some formerly resolute members of the Mission Indian Federation joined a splinter organization that disagreed with the Federation's approach to the Court of Claims over the hiring of private attorneys.

The California Indian Rights Association received its charter as a corporation on January 2, 1935.[116] Cahuilla Thomas Largo was its Sachem or president.[117] Largo was born on Cahuilla Reservation in the spring of 1885.[118] He remembered the poverty of his youth. "I don't remember ever having warm clothes and shoes to wear in winter,"[119] Largo wrote. He entered Perris Indian School where he learned English "and the ways of the paleface." Largo left the reservation and said that he never returned for any length of time.[120] Instead, like many California Indians, he migrated to the large urban areas and jobs. In 1920 he was

Second of two halves, panorama: Members of the Mission Indian Federation, ca. 1940s.
Courtesy of the Machado Family Archives

a laborer in a Los Angeles Iron Works factory. Ten years later, he made a living as a gardner and landscaper in Los Angeles.[121]

Largo's interest in native rights was triggered by meetings in 1929 concerning settlement under the Jurisdictional Act.[122] The amount being suggested at that time, as compensation for the millions of acres of land taken from Southern California Indians under the unratified treaty of 1852, was 12.8 million dollars. Largo believed the amount was too low and joined the organization led by non-Indian Frederick G. Collett, called the Indian Board of Cooperation. Collett promised to secure a settlement of 100 million dollars from the Claims Commission.[123]

Discovering what he termed "Collett's deception," he broke from the Collett's group and formed an auxiliary group of his own in 1934.[124] Largo and other local Indians were frustrated in their inability to get information from Collett concerning contractual arrangements made with three attorneys hired, by Collett, to represent the Indians.[125] Collett, said Largo, deflected inquiries by adding that the contracts would be confusing for the Indians to understand. Their frustration with Anglo intermediaries such as Collett and their suspicion of his motives led to creation of the California Indian Rights Association.[126]

Suspicion of white advisers also began to concern many members of the Mission Indian Federation. The source of this distrust, for many, was Purl Willis, the former San Diego salesman, clerk and San Diego County deputy treasurer, who was part of the three-man commission studying the condition of San Diego Indians in 1932.[127] Just when Willis officially became the white counselor for the Mission Indian Federation is not clear. However, his participation in Federation affairs seems to have intensified in a very short time. Press accounts in August and October 1932 characterize Willis as an Indian "friend" and "benefactor." By late December 1932, he is called a "militant" member of the county's Indian Affairs committee. Both Castillo and Willis represented the Mission Indian Federation at 1934 Congressional hearings in San Diego, where one newspaper called him a "professional agitator."[128]

It is likely that differences within the Mission Indian Federation, other than just over Willis, led to defections. Some of those who left, however, were important figures in the organization, such as Andrew Moro and Rupert Costo, who joined the California Indian Rights Association. Costo was the group's "delegate" to Congress. Even Buell Jones, the former "adviser" to Jonathan Tibbet and one of the accused conspirators indicted in 1922, became a director of California Indian Rights Association.[129] Others included Mission Indian Federation opponent Tómas Arviso of Rincon and Valentine Kolb (Luiseño). Two of Largo's most important lieutenants in the organization were Julia Gardner (Paiute) and Stella Von Bulow (Luiseño).[130] Their governing body was referred to as the "Yangna Council," after a central Gabrieleño village site in the Los Angeles area.[131]

Gardner, in a letter to Agent John Dady, explained an important distinction between their organization and past activist groups such as the Federation: "We have depended upon white leaders in the past whom we have found more interested in collecting money for themselves than in advancing the interests of the Indians."[132] Most, if not all, of these directors of the California Indian Rights Association were Indians living off the reservation in urban settings, where they had integrated themselves into the majority Anglo society. It is key to note how their perspective on the problems facing California Indians would naturally differ from those Indians who remained on the reservations where boundaries, allotment, water rights, dogmatic agents and sovereignty remained very real problems.

The Federation spent time, money and energy battling for legislative change to the original Indian Jurisdictional Act of 1928, which permitted Native Americans to sue the government through a Court of Claims. The Federation sought legislation that would permit Indians to choose their own attorneys (Butler Bill) to represent them before the Claims Commission for California.[133] Collier and the Indian Bureau argued that outside attorneys would simply trick their Indian clients and make off with most of any monetary settlement. The American Indian Defense Association (Collier's old group) and now the California Indian Rights Association joined Collier in this argument. Historian Garner argued that putting the California attorney general in charge of the Indians' suit was allowing the fox to guard the chickens—a clear conflict of interest since he represented the Indians and the financial interests of white Californians.[13] Garner criticized the California Indian Rights Association leadership of falling prey to government rhetoric about private attorneys. Stella Von Bulow

From left, Stella Von Bulow (Luiseño), Thomas Largo (Cahuilla) and Julia Gardner (Paiute), of the California Indian Rights Association. From *California Indian News*, newsletter of the California Indian Rights Association, April 1939

"erroneously testified,"[135] to Congress, Garner argued, that private attorneys would take fifty percent of any award given to Southern California tribes. Von Bulow and other leaders of the California Indian Rights Association journeyed to Washington to personally argue their case before Congressional committees. Their proposal was four-fold:

> Children of California Indians born since May 18, 1928 would receive an equal share of the award made by the Claims Commission.[136]

> The valuation of lands described in the eighteen treaties would be fixed at $5.70 an acre instead of $1.25 as initially stated, resulting in a settlement of $50,000,000 or $1,500 for each California Indian.[137]

> Per capital payments would be provided directly to Indian people in cash, but with an understanding that each beneficiary could receive their share in lands, buildings, cash or other equal benefit.[138]

> The California attorney general would represent California Indians, excluding involvement by private attorneys.[139]

For Castillo and Federationists on the reservations, the right to hire their own attorneys was a basic right of every American that should not be denied the American Indian. Even Olegario in the 1870s and Pablo in the 1890s were able to choose attorneys they trusted to defend their rights in court. The Federation rejected the idea of an arbitrary limitation placed by statute on the 1928 settlement. The lands surrendered under the 1851-1852 treaties were worth "not less than one hundred million dollars,"[140] Castillo declared in a 1936 statement to Congress. He also sought an amendment to the 1928 act to include "the rights of those tribes and descendents who did not sign any treaties." [141] In 1932, the Capistrano Band of Mission Indians of California signed a petition announcing their "unlimited confidence in the ability and integrity" of Castillo and Willis and authorized them "to speak and work in behalf of our people in all matters of interest to our people."[142] Castillo and the Federation sought to become a voice for the thousands of off-reservation California Indians who lived in Southern California, including members of those tribal groups most overlooked

Members of the Mission Indian Federation, ca. 1940s.
Courtesy of the Machado Family Archives

by previous government commissions such as the Juaneño and Gabrieleño. Many of these people retained a cultural unity in and around the traditional lands of their ancestors, such as San Juan Capistrano and San Gabriel, despite being situated in an increasingly urban setting. Juaneño then pointed to the signature of Cisto (Go-no-nish) of Las Flores on the original 1852 treaty as proof that they were participants in that process and entitled today to recognition and a land base for their people.[143]

Just compensation and representation for all California Indians notwithstanding, the Federation members believed a central principle of their struggle was also about making Congress acknowledge the wrong done California Indians, and getting their day in court. "Therefore, in your hands we place our last arrow,"[144] Castillo concluded. "Our final appeal is that this Congress might keep faith with the descendents of those California Indians— once so powerful and happy and prosperous—a people who have loyally stood by our America in every emergency."[145]

Years of futile litigation and Congressional hearings ended unsuccessfully for the California Indian Rights Association and the Federation. In the end, the dollar amount awarded, just under five million dollars, was almost exactly what had been estimated in 1928.[146] In 1944 the government moved to conclude the case, probably driven by a 1941 United States Supreme Court ruling, which stated that Indians' occupation of land proved their ownership.[147]

Both government and private attorneys played a role in the final decision. California Attorney General Robert Kenny, realizing the unfairness of the settlement, won federal agreement that those Indians whose ancestors did not sign the 18 treaties could bring another suit for compensation even if they benefited from the 1944 accord. This avenue was opened in August 1946 when President Truman signed legislation to settle any remaining Indian claims.[148]

Private attorneys were successful in getting agreement that the settlement would be paid directly to the Indians without going through the Indian Bureau. This only amounted to roughly $150 for each eligible Indian.[149] Most of the money was distributed by June 1955. The government also acknowledged its hypocrisy in granting Indians citizenship then denying them a basic right of personal counsel.[150] While the obstruction was removed, the Indian Bureau still tried to maintain control by insisting it must approve the attorney.[151] Perhaps the alter egos of the Mission Indian Federation and the California Indian Rights Association worked to their mutual advantage by getting as much from the respective legal representatives as could be expected and opening the door for new legal challenges for the rights of California Indians.

The mutual assaults and insults between the American Indian Federation and John Collier continued in newspapers and the halls of Congress. Alice Lee Jemison led the attack for the American Indian Federation, placing the responsibility of 'communistic' teachings among Indians upon Collier personally.[152] This was an era of heightened tension to a perceived threat from international communism and the American Indian Federation played upon the emotions of an already skeptical Congress. Collier and his associates within the Bureau were called atheistic and even Collier's former membership in the American Civil Liberties Union was cited as evidence of his leftist ideology.[153] Collier denounced Bruner and American Indian Federation leadership as falsely claiming to speak for forty tribes. Collier and Ickes publicly tied the American Indian Federation to fascist right-wing hate groups.[154] Struggling financially, the American Indian Federation unwittingly damaged itself by accepting support from such neo fascist groups as the Silver Shirts of America.[155] Ironically, the American Indian Federation came to be seen as anti-Semitic and racist in its philosophy.[156]

According to Collier, American Indian Federation "membership came substantially from the California Mission Indians and the New York Senecas."[157] By the spring of 1936, however, a split was clearly developing in the organization due to the direction the American Indian Federation had taken.[158] One headline in a 1936 edition of *The Indian* of the Mission Indian Federation declared, "The American Indian Federation Still Fighting? But For What? Off To A Good Start Last Year—Lack Of Intelligent Leadership. Not Too Late To Get Back 'On The Track'."[159] In the article, the success of 1935 was praised although the key work—abolish the BIA, repeal the Indian Reorganization Act and replace Collier—still was ahead.[160] The message was that the American Indian Federation had lost its way and the writer urged the American Indian Federation to "clean its own house, get back to earth and resume the fight for the defense of the HONOR of the American Indian."[161]

With the departure of Jemison in 1939, the American Indian Federation lost its strongest voice and most dynamic lobbyist. The organization failed after that to get the same attention from the media. Hauptman wrote that it began to decline.[162] Jemison had the same concerns as the Mission Indian Federation. The American Indian Federation had moved away from the issues that provided it with its initial pluralistic national voice for Indian people. It increasingly became a vehicle for Joseph Bruner. By 1945 only five of its nineteen leaders lived outside of Oklahoma, a change of nearly 50 percent from 1934.[163] Hauptman pointed to the paradox inherent in Jemison's life work—her "relentless, Montezumalike holy war against the BIA"[164] and years of striving for Indian self-determination. Her participation in the "red-baiting"[165] of Collier and in raising the specter of Indian reservations as strongholds of communist influence helped fuel Congressional calls for a new policy of termination in the 1950s that would wreak new havoc upon the Native American population.[166]

A similar analysis could be made of the efforts and dedication of Adam Castillo and the Mission Indian Federation. As Congress looked seriously at dissolving the Indian Bureau and the reservation system, the cure began to look as dangerous as the illness. Criticisms of Willis were growing inside and outside the Federation. Passions of many Southern California Indians were excited in 1940 by a Willis proposal that urged an end to federal subsidy of Indian education in California, arguing that the subsidy would be an offset deducted from the final settlement of the 1928 act.[167] In 1934, the Johnson-O'Malley Act basically turned over the responsibility of Indian education to the states' public school systems.[168] Castillo and Willis contended that Indian children could not be denied school services with or without the upwards of $300,000 supplied by the federal government to California from the coffers of the Indian Bureau.[169] Critics countered that without the funds, transportation and hot lunches for Indian children would be jeopardized unless supplemented by state welfare.[170]

The reaction to this was heated especially from Indian mothers, many of whom were Federation supporters. Indians, particularly those in San Diego County, were overt in their disdain for Willis and appealed to California Superintendent of Public Instruction Walter Dexter to oppose any discontinuance of federal monies.[171] "Purl Willis is a human parasite living off the uneducated and misled older people of the reservation,"[172] anti-Federationist Louise Leo Ponchetta [Ponchetti] of Santa Ysabel wrote. Others referred to Willis as an "agitator and ex-convict."[173]

This new fear undoubtedly exacerbated growing suspicions about Willis in all aspects of Federation business, particularly with the collections of funds from the reservation poor. It was reported that during a meeting at Pala, Federationists Juanita Ortega and

John Ortega Plowing near Pala, CA, undated. Courtesy of the Machado Family Archives

Winslow Couro denounced Willis when he could not account for delegate funds sent him in Washington.[174] Critic Tómas Arviso of Rincon wrote that Willis was a man without shame. Willis' theatrics before a crowd were well known and seen by many as part of a deceptive scam against those he swore he was defending. "While he sheds 'crocodile' tears supposedly for the down-trodden Indian he has his hand out in the meantime to gather in funds from the poor misled Indians,"[175] Arviso said.

The money solicited by the Mission Indian Federation became a sore point with many poor Indians on the reservations who gave from meager resources but saw little change for their sacrifices. Luiseño Max Mazzetti remembered Willis coming to fiestas on the reservation with enticements of day-old bread for tribal members who were urged to join the Federation.[176] "He was a wonderful speaker," Mazzetti said, "the envy of many attorneys....Tears would roll about how they got cheated out of their treaties."[177] Even the son of Juanita Ortega joked about whether Willis carried an onion in his pocket since the tears came so freely.[178] Manuel Machado said his mother came to greatly dislike Willis.[179] With increasing anger and doubt focused on his chief advisor, Castillo received another blow when valuable ally and Federation Vice-President Vicente Albanes died in September 1940.[180] This was followed three years later by the death of Mission Indian Federation leader John Ortega. Attorney Frederick Baker, never a friend to the Mission Indian Federation, wrote to Juanita Ortega of his regard for John. "I think he was one of the most noble men I ever knew," Baker said. "He had no hatred in his heart for anyone although he had suffered much."[181]

Willis' aim was to completely sever any ties between California Indians and the Bureau of Indian Affairs in accordance with the expressed goals of the Federation since 1920.[182] In 1944 agreement was reached on the final settlement of claims under the 1928 act but California Indians remained wards of the government with continued BIA oversight.[183] The approximately 12-million dollars withheld from native people for offsets paid for more than 90 years of government operations including existing infrastructure such as buildings as well as the land.[184] Willis, apparently undaunted from the criticism leveled in 1940, argued that by paying off the government, California Indians were free from the influence and jurisdiction of the government's Indian Service.[185] Not only did the government disagree, but the questions about what this would actually mean for the state's native population sent shock waves through the Indian communities in Southern California.

In January 1945, John Collier resigned his position as Commissioner of Indian Affairs. Willis proclaimed great joy over his departure in *The Indian*, which resumed publication in the summer of 1945 with Willis as editor.[186] Collier was branded a "traitor" to the welfare of Indians. "The Mission Indian Federation helped get Collier into the job of Indian Commissioner in 1933, and in 1945 it helped get him out."[187] The Federation had seen Collier as a voice of change and one who would finally secure the freedom for Native Americans denied them for so many years. Although sensitive to the culture of the American Indian, Collier proved to be neutralized by the very bureaucracy the Federation hoped he would dismantle.

Not everyone shared the Federation's denunciation of the Indian Reorganization Act as destructive and dangerous. Collier had stopped the tide of continuous assault on Native American life and culture if only for a few years. That temporary respite, however, was to have lasting effects even as new policies were implemented that aimed at obliterating the distinction of Indian people within the society. Scholar Clayton Koppes wrote that Collier "had achieved the first part of his dream—guaranteeing the Indian community continued existence."[188] Collier biographer Philp wrote that the Indian Reorganization Act was "a flawed product that failed to meet the needs of a diversified population"[189] but as noted by Native American activist and scholar Vine Deloria, Jr., the children of those affected by the Indian New Deal would later embrace the fight for Pan-Indianism, tribal integrity and cultural pride.[190] For that reason, Deloria said, the 1930s were "the greatest days of Indian life in the twentieth century."[191]

The Federation and others alarmed an already nervous Congress when they labeled Collier's reforms as "the very essence of communism."[192] Senator George Malone of Nevada declared that "while we are spending billions of dollars fighting Communism …we are at the same time…perpetuating the systems of Indian reservations and tribal governments, which are naturally Socialist environments."[193]

Roosevelt's New Deal was replaced with Truman's Fair Deal, which sought total integration of minority groups by "freeing the individual from supposedly invidious group identity, especially that of race,"[194] as described by historian Koppes. Assimilationist philosophy again took hold of Congressional proposals. The Fair Deal precipitated the termination policy of the Eisenhower administration. The late 1940s represented a gradualist period of phasing out federal programs and led to confusion over a transfer of Indian Bureau services from the national government to the state of California.[195]

Instead of isolating Native Americans on reservation laboratories for their conversion to Anglo cultural norms, they would be forced into the cities and mainstreamed into American life. Proposals increased to dissolve the federal Indian agency.[196] It was a new twist on Richard Pratt's idea of feeding Indians to civilization rather than civilization to Indians. This was exactly what the Federation and organizations such as the American Indian Federation had lobbied for. It surely would have had the blessing of the Federation's patron saint Carlos Montezuma. It, however, ignited a firestorm of protest among the Indian communities of Southern California.[197]

In 1947 the relationship between the Mission Indian Federation and Indians of California, Inc, headed by Frederick Collett, began to unravel. Collett's ego-driven and imperial desire to control the agenda of California Indian claims finally became apparent to Willis.[198] After a meeting late in 1946, Collett hurriedly solicited and received Castillo's signature essentially giving him the power of attorney for the Federation with the assistance of Collett's counsel, Ernest Wilkinson.[199] Upon Willis's urging, Castillo demanded the return of the disputed document and he notified the Interior Secretary that the Federation repudiated the letter and severed its contract with Wilkinson's law firm.[200] Willis discovered that Collett, without Federation knowledge, had legislation introduced that permitted him to make claims on the settlement to California Indians held by the national treasury.[201] Willis wrote that "there are literally scores of incidents showing over-stepping of authority on part of Mr. Collett…We can't afford to have our name linked in this manner with anyone."[202] Many Southern California Indians were suspicious of Collett's intention for many years. The Federation's association with Collett only provided ammunition to its enemies and undermined the credibility of the Federation with its Indian supporters.

Members of Congress and the state of California were skeptical of Collet's fund-raising activities on behalf of northern California Indians.[203] Collett maintained that he controlled all the auxiliaries of this organization through powers of attorney.[204] The California attorney general initiated its own investigation of Collett and the Federation due to its association with Indians of California, Inc.[205] The willingness of Castillo and Willis to align with any person or organization they believed might assist them in their pursuit of Federation goals gave access to the deceptive practices of Collett. The Federation's break with Collett may have been too little, too late to completely correct the damage to the Federation's reputation among many people.

Despite growing difficulties and mounting criticism, Castillo remained firm in his stand to rid California Indians of the plague represented by the federal Indian service. "We seek complete freedom from all forms of wardship," Castillo wrote to James Stewart, California Director of the Indian Bureau.[206] "Please do not come to us with an easy and gradual withdrawal," Castillo said. "We seek the blessings of a free people."[207]

However, Castillo knew that through this transition, people were suffering. He argued to Stewart that county governments in California must adhere to the state welfare code of 1937 and aid needy Indians without the need for federal involvement. San Diego County was mentioned specifically as an area refusing to abide by the welfare code. Castillo argued that no contracts should be made to reimburse such counties.[208] The Federation believed that Southern California Indians were protected under the governing laws of the state and should not be singled out as a specific minority group as done by the federal government. This special relationship is what created and continued their status as wards of the federal government without the privileges granted other Americans to define and shape their own lives.

Spurred by the concern over education for Indian children, the lines became clearly delineated between those favoring immediate termination of all Indian Bureau influence on California reservations and those who argued for a gradual reduction of wardship status. Steve Ponchetti, spokesman for Santa Ysabel, quickly became the leading voice of opposition to what newspapers termed the "Willis-led"[209] expeditions to Washington where Federationists, including Juaneños Richard and Clarence Lobo representing "free Indians" who had left the reservations, succeeded in removing more than 2 million dollars from the federal budget for Indian affairs in California.[210]

Ponchetti and a new organization loosely called the Confederation of Indians challenged the Federation's efforts. Ponchetti and allies argued that Indian education and housing along with land and mineral rights would be in jeopardy with the immediate termination of federal financial support.[211] "Our reservations are very poor," Ponchetti said, "We are asking time to get ourselves prepared before we lose the protection of the Indian Bureau."[212] The issue was highly emotional for many and the ties of past alliances were undone and remade. Willis and the Federation gained the support of an old foe, the Indian Committee of the Federation of Women's Clubs.[213] Former Federation officer Juanita Ortega now placed herself with the Ponchetti group. She told a Congressional subcommittee, "We do not want to see our young people on the roadside of this state as paupers."[214] In the end, anti-Federationists won and the federal money for California was restored.[215]

Federation leadership attempted to discredit Ponchetti and his following. The Federation, which said Ponchetti was enrolled at Mesa Grande, contested his election as chairman of Santa Ysabel.[216] This proved unsuccessful, as did future attempts to revive legislation to erase the Indian Bureau's presence in California. Controversy continued to swirl around Federation leadership. In June 1951, Federation Captain Clarence Lobo broke with the organization and made his feelings known in a letter to Commissioner of Indian Affairs Dillon Myer. "As long as the Indians have one Mr. Purl Willis with them," he wrote, "they will never get anywhere."[217] Lobo stated that the Federation kept no records and could not account for the "huge sums of money" collected over its existence.[218] "At one time, this organization covered much of the state but as their true purpose was exposed they lost ground everywhere but the reservations."[219]

Lobo also made a distinction between the concerns of reservation Indians and those of "free Indians" living off reservation. "We do not want to be classed with the reservation Indian who is forever wanting his freedom from the Bureau."[220] Both he and Ponchetti repeated a recurring theme that the Federation only represented the "old chiefs who still sign our lives away with the same little X of long ago."[221] The Federation, Lobo said, "is an old worn down unrecognized organization whose members are the very old and the most incompetent ones."[222]

The Mission Indian Federation had seen the loss of many vital founding members of the organization but none was as devastating as the loss suffered on Christmas Eve in 1953 with the death of Adam Castillo. Over the course of thirty-three years, his name became synonymous with the Mission Indian Federation. More than Jonathan Tibbet or Purl Willis, Castillo left an imprint on what the Mission Indian Federation was, what it became and its legacy of leadership in Pan-Indian activism in the twentieth century. Willis once called Castillo the "Gandhi of the Indian race."[223] Certainly like Gandhi or Martin Luther King, he used passive resistance, agitation, and an indomitable will to seek justice for a people denied. In his 1951 petition to Interior Secretary Oscar Chapman, Castillo again invoked the spirit of Luiseño General Olegario Calac: "He was an enthusiastic defender of his people and disposed to take advanced grounds on questions of their rights."[224] Adam Castillo could have been describing himself.

That same year the Federation succeeded in getting Congress to pass Public Law 280, which finally ended the long, oppressive control of Indian Service agents. Under the new law, California Indians were placed under the civil and criminal jurisdiction of the state. Scholars such as Clifford Trafzer have argued that this was a setback for native people since they lost their trust relationship with the federal government and gave jurisdiction back to the state, which historically, had shown callous disregard for its Indian population.[225] The measure also angered Federation opponents and increased hostility toward the organization.[226]

Lobo's sensitivity toward the specific problems facing non-reservation Indians in California, including federal recognition, led him to create the League of California Indians, made up of mainly Juaneño and Gabrieleño people in and around the area of San Juan Capistrano. Lobo was the first president.[227] The League, while supportive of full citizenship rights for California Indians, also sought appropriate compensation under the new Claims Commission for the land stolen from their ancestors.[228]

James Martinez, a Luiseño from La Jolla Reservation, became president of the Federation after Castillo's death. Martinez was educated at Perris and Sherman and spent part of his

Juanita Ortega (seated second from left) and delegation in Washington, undated.
Courtesy of the Machado Family Archives

youth as a baseball player in the Midwest before returning to the reservation in the 1920s when he joined the Federation.[229] Martinez worked closely with Willis and traveled with him to Washington between the years of 1953 and at least 1957. There they continued the fight to sever the ties of the Bureau of Indian Affairs in California.[230] Continued opposition came from the Ponchetti faction, which included the very vocal Max Mazzetti of Rincon, Cruz Siva of Los Coyotes and Juanita Ortega of Pala. In many ways, their protests echoed those of the early days of the Federation. They demanded better housing on the reservation, irrigation for their fields and freedom to utilize the land and resources as they saw fit—self-determination. The real thing that separated the two sides was the timeline for the transition.

As with many before him, Martinez began to question Willis' judgment and his motives: "Willis took lots of Indians to Washington but, you know, I was thinking maybe he was putting them on parade and so many people weren't necessary."[231] Again, it was the money that began to concern members. "He [Willis] went to Washington 17 straight years. He spent too much money traveling to Washington,"[232] Martinez said. Willis did some good, Martinez argued, but ultimately he "pushed for wrong and crooked people. That's how come the Federation lost its strength—because Willis, they didn't trust him anymore."[233] Martinez said the Federation's membership during this time was 500—"a formidable force against the Bureau of Indian Affairs."[234] Martinez said that by 1962, Federation members voted to terminate the services of Purl Willis.[235] However, another Federation was reconstituted under the name Mission Indian Federation, Inc. that same year.[236] Its object was to secure fair disposition of the 29 million dollars awarded by the Claims

The enactment of the 1928 Act was a partial victory only—it soon appeared that the reported offsets for ALL the Indians would almost equal the value of the promises made to the treaty Indians who comprised only from one-third to one-half of the total Indian population

Sketch, History and Proposed Settlement: Claims of California Indians, by California Attorney General Robert W. Kenny, 1944.

Commission established in 1946. President Dan Pico of Pechanga led this incorporated Federation.[237] Its membership and Board appear to be primarily Juaneño, some who were part of the League of California Indians.[238] The idea for a newly incorporated Federation, however, came from Willis. A puzzled Clarence Lobo wrote Pico about the "new Junior Organization" but was skeptical of its purpose and of the tactics used by Willis to secure membership, implying that people only signed to "get their hands on some of that green folding stuff."[239] Lobo cautioned that such methods would only hurt the Indian cause. "It would have been a great victory if the Old Federation name could have been restored and kept in honor of the many, many Indians who fought and died as members of that once powerful and respected organization composed of American Indians."[240] The Federation (or Federations) disbanded shortly afterwards, according to Martinez.[241]

In September 1966 there was a convention in San Francisco of the United Indian War Veterans of the United States.[242] The outgoing national commander of the organization was Purl Willis. A keynote speaker of the event was Cahuilla leader and assistant engineer with the state department of highways Rupert Costo.[243] "You have ended your war," Costo told the small aged group of men before him. "Indians still must win our great battle—a battle for justice, release from autocratic government controls…the chance to shape our own destiny."[244] Purl Willis died in 1972 at the age of 92. Max Mazzetti reported that only two Indians attended his funeral.[245]

The Mission Indian Federation continued the war started by Antonio Garra in 1851—a war for a whole life. The Federation sought the same thing Garra, Olegario and Pablo fought for—a chance to lead their lives as they saw fit without the interference of the government, recognition of tribal sovereignty, and to have the historic injustice done them acknowledged and corrected fairly. To accomplish these goals, the Federation used the only tools available—resistance. The history of resistance is a rich one among Indians in Southern California. It was a war worth fighting in 1851 and is one worth fighting today.

Notes:

[1] *The Indian,* Magazine of the Mission Indian Federation (April 1922), 11.

[2] Kenneth Philp, *John Collier's Crusade for Indian Reform, 1920-1954* (Tucson, Arizona: University of Arizona Press, 1977), 46.

[3] Ibid., 28-31.

[4] Ibid., 47, 62.

[5] Ibid., 4, 10-16.

[6] Ibid., 17.

[7] Ibid., 10.

[8] Ibid., 26.

[9] Ibid., 1-3.

[10] Ibid., 26.

[11] Ibid., 27-28.

[12] Ibid., 46-47.

[13] Ibid., 53.

[14] Trafzer, *As Long As the Grass Shall Grow,* 345.

[15] Ibid.

[16] Philp, *John Collier's Crusade for Indian Reform*, 90.

[17] Ibid., 91.

[18] Ibid., 117.

[19] *The Indian*, Magazine of the Mission Indian Federation, (April 1922), 10.

[20] *The Indian*, Magazine of the Mission Indian Federation, v. 1, no. 3 (April 1921), 6.

[21] *The Indian*, Magazine of the Mission Indian Federation (March 1922, 3.

[22] *The Indian*, Magazine of the Mission Indian Federation (April 1922), 10.

[23] *The Indian*, Magazine of the Mission Indian Federation, v. 1, no. 3 (April 1921), 6.

[24] John Baptist Ortega was born at Agua Caliente on June 29, 1876—in the "Canyon of the Warm Waters" or "Kopa" (Warner Ranch) as it was called by its inhabitants. He was a full-blood Cupeño. John Ortega knew the feeling of being dispossessed. His people were driven from their homes at the warm springs and relocated at Pala in San Diego County in 1903. In 1927, John represented the Federation at a meeting in San Juan Capistrano where the government was enrolling local Indians who lived off the reservations, mostly Juaneño and Gabrieleño, under compliance with the Jurisdiction Act. There he met Juanita Machado and her eight children who were living through difficult times in the Watts section of L. A. Her husband had given in to the pressures of providing for the family and left. Juanita cared for her family with the help of her mother-in-law Teresa Morales. John hired a truck to carry Juanita, her children and all they owned to Pala where they were enrolled in the tribe as Juaneño/Gabrieleño and Juanita joined the Federation. Juanita was Juaneño; her children Juaneño and Gabrieleño. She was a direct descendent of the medicine woman Clara Sitales who fled to the ghettos of Los Angeles after her village near the San Juan mission was burned in the nineteenth century. Juanita's mother and father died when she was very young and she was raised by her grandmother who taught her the "ways" of healing. She and her children, however, continued to live in the Los Angeles area while making frequent visits to the San Diego County reservation. In 1932, she and her family are still listed on the rolls of the Capistrano Band of Mission Indians which met in San Juan. It is probable that between 1934 and 1935 Juanita and her children settled permanently in the Pala valley. Juanita

Ortega is remembered as very stern and smart and someone who always spoke her mind. Her voice and opinions would be well known in the years ahead as the Federation adapted to the various challenges facing Indian people of Southern California. The Juaneño and Gabrieleño tribes are not recognized by the federal government although individual members were enrolled under the 1928 act. Richard Hanks interview with Dorothy Mathews, Susan Frank, Debra McIntire and Valkyrie Houston, Tribal council of the Gabrieleño Band of Mission Indians, September 19, 2004. Interview with Manuel Machado, transcript from archives, Gabrieleño Band of Mission Indians. This Manuel Machado should not be confused with his Great-Uncle Manuel Machado who was a Federation member on the Morongo Reservation. John Ortega may have been related to Ambrosio Ortega, the highly respected spokesman for the Cupeño during their forced removal in 1903. This writer could not determine the parentage of Cupeño leader Ambrosio Ortega but in 1920 this Ambrosio was living with his brother Jesus and Jesus' family at Pala. All three men, Ambrosio, Jesus and John, were born within six years of each other, between the years of 1870 and 1876. Family history says that John Ortega's father was also named Ambrosio Ortega.

[25] Letter, Adam Castillo to Marcus Forster and Juanita Ortega, May 21, 1935, in Sandoval Collection, Archives of Juaneño Band of Mission Indians, Acjachmemem Nation, San Juan Capistrano, California.

[26] Letter Juanita Ortega to Roy Manuel, January 24, 1935, Gerald Smith Collection.

[27] Letter Adam Castillo to Charles Rhoads, April 19, 1930, National Archives, Pacific Region (Laguna Niguel), RG 75 Mission Indian Agency Central Classified Files, 1920-1953, Box 16.

[28] Ibid.

[29] Ibid.

[30] Ibid.

[31] Resolution, Mission Indian Federation, October 1930, National Archives, Pacific Region (Laguna Niguel), RG 75 Mission Indian Agency Central Classified Files, 1920-1953, Box 16.

[32] Unidentified clipping, September 22, 1931 in National Archives, Pacific Region (Laguna Niguel), RG 75 Mission Indian Agency, Central Classified Files, 1920-1953, Box 24.

[33] Newspaper clipping, n.d. (ca. 1931) National Archives, Pacific Region (Laguna Niguel), RG 75 Mission Indian Agency, Central Classified Files, 1920-1953, Box 24.

[34] *San Diego Sun* newspaper, December 22, 1932, National Archives, Pacific Region (Laguna Niguel), RG 75 Mission Indian Agency, Central Classified Files, 1920-1953, Box 24.

[35] Letter, Tomas Arviso to Dr. Walter Dexter, July 27, 1940, National Archives, Pacific Region (Laguna Niguel), RG 75 Mission Indian Agency Central Classified Files, 1920-1953, Box 88.

[36] *Washington Post* newspaper, February 18, 1906, p. 11.

[37] *Christian Science Monitor*, May 14, 1932, National Archives, Pacific Region (Laguna Niguel), RG 75 Mission Indian Agency, Central Classified Files, 1920-1953, Box 24.

[38] News clipping, August 22, 1932, National Archives, Pacific Region (Laguna Niguel), RG 75 Mission Indian Agency, Central Classified Files, 1920-1953, Box 24.

[39] Fact Finding Study of Social and Economic Conditions of Indians of San Diego County, California and Reports from Specialists in Allied Fields, 74.

[40] Ibid., 17.

[41] Ibid.

[42] Ibid.

[43] Ibid., 18.

[44] Ibid., 58.

[45] DePorte, *To the Hon. Commissioner of Indian Affairs*, Exhibit G, 12.

[46] Edward H. Davis, San Diego Evening Tribune, newspaper, December 28, 1932, National Archives, Pacific Region (Laguna Niguel), RG 75 Mission Indian Agency, Central Classified Files, 1920-1953, Box 24.

[47] Ibid.

[48] News clipping, n.d. (ca. 1933) National Archives, Pacific Region (Laguna Niguel), RG 75 Mission Indian Agency, Central Classified Files, 1920-1953, Box 24.

[49] Philp, *John Collier's Crusade for Indian Reform*, 38.

[50] Ibid., 131-133.

[51] Ibid., 134

[52] *The Indian*, Magazine of the Mission Indian Federation v. 4, no. 3 (July-August 1934), 1. At this time 28-year-old Cahuilla, Rupert Costo is listed as a contributor to *The Indian* magazine.

[53] Garner, *The Broken Ring*, 127-128.

[54] Ibid., 127.

[55] Ibid., 129.

[56] *San Diego Sun* newspaper, February 15, 1933, p. 9, clipping in National Archives, Pacific Region (Laguna Niguel), RG 75 Mission Indian Agency, Central Classified Files, 1920-1953, Box 24.

[57] Ibid.

[58] Ibid.

[59] Ibid.

[60] Philp, *John Collier's Crusade for Indian Reform*, 2.

[61] Philp, *John Collier's Crusade for Indian Reform*, 141-143.

[62] Ibid., 146-154, 159.

[63] *The Indian*, Magazine of the Mission Indian Federation v. 4, no. 3 (July-August 1934), 3.

[64] Philp, *John Collier's Crusade for Indian Reform*, 147-154.

[65] Ibid., 153.

[66] Ibid.

[67] Ibid., 153-154.

[68] Ibid., 163.

[69] Ibid., 156.

[70] John Collier, *Hearings before the Committee on Indian Affairs, House of Representatives Seventy-third Congress, Second Session on H. R. 7902, Part 7*, 272-277; *Los Angeles Times* newspaper, April 17, 1934, clipping in National Archives, Pacific Region (Laguna Niguel), RG 75 Mission Indian Agency Central Classified Files, 1920-1953, Box 16. Collett and the Indian Board of Cooperation should correctly be credited with the pressure it was able to bring on Congress to secure passage of the Jurisdictional Act of 1928. Writer Terri Castaneda, stated that during the first two decades of the 20th century, "Collett moved quickly to establish himself in both Washington and California as the representative authorized to speak for all Indians in California." He created extensive auxiliaries throughout northern and central California "by which he was able to collect yearly and even monthly dues from individual Indians, most of whom were landless and destitute." According to Casteneda, Collett's "fund-raising tactics became particularly ruthless" after passage of the 1928 act. See Terri Castaneda, "Making News, Marie Potts and the Smoke Signal of the Federated Indians of California," in *Women in Print, Essays on the Print Culture of American Women from the Nineteenth and Twentieth Centuries* (Madison, Wis.: University of Wisconsin Press, 2006), 81.

[71] Ibid., 275.

[72] Ibid.

[73] Ibid.

[74] *Los Angeles Times* newspaper, April 17, 1934, clipping in National Archives, Pacific Region (Laguna Niguel), RG 75, Mission Indian Agency, Central Classified Files, 1920-1953, Box 16.

[75] Collier, *Hearings before the Committee on Indian Affairs*, 282.

[76] Ibid.

[77] Ibid.

[78] Ibid., 281, 292.

[79] Philp, *John Collier's Crusade for Indian Reform*, 159.

[80] Lawrence Kelly, "The Indian Reorganization Act: The Dream and the Reality," *Pacific Historical Review* (August, 1975), 298

[81] Ibid.

[82] Philp, *John Collier's Crusade for Indian Reform*, 198-199.

[83] Tomas Amalio Salinas, *Pearl Chase, John Collier, and Indian Reform through the New Deal: Native American Affairs in California and the West, 1880-1937*, unpublished Ph.D dissertation, University of California, Santa Barbara, 1995, fn 270.

[84] Kelly, "The Indian Reorganization Act," 296.

[85] Adam Castillo, *The Indian*, Magazine of the Mission Indian Federation (April-May, 1936), 18.

[86] Laurence M. Hauptman, "The American Indian Federation and the Indian New Deal: A Reinterpretation," *Pacific Historical Review*, (November 1983), 378.

[87] Castillo, *The Indian*, Magazine of the Mission Indian Federation (April-May, 1936), 18.

[88] Ibid.

[89] Hauptman, "The American Indian Federation and the Indian New Deal," 381-382.

[90] Ibid., 378-379.

[91] Ibid., 378.

[92] Ibid., 380-381.

[93] Ibid., 383-384. Ironically, considering their views on assimilation, Bruner, Sloan and Lone Wolf were all defenders of and practicing peyotists. See Hauptman, 381; Hertzberg, *Search for an American Indian Identity*, 174, 149. See also, fn 26, this chapter. The letter sent by Castillo is sent to Juanita Ortega and Vivian Banks as representatives of the American Indian Federation.

[94] Table I: 6: 1, Action by Tribes on the Indian Reorganization Act (December 15 and 18, 1934) in Gerald Smith Collection, A.K. Smiley Public Library

[95] Garner, *The Broken Ring*, 127.

[96] Ibid., 128-129.

[97] Ibid., 129.

[98] Ibid., 129-130.

[99] Ibid., 130.

[100] Ibid., 128.

[101] Ibid., 130.

[102] Ibid.

[103] Ibid., 131.

[104] Ibid., 128.

[105] Ibid., 133. The spelling of Indian storeowner "Marcos Pete," is probably incorrect and the writer believes that this is Marcus J. Pete, son of Joe Pete who testified to a Congressional committee on behalf of the Federation as Secretary of the Agua Caliente Mission Indians in March 1934 and is listed as a member of the Mission Indian Federation in *The Indian*, the Federation's publication, (July-August 1934). The 1930 census for the San Gorgonio of Riverside County does not show a listing for "Marcos Pete" or anyone of a similar spelling besides Marcus Pete.

[106] Ibid.

[107] Ibid.

[108] *Los Angeles Times* newspaper, November 21, 1937, p. B 14; *Reno Evening Gazette* newspaper, November 23, 1937, p. 6

[109] Ibid.

[110] Garner, *The Broken Ring,* 134.

[111] Ibid., 135.

[112] Garner wrote that the "ferocity" of the government's oppressive tactics in 1937 crushed the idea of a true reservation for the Palm Springs area. Half of the Cahuilla held out for valuable allotments while the Mission Indian Federation acquiesced to Indian involvement in securing a decent price for the land under contention. Acrimonious Congressional hearings followed where the Federation worked to defeat any compromise measures. In 1938 the city of Palm Springs incorporated Indian lands in complete disregard of Indian wishes. Suit was brought and delayed but in 1943 the Court of Appeals ruled against the Cahuilla case of Lee Arenas et al vs. United States. This was reversed a year later by the United States Supreme Court. Additional suits and appeals followed without satisfaction to the tribe until 1956 when the courts mandated a new equitable distribution of allotted land to the Cahuilla. Garner noted that the decision was made easier since many of the original awardees were no longer living. This seeming victory was challenged, however, and continued into the 1960s and 1970s. For details of this torturous struggle by the Cahuilla see Garner, 136-149.

[113] Letter, Adam Castillo to members of the American Indian Federation, January 1, 1936, in Gerald Smith Collection.

[114] Ibid.

[115] Ibid.

[116] Group letter, Sam Collins to "Dear Indian Friends," March 4, 1935, National Archives, Pacific Region (Laguna Niguel), RG 75 Mission Indian Agency, Central Classified Files, 1920-1953, Box 16. This letter announced the formation and incorporation of the California Indian Rights Association.

[117] *California Indian News*, newsletter of the California Indian Rights Association, (July 1936), 14.

[118] Federal census records Riverside County, Perris twp., for 1900 show Thomas Largo a student there, born April 25, 1885.

[119] Thomas Largo, "Early Cahuilla Reminiscences," *California Indian News* (February 1937), 12-13.

[120] Ibid., 13.

[121] Federal census records for Los Angeles, 1920 and 1930.

[122] Thomas Largo, "Why We Organized," *California Indian News*, newsletter of the California Indian Rights Association, (July 1936), 4.

[123] Ibid.

[124] Ibid.

[125] Ibid.

[126] Ibid.

[127] Willis was born around 1880 in Ohio. By 1910 Willis, his wife Ruth, son Richard and a brother are living in San Diego where Willis is a clerk at the city hall. Ten years later the growing family moved to El Centro and Willis stated he was an automobile dealer. At the time of Jonathan Tibbet's death in 1930, Willis was living again in San Diego, making a living by selling real estate. His transition back to county government must have been shortly after the 1930 census since he is shown in 1931 newspapers as a member of the county's committee on Indian affairs and a deputy treasurer. Willis, like Tibbet before him, was a member of the United Indian War Veterans of the United States. See Federal Census records, San Diego County area, 1910, 1920, 1930.

[128] News clipping, August 22, 1932; October 5, [1932]; *San Diego Sun* newspaper, December 22, 1932, National Archives, Pacific Region (Laguna Niguel), RG 75, Mission Indian Agency, Central Classified Files, 1920-1953, Box 24; *Los Angeles Times* newspaper, June 29, 1934, p. 4.

[129] *California Indian News*, Newsletter of the California Indian Rights Association (July 1936), (September 1936).

[130] Ibid.

[131] *California Indian News*, Newsletter of the California Indian Rights Association, (September 1936), 9.

[132] Letter, Julia Gardner to John Dady, April 24, 1935, National Archives, Pacific Region (Laguna Niguel), RG 75 Mission Indian Agency Central Classified Files, 1920-1953, Box 16.

[133] Garner, *The Broken Ring*, 155-157.

[134] Ibid., 157.

[135] Ibid.

[136] *California Indian News*, Newsletter of the California Indian Rights Association, (October 1936), 4.

[137] Ibid.

[138] Ibid.

[139] Ibid.

[140] Statement of Adam Castillo, April 10, 1936, copy in the Gerald Smith Collection and printed in *The Indian*, Magazine of the Mission Indian Federation (April-May, 1936).

[141] Ibid.

[142] Resolution, 1932, signed by members of the "Capistrano Band of Mission Indians of California," copy from the Sandoval Collection, Archives of Juaneño Band of Mission Indians Acjachmemem Nation San Juan Capistrano, California.

[143] Indian Treaties Made at Temecula, California, January 5, 1852, and Santa Ysabel, California, January 7, 1852, Issued by the Mission Inn Indian Federation, 171 E. Prospect Avenue, Riverside, California, 1920, copy provided the writer by Archives, Gabrieleño Band of Mission Indians.

Scholar Heather Valdez Singleton wrote of the viable Gabrieleño communities which existed at the time of the 1891 Smiley Commission. "While [Helen Hunt] Jackson noted the impoverished status of the Gabrieleno, A. K. Smiley, the head of the Mission Indian Relief Act Commission, overlooked the Gabrieleno when he visited various Indian communities and villages in 1891. Smiley's diary fails to indicate why he did not visit San Gabriel. He apparently saw no reason to change the established policy of federal neglect for the Gabrielenos." According to Singleton, anthropologists J.P. Harrington and C. Hart Merriam had Gabrieleño informers and groups of Gabrieleño lived at the Tejon Reservation. Despite Alfred Kroeber's declaration that Gabrieleno culture and people "have melted away," federal officials encouraged Gabrieleno children to enroll at Riverside's Sherman Indian Institute. "From 1890 to 1920 Sherman Indian School registered at least fifty Gabrieleno students," noted Singleton. Over 150 Indians enrolled under the 1928 act identified themselves as Gabrieleño. See Singleton, "Surviving Urbanization: The Gabrieleno, 1850-1928," *Wicazo Sa Review* (Fall 2004). The Village site of Las Flores in the Los Angeles basin is today claimed by both Juaneño and Gabrieleño people.

[144] Statement of Adam Castillo, April 10, 1936, copy in the Gerald Smith Collection and printed in *The Indian*, Magazine of the Mission Indian Federation (April-May, 1936).

[145] Ibid.

[146] Garner, *The Broken Ring*, 162.

[147] Ibid., 163. The case mentioned was filed by the Walapai Indian tribe in the 1970s.

[148] Ibid, 162-164.

[149] Ibid., 166.

[150] Ibid, 164

[151] Ibid., 165.

[152] Laurence M. Hauptman, *The Iroquois and the New Deal* (Syracuse, New York: Syracuse University Press, 1981), 51.

[153] Philp, *John Collier's Crusade for Indian Reform*, 173.

[154] Hauptman, "The American Indian Federation," 397.

[155] Hauptman, *The Iroquois and the New Deal* , 51-52.

[156] Ibid., 395.

[157] Philp, *John Collier's Crusade for Indian Reform*, 173.

[158] Hauptman, *The Iroquois and the New Deal*, 53.

[159] The Indian, Magazine of the Mission Indian Federation (April-May, 1936), 20.

[160] Ibid.

[161] Ibid.

[162] Hauptman, "The American Indian Federation," 383.

[163] Ibid., 400.

[164] Hauptman, *The Iroquois and the New Deal*, 51.

[165] Ibid., 51.

[166] Ibid., 54.

[167] Garner, *The Broken Ring*, 165; Letter, Edward H. Davis to California Superintendent of Instruction Dr. Walter Dexter, August 9, 1940. Von Bulow noted Federation defections "because of Willis" in a 1940 open letter in the *California Indian News*, Newsletter of the California Indian Rights Association (July 1940), 13.

[168] Trafzer, *As Long As the Grass Shall Grow*, 356.

[169] Letters Castillo to James Stewart, July 25, 1949, October 18, 1949, National Archives, (San Bruno), Record Group 75, BIA California Sacramento Office, Coded Records, 1910-1958 of Program and Administration, 1950-1958, Box 27.

[170] Letter, Tómas Arviso to Dr. Walter Dexter, n.d.; Letter, Harry Coonradt to John Dady, August 17, 1940, National Archives, Pacific Region (Laguna Niguel), RG 75 Mission Indian Agency Central Classified Files, 1920-1953, Box 88.

[171] Letter, Louise Leo Ponchetta to Dr. Walter Dexter, August 10, 1940, National Archives, Pacific Region (Laguna Niguel), RG 75 Mission Indian Agency Central Classified Files, 1920-1953, Box 88.

[172] Letter, Louise Leo Ponchetta to Dr. Walter Dexter, August 10, 1940.

[173] Letter, Harry Coonradt to John Dady, August 17, 1940.

[174] *California Indian News*, Newsletter of the California Indian Rights Association (July 1940), 13.

[175] Letter, Tómas Arviso to Dr. Walter Dexter, n.d. Arviso was a member of the Valley Center school board at the time. In his condemnation of Willis, Arviso also alleged that Willis' son Robert was serving time in San Quentin prison for burglary and that Willis had a reputation of dishonesty in his business dealings and was on a blacklist with creditors for inability to pay his debts.

[176] Interview with Luiseño Max Mazzetti, June 14, 2000, Rincon Reservation, conducted by Ron Ampie and Tanis Thorne, online transcription provided at, http://eee.uci.edu/clients/tcthorne/idp/MaxInterview.htm.

[177] Ibid.

[178] Richard Hanks interview with tribal council of Gabrieleño Band of Mission Indians, September 19, 2004, Banning, California.

[179] Ibid.

[180] *Los Angeles Times*, newspaper, September 12, 1940, p. B2. His obituary listed the age of Albanes as only 55. Vicente Albanes was also captain of the La Jolla Reservation and had accompanied Castillo and Willis to Washington to lobby for Southern California Indians.

[181] Letter Frederick Baker to Juanita Ortega, March 11, 1945, Rupert and Jeanette Costo Collection, Box 6. Frederick Baker was appointed special counsel to represent California Indians in their suit by the California Attorney General.

[182] Letter Castillo to James Stewart, October 18, 1949.

[183] Ibid.

[184] Kenny, Attorney General of California, *History and Proposed Settlement Claims of California Indians*, 42-49.

[185] Garner, *The Broken Ring*, 165; Letter Castillo to James Stewart, October 18, 1949, p. 2.

[186] *The Indian*, Magazine of the Mission Indian Federation (November 1945), 3.

[187] Ibid.

[188] Clayton R. Koppes, "From New Deal to Termination: Liberalism and Indian Policy, 1933-1945," *Pacific Historical Review* (1977), 555.

[189] Philp, *John Collier's Crusade for Indian Reform*, 244.

[190] Ibid.

[191] Koppes, "From New Deal to Termination," 555.

[192] *The Indian*, Magazine of the Mission Indian Federation (November 1945), 3.

[193] Koppes, "From New Deal to Termination," 556.

[194] Ibid., 558.

[195] Ibid., 557-559.

[196] Ibid.

[197] *San Diego Union* newspaper, October 19, 1950, "Accusations Hurled at Indian Hearing," National Archives, (San Bruno), Record Group 75, BIA California Sacramento Office, Coded Records, 1910-1958 of Program and Administration, 1950-1958, Box 27; *San Diego Union* newspaper, March 22, 1950, "Alarmed Indians Call Meeting to Protest Wardship Fund Cut."

[198] Letters, Purl Willis to Adam Castillo, March 11, 1947, April 3, 1947, Rupert and Jeanette Costo Collection, Box 6.

[199] Castillo to F.G. Collett, April 5, 1947, Rupert and Jeanette Costo Collection, Box 6.

[200] Letter, Willis to Castillo, April 3, 1947.

[201] Letter, Willis to Castillo, March 11, 1947.

[202] Ibid.

[203] Ibid.

[204] Ibid. Castaneda, "Making News and the Smoke Signal of the Federated Indians of California," 81.

[205] Letter, Willis to Castillo, March 11, 1947.

[206] Letter Castillo to James Stewart, October 18, 1949, National Archives, (San Bruno), Record Group 75, BIA California Sacramento Office, Coded Records, 1910-1958 of Program and Administration, 1950-1958, Box 27.

[207] Ibid.

[208] Ibid.

[209] *San Diego Union* newspaper, March 5, 1950, clipping in Tribal Archives, Soboba Band of Luiseño Indians.

[210] *San Diego Journal* newspaper, February 28, 1950, clipping in Tribal Archives, Soboba Band of Luiseño Indians.

[211] *San Diego Union* newspaper, October 19, 1950, A-10, clipping in Tribal Archives, Soboba Band of Luiseño Indians.

[212] *San Diego Evening Tribune* newspaper, October 19, 1950, A-14, clipping in Tribal Archives, Soboba Band of Luiseño Indians.

[213] Ibid.

[214] Ibid.

[215] *San Diego Union* newspaper, May 9, 1950, clipping in Tribal Archives, Soboba Band of Luiseño Indians.

[216] Petition To The Honorable Oscar L. Chapman, Secretary of the Interior On Behalf of The Undersigned Delegation of Mission Indian Citizens of California, Tribal Archives, Soboba Band of Luiseño Indians.

[217] Letter Clarence Lobo to Dillon Myer, June 11, 1951, National Archives, (San Bruno), Record Group 75, BIA California Sacramento Office, Coded Records, 1910-1958 of Program and Administration, 1950-1958, Box 27.

[218] Ibid.

[219] Ibid.

[220] Ibid.

[221] Ibid.

[222] Ibid.

[223] News clipping, August 22, 1932, National Archives, Pacific Region (Laguna Niguel), RG 75, Mission Indian Agency, Central Classified Files, 1920-1953, Box 24.

[224] Petition To The Honorable Oscar L. Chapman, Tribal Archives, Soboba Band of Luiseño Indians.

[225] Trafzer, *As Long As the Grass Shall Grow*, 391.

[226] Monguia, *The Mission Indian Federation*, 22.

[227] Minutes of the League of California Indians, July 8, 1951, August 26, 1951, Yolanda Sandoval Collection.

[228] Letter Clarence Lobo to Dillon Myer, June 11, 1951.

[229] Talley, *The Life History of a Luiseño Indian*, 82-83.

[230] Ibid., 86-87

[231] Ibid.

[232] Ibid.

[233] Ibid.

[234] Ibid., 87.

[235] Talley, *The Life History of a Luiseño Indian*, 35.

[236] Roster of Mission Indian Federation, Inc., 1962, Yolanda Sandoval Collection.

[237] Letter, Dan Pico and Purl Willis to Congressman James Haley, April 17, 1966, Yolanda Sandoval Collection.

[238] Roster of Mission Indian Federation, Inc., 1962, Yolanda Sandoval Collection.

[239] Letter, Clarence Lobo to Dan Pico, March 7, 1962, Clarence Lobo Collection/ David Belardes Collection, San Juan Capistrano.

[240] Ibid.

[241] Talley, *The Life History of a Luiseño Indian*, 35.

[242] *Reno Evening Gazette* newspaper, September 16, 1966, p. 23.

[243] Ibid.

[244] Ibid.

[245] Max Mazzetti interview, 35.

Conclusion

The Mission Indian Federation was created by the aged Cahuilla leaders from the arid deserts of Southern California who were the masters of these traditional lands. It sputtered out of existence in the coastal plains of Southern California while in the hands of a different generation of dispossessed Juaneño and Luiseño leaders who sought justice for their "free" Indians—people not recognized by the federal government but Indians nonetheless. The Federation answered a need for a people who fought for respect and self-determination since contact with the first Europeans who had invaded their homelands. During the Federation's existence it was a force for change in American Indian policy. It was instrumental in securing or altering the Indian Citizenship Act of 1924, the California Indians' Jurisdictional Act in 1928, the creation of the Claims Commissions in 1928 and 1946, and the Indian Reorganization Act of 1934.

The Federation had its critics. This would not be unusual for an organization that survived for so long in a time of such momentous change in Native American history. Some of its legislative successes and political choices led to greater challenges for California's first peoples. But for nearly half a century it provided a strong voice for Southern California Indians who were shackled to an insensitive and often hostile bureaucracy. For many, it was and has become a symbol of what is possible when oppressed people organize for the greater good of their lives and their future. It is a symbol of resistance, but with its origins deep in the past of native California. Members of the Mission Indian Federation are inextricably part of those Indians of Southern California who, prior to the first contact with the strange white invaders, lived together, traded, sang the ancient songs, prayed to their gods, mourned their dead, and lived in relative peace. James Martinez noted that for all its mistakes, without the Mission Indian Federation, the Bureau of Indian Affairs would still be the dominant force in the lives of Native Americans.

The Federation drew upon the spirit of dynamic leadership. During its existence these leaders included such men as Carlos Montezuma. But, it also remembered the sacrifices of those California Indians who paid dearly to maintain the homelands and culture of a people besieged by an Anglo society indifferent or angry at their very existence.

Federation President Adam Castillo invoked the memory of Luiseño General Olegario Calac in his dealings with Congress. Castillo joined Calac and the many others who gave of themselves for the betterment of the Indian race.

History has proven unkind to the story of California Indians. Seen as merely early and docile victims to the juggernaut of European and American imperialism, their struggle fades quickly from the texts of basic school curriculum and serious scholarship. This is a grave mistake. Indians of Southern California not only fought, they led. They not only changed their lives but also the policies that controlled the lives of Native Americans across the United States.

Their communities did not have the legendary warrior societies of the Great Plains but there were warriors just the same. Warriors often rise from within the moment when the threat is greatest to loved ones and neighbors. This is not race specific but a basic human response. The names of those warriors of Southern California Indians are not mentioned in the same breath as those of the legendary figures from the Indian Wars such as Crazy Horse, Red Cloud or Quanah Parker, but they should be. Antonio Garra, Juan Antonio, Manuel Largo, Olegario Calac, Leonicio Lugo, William Pablo, Joe Pete, and Adam Castillo—all were men of extraordinary faith and dedication to the survival of their race and California Indian culture.

Historian Frederick Hoxie wrote that often, "scholars and bureaucrats viewed Indians as people from another time, they did not recognize that even when conquered, Native Americans could still act and make choices....Those choices were limited but individuals continued to shape their own futures."[1] In the case of Southern California Indians, they never surrendered to the invaders but adapted to the conditions imposed upon them and resisted the assault on their culture and families. Their unwavering struggle for self-determination in the face of unrelenting hardship and injustice revealed a courage too often overlooked but worthy of our respect.

Notes:

[1] Frederick E. Hoxie, "Exploring A Cultural Borderland: Native American Journeys of Discovery In The Early Twentieth Century," in *American Nations: Encounters in Indian Country, 1850 to the Present*, Frederick E. Hoxie, Peter C. Mancall and James H. Merrell, eds. (New York: Routledge, 2001), 270.

Sources

Beattie, George and Helen Pruitt Beattie, *Heritage of the Valley; San Bernardino's First Century* (Pasadena, Calif.: San Pasqual Press, 1939).

Beebe, Rose Marie and Robert M. Senkewicz, eds., *Lands of Promise and Despair: Chronicles of Early California, 1535-1846* (Berkeley, CA: Heyday Books, 2001).

Bingham, Edwin R., *Charles F. Lummis, Editor of the Southwest* (San Marino, California: The Huntington Library, 1955).

Brown, John Jr., and James Boyd, eds., *History of San Bernardino and Riverside Counties with Selected Biography of Actors and Witnesses of the Period of Growth and Achievement, vols. I and II* (Madison, Wis.: The Western Historical Association, 1922).

Cardozo, Christopher and Joseph D. Horse Capture, Sacred Legacy: Edward S. Curtis and the North American Indian (New York: Simon & Schuster, 2000).

Carrico, Richard L., *Strangers in a Stolen Land: Americans Indians in San Diego, 1850-1880* (Newcastle, California: Sierra Oaks Publishing Co., 1987).

Casebier, Dennis G., *Carleton's Pah-Ute Campaign* (Norco, California: Dennis G. Casebier, June 1972).

Caughey, John Walton, ed., *The Indians of Southern California In 1852: The B.D. Wilson Report* (San Marino, California: Huntington Library, 1952).

Chalfant, Willie A., *The Story of Inyo* (Los Angeles: Privately Published, 1933).

Collier, John, *From Every Zenith: A Memoir and Some Essays on Life and Thought* (Denver, CO: Sage Books, 1963).

Costo, Rupert and Jeannette Henry Costo, eds., *The Mission of California: A Legacy of Genocide* (San Francisco, CA: Indian Historian Press, 1987).

Dankey, James P. and Wayne A. Wiegand, eds., *Women in Print: Essays on the Print Culture of American Women from the Nineteenth and Twentieth Centuries* (Madison, Wis.: University of Wisconsin Press, 2006).

Danziger, Edmund Jefferson, Jr., Indians and Bureaucrats, Administering the Reservation *Policy during the Civil War* (Urbana, Chicago, London: University of Illinois Press, 1974). Duhaut-Cilly , Auguste, *A Voyage to California, the Sandwich Islands, & Around the World in the Years 1826-1829*, August Frugé and Neal Harlow, eds., (San Francisco: The Book Club of California, 1997).

Engelhardt, Fr. Zephyrin, *San Juan Capistrano Mission* (Los Angeles, Cal.: The Standard Printing Co., 1922).

Garner,Van H., *The Broken Ring: The Destruction of the California Indian* (Tucson, Arizona: Westernlore Press, 1982).

Guinn, J.M., *A History of California and an Extended History of Its Southern Coast Counties*, v. 1 (Los Angeles, Cal.: Historic Record Company, 1907).

Haas, Lisbeth, *Conquests and Historical Identities in California, 1769-1936* (Berkeley and Los Angeles, California: University of California Press, 1995).

Hauptman, Larence M., *The Iroquois and The New Deal* (Syracuse, N.Y.: Syracuse University Press, 1981).

Heizer, Robert F., ed., *Federal Concern about Conditions of California Indians, 1853 to 1913* (Ramona, California: Ballena Press Publications in Archaeology, Ethnology and History No. 13, 1979).

_____, ed. *Some Last Century Accounts of the Indians of Southern California* (Ramona, California: Ballena Press, 1976).

_____, ed. *The Indians of Los Angeles County: Hugo Reid's Letters of 1852* (Highland Park, CA: Southwest Museum, 1968).

Hayes, Judge Benjamin, *Pioneer Notes From the Diaries of Judge Benjamin Ignatius Hayes, 1849-1875* (Los Angeles: Privately printed, 1929).

Hertzberg, Hazel W., *The Search For An American Indian Identity: Modern Pan-Indian Movements* (Syracuse, N.Y.: Syracuse University Press, 1971).

Hoxie, Frederick E., Peter C. Mancall and James H. Merrell, eds., *American Nations: Encounters in Indian Country, 1850 to the Present* (New York: Routledge, 2001).

Hoxie, Frederick, *A Final Promise: The Campaign to Assimilate the Indians, 1880-1920* (Lincoln, Nebraska: University of Nebraska Press, 2001).

Hughes, Tom, *History of Banning and San Gorgonio Pass* (Riverside, California: Banning Record Print, 1939).

Hurtado, Albert L., *Indian Survival on the California Frontier* (New Haven and London : Yale University Press, 1988).

Ingersoll, Luther A., *Ingersoll's Century Annals of San Bernardino County, 1769-1904 : Prefaced with a Brief History of the State of California : Supplemented with an Encyclopedia of Local Biography and Embellished with Views of Historic Subjects and Portraits of Many of its Representative People* (Los Angeles: L.A. Ingersoll, 1904).

Jackson, Helen Hunt, *Glimpses of California and the Missions* (Boston: Little, Brown & Company, 1923).

Jackson, Robert H. and Edward Castillo, Indians, *Franciscans, and Spanish Colonization: The Impact of the Mission System on California Indians* (Albuquerque, NM: University of New Mexico Press, 1995).

Johnson, Kenneth M., *K-344 or the Indians of California vs. The United States* (Los Angeles, CA: Dawson's Book Shop, 1966).

Johnston, Bernice Eastman, *California's Gabrielino Indians* (Los Angeles, California: Southwest Museum, 1962).

Johnston, Francis J., The Bradshaw Trail (Riverside, California: Historical Commission Press, 1987).

Littlefield, Alice and Martha C. Knack, eds., *Native Americans and Wage Labor, Ethnohistorical Perspectives* (Norman and London: University of Oklahoma Press, 1996).

Mathes, Valerie Sherer, ed., *The Indian Reform Letters of Helen Hunt Jackson, 1879-1885* (Norman, OK: University of Oklahoma Press, 1998).

McMurtry, Larry, *Oh, What A Slaughter: Massacres in the American West, 1846-1890* (New York: Simon & Shuster, 2005).

Miller, Bruce W., *The Gabrielino*, (Los Osos, California: Sand River Press, 1991).

Milner, Clyde A. and Floyd A. O'Neil, *Churchmen and the Western Indians, 1820-1920* (Norman and London: University of Oklahoma Press, 1985).

Murillo, Pauline, *Living in Two Worlds, The Life of Pauline Ormego Murillo* (Highland, CA: Dimples Press, 2001)

Patencio, Francisco, *Stories and Legends of the Palm Springs Indians*, Margaret Boynton, ed., (Los Angeles: Times-Mirror, 1943).
_____, *Desert Hours with Chief Patencio As Told to Kate Collins*, Roy F. Hudson, ed. (Palm Springs: Palm Springs Desert Museum, 1971).

Philp, Kenneth, *John Collier's Crusade for Indian Reform: 1920-1954* (Tucson, Arizona: University of Arizona Press, 1977).

Phillips, George Harwood, *Chiefs and Challengers: Indian Resistance and Cooperation in Southern California* (Berkeley: University of California Press, 1975).

La Potin, Armand S., ed., *Native American Voluntary Organizations* (New York: Greenwood Press, 1987).

Prucha, Francis Paul, *American Indian Policy in Crisis, Christian Reformers and the Indian, 1865-1900* (Norman: University of Oklahoma Press, 1976).

_____, *The Churches and the Indian Schools, 1888-1912* (Lincoln and London: University of Nebraska Press, 1979).

Prucha, Francis Paul, ed., *Americanizing the American Indians: Writings by the "Friends of the Indian," 1880-1900* (Cambridge, Massachusetts: Harvard University Press, 1973).

Robinson, John W. and Bruce D. Risher, *The San Jacintos: The Mountain Country from Banning to Borego Valley* (Arcadia, California: Big Santa Anita Historical Society, 1993).

Romero, John Bruno, *The Botanical Lore of the California Indians with Side Lights on historical Incidents in California* (New York: Vantage Press, Inc., 1954).

Shipek, Dr. Florence, *Pushed Into The Rocks: Southern California Indian Land Tenure, 1769-1986* (Alpine, CA: Viejas Band of Kumeyaay Indians).

Sandos, James A., *Converting California: Indian and Franciscans in the Missions* (New Haven & London: Yale University Press, 2004).

Smythe, William Ellsworth, *History of San Diego, 1542-1907: An Account of the Rise and Progress of the Pioneer Settlement on the Pacific Coast of the United States*, (San Diego: San Diego History Co., 1907).

Speroff, Leon, *Carlos Montezuma, M.D.: A Yavapai American Hero* (Portland, OR: Arnica Press, 2005).

Stanley, Samuel L., ed., *American Indian Economic Development* (The Hague: Mouton Publishers, 1978).

Strong, William Duncan, *Aboriginal Society in Southern California* (Banning, California: Malki Museum Press, 1972).

Sturtevant, William C., ed., *Handbook of North American Indians*, vol. 8, *California*, Robert F. Heizer, ed., (Washington, D.C.: Smithsonian Institution, 1978).

Thompson , Mark, *American Character: The Curious Life of Charles Fletcher Lummis and the Rediscovery of the Southwest* (New York: Arcade Publishing, 2001).

Trafzer, Clifford E., *The People of San Manuel* (Patton, California: San Manuel Band of Mission Indians, 2002).

_____, *As Long As The Grass Shall Grow And Rivers Flow* (Belmont, CA: Wadsworth Group: 2000).

Webb, Edith Buckland, *Indian Life at the Old Missions* (Lincoln and London: University of Nebraska Press, 1982).

Unpublished Manuscripts:

Salinas, Tomas Amalio
Pearl Chase, John Collier, and Indian Reform through the New Deal: Native American Affairs in California and the West, 1880-1937
Ph.D Dissertation, University of California, Santa Barbara, 1995

Talley, Robin Paige
The Life History of a Luiseño Indian: James (Jim) Martinez
Masters Thesis, San Diego State University, 1982

Monguia, Anna Rose
The Mission Indian Federation: A Study in Indian Political Resistance
Masters Thesis, University of California, Los Angles, 1975

Periodicals:

American Indian Culture and Research Journal

California History

California Indian News

Canadian Bulletin of Medical History, Bulletin Canadien d'Histoire de la Médicine

Historical Society of Southern California Quarterly

The Indian Magazine

The Indian Reporter

Journal of California and Great Basin Anthropology

Journal of San Diego History

Land of Sunshine

The Masterkey

The Outlook

Out West

Pacific Historical Review

Proceedings of the Lake Mohonk Conferences

San Bernardino County Museum Association Quarterly

Sunset, Magazine of the Pacific

Western Historical Quarterly

Wicazo Sa Revie

Primary Resources:

Constance Goddard DuBois Papers
Cornell University

Richard Henry Pratt Papers
Yale Collection of Western Americana, Beinecke Rare Book and Manuscript Library

The Rupert and Jeannette Costo Archive of the American Indian
University of California, Riverside

Horatio Nelson Rust Papers
Huntington Library, San Marino, California

Records of the Bureau of Indian Affairs
Records of the Mission Indian Agency
The National Archives, Pacific Region
Laguna Niguel and San Bruno, California

Carlos Montezuma Papers
University of California, Riverside

Pearl Chase Collection
University of California, Santa Barbara

Samuel Cary Evans Papers
Riverside Metropolitan Museum

John Peabody Harrington Papers
University of California, Riverside

Tribal Archives
Soboba Band of Luiseño Indians

Gerald Smith Collection
A.K. Smiley Public Library, Redlands, CA

Scrapbook of Ben de Crevecoeur
A.K. Smiley Public Library, Redlands, CA

Charles T. Beach Collection
A.K. Smiley Public Library, Redlands, CA

Myron Crafts Collection
A.K. Smiley Public Library, Redlands, CA

C.O. Barker Collection
A.K. Smiley Public Library, Redlands, CA

Burr Belden Collection
A.K. Smiley Public Library, Redlands, CA

Yolanda Sandoval Collection
Clarence Lobo Collection
Archives of Juaneño Band of Mission Indians
Acjachmemem Nation
San Juan Capistrano, California

Oral Interviews:

Joe Guacheno—Diegueño (Kumeyaay) elder of Santa Ysabel Reservation

Gloria Wright—Juaneño/Gabrieleño/Luiseño/Cahuilla member, Pechanga Reservation

Mary Magee—Luiseño/Juaneño member of the Pechanga Reservation

Pauline Murillo—Elder of the San Manuel Band of Serrano Indians

Francis De Los Reyes—Elder of the San Manuel Band of Serrano Indians

Robert Levi—Cahuilla elder and Bird Singer

Paul Cuero—Tribal Chairman of the Campo Band of Kumayaay Indians

Manuel Hamilton—Tribal Chairman of the Ramona Band of Cahuilla Indians

Ann Hamilton—Elder of the Cahuilla/ Ramona Band of Cahuilla Indians

Virginia Scribner—Elder of the Santa Rosa Band of Cahuilla Indians

JoMay Modesto—Elder of the Cahuilla Band of Cahuilla Indians

Ernest Siva—Cahuilla-Serrano Elder/Morongo Band of Mission Indians

Dorothy Mathews—Tribal council of the Gabrieleño Band of Mission Indians
Susan Frank,
Debra McIntire
Valkyrie Houston

Willie Pink—Pala Band

Harold Mathews—Cahuilla of the Morongo Reservation

Lowell Bean—Professor Emeritus, California State University, Hayward

Ray Reeder—Anglo resident of Soboba Indian Reservation, Riverside, County

Max Mazzetti—Elder with the Rincon Band of Luiseño Indians
Interview conducted by Ron Ampie and Tanis Thorne, June 14, 2000. Online transcription
provided at, http://eee.uci.edu/clients/tcthorne/idp/MaxInterview.htm.

Sisters (from left) Debra McIntire, Susan Frank, and Dorothy Mathews of the Gabrieleño Band of Mission Indians, with anthropologist Lowell J. Bean.

ILLUSTRATIONS

INDEX